FROM PETER TO JOHN PAUL II

DEDICATION

In Loving Memory of Two Friends
    Cosimo Gatto
        (Who happened also to be my father-in-law)
    June Palmieri Crincoli
        (Who happened also to be my niece)

ACKNOWLEDGMENTS

To every member of my household, viz.
    To my three sons, Frank, Ron and John for
        accompanying me to Rome for the research;
    To my wife, Camille, for her suggestions, proof-
        reading, and typing;
    To my wife's mother, Emma Gatto, for her
        constant encouragement;
    And to my dog, Princess, for keeping me
        company, snuggled at my feet while I wrote.

From Peter
to John Paul II

An Informal Study of the Papacy

FRANK J. KORN

ALBA·HOUSE　　NEW·YORK

SOCIETY OF ST. PAUL, 2187 VICTORY BLVD., STATEN ISLAND, NEW YORK 10314

Library of Congress Cataloging-in-Publication Data

Korn, Frank J.
  From Peter to John Paul II.
    ISBN 0-8189-1161-1

Library of Congress Catalog Card Number: 80-65721

Nihil Obstat:
James A. Clarke
Chancellor

Imprimatur:
✠ James W. Malone
Bishop of Youngstown
April 24, 1980

ISBN: 0-8189-1161-1

Printing Information:

Current Printing - first digit   4   5   6   7   8   9   10

Year of Current Printing - first year shown

1994   1995   1996   1997   1998   1999

CONTENTS

PART I

A History of the Papacy up to

the Twentieth Century

INTRODUCTION

Vatican City
April 15, 1979

Easter Sunday, 1979 A.D. is about to pass into history. Night's purple mantle has descended upon the shoulders of the Eternal City. Rome's marble glories the Colosseum, the Forum, the fountains, are bathed in a blend of moonlight and floodlight. The trees in their new spring garb, silhouetted against soiled white baroque churches or burnt siena Renaissance palaces, look down upon the Romans in their paschal finery returning home from vespers, from relatives' apartments, from a family feast at a local *trattoria*.

While I struggle with these opening lines in my flat not too far from the Vatican, my wife, who has accompanied me to Rome on my annual pilgrimage here to celebrate the Resurrection, sips *cappuccino* with our landlady as they chat and watch a film on television. With the words refusing to come, I begin to muse. I wonder what a neighbor of mine, Pope John Paul II, is doing at this precise moment. Such wondering is customary for me, for the popes and their holy office have held a profound fascination for me since my days as an altar boy in the 1940's. Perhaps what I have to say on this subject (and how I say it) in the pages to follow will arouse or renew in you, too, a keen interest in Peter, the first pope, and in the 263 men who have occupied his episcopal throne in the nineteen and a half centuries since. At least that is my hope and prayer.

This morning, in balmy spring weather under limpid blue Italian skies, my fellow pilgrim and I witnessed the Holy Father's Easter Mass in the great square of St. Peter, from a marvelous vantage point atop Bernini's colonnade. Thanks to the influence of a friend of mine in the service of the Vatican *Vigilanza*, we were able to obtain passes to the *tribuna* as this particular point is known. From our seats along the balustrade, Camille and I watched in awe as the centuries-old pageantry unfolded down in the vast *piazza*. Though the Mass was to begin at eleven o'clock, we had arrived two hours earlier to enjoy the colorful and spectacular preliminaries.

With every minute the square continued to be filled with representatives of every continent and practically every nation, attesting vividly to the international and universal character of the Church. Pilgrim groups proudly displayed their national colors and held up enormous banners in an array of languages. Swiss guards in their fairy-tale red, yellow and blue uniforms—halberds and helmets gleaming in the copper sun—were working with the Vatican gendarmes in directing the swelling tide of pedestrian traffic. By ten-thirty a quarter of a million people had arrived and we could see thousands more making their way up the Via della Conciliazione, the graceful boulevard that begins at the banks of the Tiber and climbs directly to St. Peter's. There was a happy, festive, yet reverential air about the place with some groups raising their voices in folksong above the pleasant patter, children releasing their helium-filled balloons into the azure heavens, priests pointing out things of interest to their flocks, vendors hawking religious articles, television crews making their last minute checks, an occasional plane passing over on the way to Fiumicino, the bells of St. Peter's joyously ringing out the happy tidings of the day.

At ten forty-five there was a sudden hush and all heads turned toward the right colonnade from which emanated a group of about a hundred back-packers led by a bearded youth carrying a large, rugged cross fashioned out of the trunks of two small trees. The hush turned to a murmur as the young travelers (we later learned they had days earlier set out from Assisi and had walked all the way to Rome) strode the path cleared for them by the guards. The murmur changed to applause and the applause crescendoed to a tumultuous ovation as the hikers ascended the *sagrato* and took the seats reserved for them just to the left of the altar.

Again all eyes turned toward the same colonnade through which this time marched, to the cadenced beating of drums, the Palatine Guard in their impressive black and white uniforms. They came to a halt in the center of the *piazza*, in the lane between the barricades that demark the seating section and those that indicate the standing area, and were joined there moments later by a detachment of the little Swiss legion. For the next few minutes the military band of the Palatine delighted the crowd with a medley of marching tunes.

At a minute to eleven the Sistine Choir, stationed to the left and rear of the altar, raised their voices in the papal hymn, *Tu Es Petrus.* Another ripple of applause began up in the *tribuna* as we were the first to notice Pope John Paul II, clad in a white embroidered mitre and chasuble, carrying in his left hand a crucifix-crowned crosier, already raising his right hand in the traditional pontifical gesture of blessing, striding vigorously in the company of Monsignors Virgilio Noe and Horacio Cocchetto to the temporary wooden altar set up at the top of the steps in front of the immense church.

My mind raced back to Easter Sunday last when my son John and I sat in this same place to participate in the outdoor Mass celebrated by His Holiness, Pope Paul VI, who had, against the wishes of his doctors, left a sick bed so as not to disappoint the hundreds of thousands of pilgrims who had journeyed to the Eternal City principally for this event.

But time is a restless river whose ceaseless flow changes and sweeps along everything in its course. And in the year just past that river has been particularly inexorable, for things are very different now. Last year the same two *monsignori* had to support the aging, arthritic, and (as we now realize) dying pope, virtually holding him up by the elbows throughout the Mass.

Today, not one but two Supreme Pontiffs later, I sit here with my priceless memories. Papa Montini is gone. The last time we pulled out of Rome early last September, John Paul I, *Il Papa del Sorriso* (the pope of the smile), was clutching the keys. Now Papa Luciani, too, is gone. So this morning we had our first glimpse of the new young pope, young, that is, by the standards of the chair of Peter. Long live Papa Wojtyla!

When the full throng realized that the pope had arrived, wave upon wave of thunderous applause, punctuated by shouts of *"Viva Il Papa!"*, rolled in from the edges of the square, crested at the barricades separating the reserved section from the rest of the splendid churchyard, and pounded resoundingly at the feet of the Holy Father. But as the pope began the Mass, his strong voice booming out the ancient prayers in Latin, the multitude fell into a reverent, filial silence. The people watched in near perfect stillness as the pontiff walked around the altar, preparing it with incense for the Holy Sacrifice. Then they burst into thunderous applause again at the emotional opening words of John Paul's homily: *"Fratres et filii carissimi, Christus surrexit!"*

After the hour-long liturgy, *Il Papa* appeared (it was noon and the great bells were ringing out their triumphant message) on the central balcony over the entrance to the basilica to deliver his apostolic blessing, *Urbi et Orbi* (to the city and to the world). A tapestry with the papal coat of arms—in the lower right corner a large *M* joined to a cross symbolizing Karol Wojtyla's special devotion to the Blessed Virgin Mary—hung, flapping in the breeze, from the balcony railing. The overflow crowd now numbering more than 300,000 (Monsignor D'Arcy, rector of the North American

College on the Janiculum hill, said it was the largest he had ever seen in all his years in Rome and put it at 350,000) listened intently as the pope prefaced his blessing with a few spiritual thoughts in slightly accented but beautiful Italian: *"Prima di tutto, la parola, 'Alleluia!'"* he exclaimed ("First of all, the word, 'Alleluia!'"). While birds fluttered softly in the campanile and flew to and fro midst the statues of Christ and the apostles lining the top of the facade, John Paul II, in an appealing sing-song voice that seems to have been a mutual characteristic of our most recent popes, went on to extend his fervent felicitations for the day: *"Buona Pasqua! Buona Pasqua! Buona Pasqua!"* ("Happy Easter! Happy Easter! Happy Easter!") as the crowd roared back its heartfelt sentiments: *"Viva Il Papa! Viva Il Papa! Viva Il Papa!"*

Following the benediction the excited, and at this point ecstatic, throng slowly, very slowly, and almost reluctantly, began to disperse. As the sea of humanity reversed its tide and began to flow back toward the Tiber, large segments of it began to gather under the window of the pope's study overlooking the square from behind the right colonnade. After twenty minutes or so had passed, the faithful began to clap rhythmically and to call for the Holy Father. Then, magically, the curtains of the second window from the right on the top floor of the Apostolic Palace parted and suddenly there appeared a figure in white, waving to his flock below. A microphone was hastily set up for this unexpected appearance and over the speakers soon came the wonderful paternal voice again, thanking us for calling him and waiting so patiently for him. Then, after urging us all to enjoy Rome and the splendid Easter weather, he once again wished us all: *"Buona Pasqua! Buona Pasqua! Buona Pasqua!"* Waving, applauding and shouting to him affectionately, the people tried to persuade him to stay but he laughingly demurred with a single word, *"Basta,"* ("Enough") and slipped from view. It was a beautiful, unforgettable closing to a beautiful, unforgettable morning, a thrilling vignette that we shall recall again and again for the rest of our days.

Following this, my wife and I, in the company of a few friends, made our way to a favorite *trattoria* in the Trastevere for a light Easter lunch and some picture-taking. While I have had the intention of writing a small volume on the papacy for some time, it was there this afternoon, over a glass of Orvieto and a sandwich of *prosciutto e formaggio*, that I resolved to begin writing this very evening. And so, while I sit here at my desk and reflect on the inspiring and thrilling events of a few hours ago and wonder what John Paul II is doing with his Easter Sunday evening, I simultaneously wonder how Peter celebrated those early Easters, and where he resided in those turbulent times.

Surely, we know, there was no official papal residence back then. Indeed, Peter and his successors in the first three centuries of the Christian era often had to live wherever courageous friends would harbor them. Since Christianity had become a serious violation of Roman law, they had to be frequently on the run from the authorities, sometimes changing residence on minutes' notice to elude the imperial police. There were no out-door Easter Sunday Masses then, amidst such panoply and architectural grandeur. No wave upon wave of applause crashed round the feet of Peter. No *"Viva Il Papa"* serenaded him.

Rather, this is how it all began.

CHAPTER I

ORIGIN OF THE PAPACY

Nearly two millennia have passed since the reign of Caesar Tiberius, the second emperor of Rome. It was during the fifteenth year of Tiberius' occupancy of the throne that Jesus of Nazareth, Son of God and Savior of the world, ventured out beyond the city limits of his home town to begin his public ministry. His messianic message caused quite a stir throughout Galilee and Palestine in the province of Judea, but the Roman officials showed little or no reaction or concern. The Nazarene's growing following was dismissed as nothing more than another eccentric cult, much like those of Mithras and Isis and Cybele. Religious cults were certainly nothing new in the province of Judea or anywhere else in the Roman world. But as Christ supported his claims of divinity with wondrous and miraculous deeds, great numbers of provincials entered the ranks of his disciples.

From among these disciples twelve men were selected by Jesus as his apostles. On these he would rely to take his message to the corners of the known world. One of the twelve was the rugged Simon Bar-Jona, a Galilean fisherman. He had been influenced by his brother, Andrew, to embrace the teachings of Christ and to assist in their propagation.

At one gathering of the twelve, Jesus posed the question: "Who do you say that I am?" All failed to impress him with their responses except Bar-Jona who answered: "You are the Messiah, the son of the living God." More than the others, albeit at first imperfectly, Peter had grasped something of the reality of Christ's divinity.

"Blessed are you, Simon son of Jona," the Lord said to Peter. "No mere man has revealed this to you but my Father in heaven."

Thus the interviews for the greatest possible position on earth, that of vicar of Christ, had been conducted and concluded, for it was at this juncture that Jesus, recognizing a fiery zeal and total commitment on Peter's part, made him the head of his Church on earth. In less than a year Christ would die on the cross, rise from the tomb, and ascend to his Father in heaven. Now was the hour to reveal his choice to the twelve, a choice that was immediately accepted without challenge or reservation by Simon's colleagues.

The first papal election and coronation were then consumated in a terse, impromptu and modest ceremony by the Divine Master himself with these words: "You are 'Rock' and on this rock I will build my Church, and the gates of hell shall not prevail against it. I will entrust to you the keys of the kingdom of heaven. Whatever you declare bound on earth shall be bound in heaven, and whatever you declare loosed on earth shall be loosed in heaven" (Mt. 16:18).

Jesus had not only bestowed new and awesome responsibilities on Simon, he had also chosen for his vicar (i.e. representative) on earth a new name: Peter. It was the contemporary word for rock and this 'rock' was to be the unshakable foundation for Christ's universal Church, unshakable in the face of relentless and powerful assaults from the legions of hell.

After Jesus' resurrection from the dead and just prior to his ascension into heaven, the Lord reconfirmed Peter's apostolic primacy with the mandate: "Feed my lambs; feed my sheep" (Jn. 21:17). To extend Christ's own metaphor, Peter was without question the Shepherd of the flock. In the writings of the Evangelists any listing of the apostles always begins with Peter. Matthew, Mark, Luke and John were in this manner also supporting the primacy of Peter. Following our

Lord's ascension into heaven, Peter presided at a meeting of all the apostles in Jerusalem. On top of the agenda was the selection of a replacement (Matthias) for the apostate Judas. Peter himself had no doubt about his special role and, early on in all matters of the primitive Church, assumed a unique and unchallenged leadership. The papacy had begun. Peter had taken charge of the infant Church.

Nine days after Christ ascended to the right hand of the Father, Peter preached his first sermon under the influence of the Holy Spirit. Thousands assembled to hear the simple, faith-filled, fiery eloquence of the apostolic prince. Jerusalem was, on that occasion, bulging with devout pilgrims come to observe the Judaic rites of the Pentecostal season. Peter's sermon resulted in the conversion and baptism of three thousand, most of them Jews. Within weeks, the number had doubled. Upon completion of the festival many returned to their home lands eager to propagate the new faith. Those who remained in Jerusalem assisted the apostles in establishing a Christian community, the first parish, the first diocese of the Church. But the "gates of hell" here made their first futile attempt to "prevail against it."

Excitement begot commotion, commotion begot unrest, unrest begot friction between the believers and non-believers. Peter and the others were arraigned by the authorities on charges of disturbing the peace. They were ordered to cease and desist in their quest for converts. The Christian leaders respectfully replied that they could not obey the order, for they were obligated only to obeying the laws of God whenever they were in conflict with the laws of men.

While the pharisees and priests deliberated, Gamaliel, the outstanding legal mind of the day, advised his comrades to take no steps just yet. "Nothing is necessary on our part," the noted jurist suggested, "for if this movement be merely of man it will evaporate; but if it be of God, then there is nothing we can do about it anyway."

And so the accused were released. But they continued to be harassed and persecuted in their own home land. Because of this harassment the early administration of the Church had to be, for the most part, clandestine. But the preaching and teaching and quest for conversions went on, in the streets and squares, the fields and farms, and from house to house.

While the apostles were fully prepared, indeed eager, to give their lives for the Church, the cloak of martyrdom enfolded first a young man named Stephen who had been one of the first seven deacons ordained by them. These deacons were assigned to administer the Church's common fund for the poor. But in addition to these duties Stephen applied himself also to preaching. We are told that he received a Greco-Roman education and that he was fluent in Greek. He is reported to have directed his proselytizing efforts toward the Greek-language synagogues of his homeland. One of the congregations reported him to the Sanhedrin (in the time of Christ, the supreme court of the Jews) as a heretic.

At his trial, Stephen, unintimidated, charged his accusers with the murder of the Messiah. This so enraged the court that Stephen was sentenced to death by stoning. Saul of Tarsus, while he did not participate in the stoning, tacitly approved the execution. He could never have imagined at that moment that within a couple of decades he, too, would be martyred for the faith, and that by that time the Christian world would know and revere him as Paul of Tarsus, one of the greatest of all the apostles of Christ.

In spite of the oppressive tactics of the provincial political chiefs, the spread of Christianity continued. It was inevitable that the religion should eventually reach Rome, seat of imperial splendor to which all roads led and, in the Catholic world today, still do. And so it was that shortly after the crucifixion the new faith was swiftly carried to the Eternal City, for some among the crowds that had attended the Pentecostal sermon of Peter were Jewish pilgrims from Rome. Upon their return these inspired and enlightened converts formed the first Christian community in the capital.

While for some time after the death of Christ Peter lived and taught in Jerusalem and then in Antioch, he fully acknowledged that Rome was the center of the world stage. Thus he ultimately decided to move his episcopal chair to the imperial metropolis of the western world, the better to propagate the word of God. Some scholars place his arrival in Rome as early as the second year of the reign of Claudius, that is in 42 A.D., when he assumed the leadership of the growing Christian community there.

In the meantime, Saul of Tarsus, who had been one of the fiercest enemies of Christianity, had been converted to the cause while on his way to Damascus to prosecute Christians there. In a flash he had gone from antagonist to apostle, from bitter foe to most loyal defender of the faith. And in Acts 19:21 he echoes the sentiments of Peter regarding the new seat of Christianity with the words, "I must go on and see Rome." His arrival is placed at some time soon after Peter's.

Rome, then, was where Peter established his see (or diocese), evidently believing that here was where the Church was destined to grow, mature and spread. At Rome, Peter exercised his role as chief Shepherd of the flock. He was its first bishop. Though Peter traveled to various provinces to settle ecclesiastical and doctrinal disputes, he would return again and again to Rome, *Caput Mundi et Urbs Aeterna.* On one excursion from Rome he presided over the first Church council, held in Jerusalem and attended by all the other apostles, circa 51 A.D.

Throughout the Christian world, as Christ had hinted they would, there erupted divisions, heresies, and controversies, all of which saddened Peter and his successors very much. Many of these problems the bishop of Rome was called upon to resolve, for it was to Rome that the rest of the Christian world most frequently looked for a verdict in any moral or doctrinal dispute. Ecclesiastical problems of the greatest moment were often referred to Rome, the see of Peter, for final disposition. This dependency on Rome as the supreme arbiter in Church affairs was the basis for Augustine's phrase three centuries later, *"Roma locuta est, causa finita est."* ("Rome has spoken, the case is settled").

Thus ever since, the popes, as bishops of Rome, successors of Peter, heirs to his mandate from Christ, have served as the promoters of ecclesiastical unity and guardians of the faith during serious doctrinal controversies. In the Catholic Church to this day the powers conveyed to Peter by Jesus are held to be continued in full measure to his duly appointed successors in the Roman bishopric. The origin, then, of the primacy of Rome is to be found in the role of Peter in that diocese. And all of this is attested to in New Testament passages and in other contemporary writings.

Peter's early years in Rome were generally free from government harassment. The Christians were regarded then as harmless though fanatical cultists. Their rites and beliefs were in fact a source of amusement and fascination to the pagans. Though very little is recorded, there are some things we can say with relative certitude about the Galilean's pontificate. We know that he enjoyed an active and rewarding ministry in Rome. His duties included appointing, blessing and consecrating new bishops and deacons to help with the growing Church, visiting the sick, feeding the poor, burying the dead— all the corporal and spiritual works of mercy—as well as converting great numbers.

There is in Rome a little inn on the southeastern slope of the Aventine hill. It adjoins the ancient church of Santa Prisca and many scholars hold that the foundations of this church and inn belong to the first century house of the Jewish expatriates, Aquila and his wife Priscilla. They also contend that this couple, converts, hosted Peter and aided him in his ministry. Because of their knowledge of the city and their association with many Roman citizens the couple were able to help Peter to number, among his multitude of converts, nobles, military officers, political luminaries, and even relatives of the future emperor, Domitian.

Tradition also tells us that Peter at times resided crosstown on the Esquiline with a certain Senator Pudens and his family (where today on Via Urbano stands the church in honor of the senator's daughter, St. Pudentiana). A fragment of the wooden table on which Peter may have celebrated Mass, the first papal altar, is still preserved in this church. The wooden *cathedra* (Latin for chair) which Pudens gave to Peter for use as his episcopal throne serves now, according to an ancient tradition, in its bronze-gilt, baroque-ornamented state, as the backdrop for the high altar in St. Peter's basilica. Peter is said to have used this chair in the conduct of all important and official Church business. (Hence we have today the term *ex cathedra* applied to any occasion wherein the pope speaks "from the chair" and with infallibility on a matter of doctrine or morals.)

But this period of relative serenity during Peter's reign was to come to a sudden and horrible end in the year of our Lord 64. We can pinpoint the very day it happened: July 19. At dusk on that sultry summer day a fire broke out in the great chariot race track, the *Circus Maximus*. For more than a week the conflagration raged. And when it had finally spent itself, eleven of Rome's fourteen political precincts were but charred shadows of their former selves.

While the story of the emperor, the mentally unbalanced Nero, fiddling as Rome burned was probably apocryphal, the suspicion that he had ordered the fire was well-founded. His unhappiness with the hopeless jumble that was old Rome, his well-known grandiose plan for a new and splendorous capital, combined with all the grain and prefabricated tents and other essentials he was so quickly able to produce for the survivors fueled that suspicion. People suddenly recalled having seen, for weeks before the fire, ships in the nearby port of Ostia laden with grain, tent material and the like. It thus appeared to many that the machinery for both the fire and its aftermath had been set in motion a considerable time in advance.

The theory that Nero had indeed planned the fire gained wider and wider acceptance until one day the surviving populace, bereaved by the loss of their loved ones, distraught over the devastation to their property, embittered by their cruel fate, mobilized and began to march, infuriated, on the imperial palace. Informed of the ugly mood of the fast approaching mob, the by-now maniacal ruler—fearful that his vaunted Praetorian guard would be unable to stem the tide and save him—concocted a story of Christian arsonists being responsible for the holocaust. Stepping out onto his balcony he defused the assassination plans of the rabble with his demonic fabrication and in so doing provoked an hysterical witch hunt for all known Christians. The murderous notions of the masses were now unleashed upon those innocent and defenseless Christians who had survived the fire. (The fact that the death toll and material losses were proportionately high for the Christians as well was lost on the poisoned minds of their non-Christian neighbors.) Dragged into the ravaged, narrow, twisting streets, these early followers of Jesus —men, women, children—were knifed, stoned, pummeled or stomped to death.

Nero joined in the massacre with official condemnations of the entire Christian community and warrants for the arrest of all its members. Suddenly the practice of Christian worship, once viewed as a silly fetish, became a crime of the most serious dimension. This new ruling also put a new weapon of tyranny into the hands of the wicked Nero. He could now crush any out-spoken opponents to his regime merely by adding their names to the list of Christian suspects.

The awful persecutions of the Church had begun. And they would flare up and rage again and again, with varying degrees of intensity and savagery, for the next three centuries. This first pogrom continued for more than five years without letup and in the course of it Peter and Paul, as leaders of the tiny persecuted community, were proscribed as public enemies numbers one and two. Heartsick over the pagan bestiality toward their flock but unconcerned over the grave peril to their own lives, the two apostles went on daily with their sacred ministry. But they had to find new ways of eluding the police network closing in on them. They rarely stayed in the same residence for more than a couple of nights.

One persistent tradition has his dearest friends persuading Peter at length to flee from Rome to save his life. The story relates that Peter reluctantly departed from Rome one cold, dreary night by way of the Via Appia, the great highway south opened in 312 B.C., hoping to go to Brundisium, the Adriatic port, and from there to Greece. At the second mile marker Peter had an apparition of Christ who was walking toward the city. Astonished, with his poor heart pounding, the bishop of Rome inquired of Jesus: *"Quo vadis, Domine?"* ("Where are you going, Lord?"), to which the Savior responded: *"Venio Roman iterum crucifigi"* ("I am coming to Rome to be crucified all over again"). Sensing that Jesus was disappointed by his apparent abandonment of his flock, Peter wept bitterly, asked forgiveness, turned and re-entered the city to resume his ministry and eventually suffer his own crucifixion there.

Peter and Paul were arrested within days of each other. They were taken to Rome's municipal jail, the

Mamertine prison. There they suffered nine months of starvation and beatings in the foul subterranean section of the prison, the Tullianum dungeon. Word then came from the palace that the two apostles had been sentenced to hideous, violent deaths. Rome's first bishop was removed to the Circus of Nero on *Mons Vaticanus* where before a howling throng he was crucified (head down at his own request, since he considered himself unworthy to die in the fashion of his Master). Paul's father's provincial Roman citizenship entitled Paul to lesser final indignities. He was escorted by a small execution group to a place on the road to the sea, Via Ostiense, about a mile beyond the city walls where he was decapitated.

With the deaths of the two apostles the episcopate of Rome was vacant, the local church leaderless, the flock without a shepherd. It was the darkest hour for the followers of Christ since Golgotha. Fortunately, however, the members of the Roman community of believers were guided by the Holy Spirit in the selection of a successor to Peter. A certain Linus from Tuscany, who had worked closely with Peter over the years in Rome was soon after chosen bishop and the Church was on the move again. There was widespread belief that Linus had been handpicked by Peter to succeed him. Linus was thenceforth addressed, as were all other bishops at the time, as *Papas* (a Greek term of endearment for Father). In time the term would be reserved solely for the Holy Father, the bishop of Rome, whom all the other prelates recognized as *primus inter pares* (first among equals).

Thus the primacy of Peter was considered transferable to and conferable on his immediate successor and on every future occupant of the episcopal throne of Rome. Some of the apostles were still alive when this primacy was extended to Linus and they raised no objections to the idea. This tacit apostolic endorsement of Petrine succession led early theologians to embrace it also. From the very beginning then believers of all ranks and backgrounds held that all the statements in the New Testament alluding to Peter as head of the Church apply as well to all his successors; that the inheritors of Peter's see *(Petri sedes)* gain with their election to the pontificate all of his prerogatives.

This concept was reenforced and propagated throughout the early centuries. In the records of the Council of Nicea, for example, it is recorded that *"Ecclesia Romana semper habuit primatum"* ("the Church in Rome always holds primacy").

These then are the roots of the holy office of Supreme Pontiff, the institution of the papacy, the formal leadership of Christ's Church on earth. With respect to the papacy's influence and impact on civilization ever since, with respect to its sanctity, to its divine mandate, to its longevity, I think Mac Cauley said it most eloquently:

"There is not now, and there never was on this earth, a work of human policy so well deserving of examination as the Roman Catholic Church. The history of that Church joins together the two great ages of human civilization. No other institution is left standing which carries the mind back to the times when the smoke of sacrifice rose from the Pantheon, and when camels, leopards, and tigers bounded in the Flavian amphitheatre. The proudest royal houses are but of yesterday, when compared with the line of the Supreme Pontiffs. That line we trace back in an unbroken series from the pope who crowned Napoleon in the nineteenth century to the pope who crowned Pepin in the eighth; and far beyond the time of Pepin the august dynasty extends, till it is lost in the twilight of fable. The republic of Venice came next in antiquity. But the republic of Venice was modern when compared with the papacy; and the republic of Venice is gone, and the papacy remains. The papacy remains, not in decay, not a mere antique, but full of life and useful vigor. The Catholic Church is still sending forth to the farthest ends of the world missionaries as zealous as those who landed in Kent with Augustine, and still confronting hostile kings with the same spirit with which she confronted Attila. The number of her children is greater than in any former age. Her acquisitions in the New World have more than compensated for what she lost in the Old. Her spiritual ascendency extends over the vast countries which lie between the plains of the Missouri and Cape Horn, countries which a century hence may not improbably contain a population as large as that which now inhabits Europe. The members of her communion are certainly not fewer than a hundred and fifty millions; and it will be difficult to show that all other Christian sects united amount to a hundred and twenty millions. Nor do we see any sign which indicates that the term of her long dominion is approaching. She saw the commencement of all the governments and of all the ecclesiastical establishments that now exist in the world; and we feel no assurance that she is not destined to see the end of them all. She was great and respected before the Saxon had set foot on Britain, before the Frank had passed the Rhine, when Grecian eloquence still flourished in Antioch, when idols were still worshipped in the temple of Mecca. And she may still exist in undiminished vigor when some traveller from New Zealand shall, in the midst of a vast solitude, take his stand on a broken arch of London Bridge to sketch the ruins of St. Paul's."

Tu es Petrus !

CHAPTER II

THE EARLY POPES AND THE PERSECUTIONS

Pope Linus began and completed his reign in the same ugly climate that caused the brutal end to the reign of his predecessor. The second pontiff, like Peter, toiled in the vineyard of Christ under the dark, low-lying clouds of the rabble's fury, the clangor of arms, the emperor's whims. If the entire Christian community was the target of pagan violence, Linus was, to continue the metaphor, the bulls-eye. In their own savage way, the non-Christian citizenry and the government authorities were thus also attesting to the preeminence of the bishop of Rome, and the leadership position of the Roman see was the theme of documents still extant from the earliest times.

In the early 100's Ignatius, the bishop of Antioch, was sentenced to death by being devoured by beasts in the arena at Rome. While awaiting execution he wrote a series of letters regarding the new Church. In an epistle to the reigning pontiff, Alexander I, Ignatius acknowledged the special authority and factual preeminence of the community of believers in Rome over whom Alexander presided.

During the final decades of the second century the very learned and holy Irenaeus served as bishop of Lyons in Gaul (now southern France). He wrote: "All churches everywhere must agree with this Church (of Rome) because of its more effective leadership, since in it Christians everywhere have preserved intact the apostolic tradition."

This pagan and Christian recognition of the bishop of Rome as head of the universal Church made the chair of Peter a particularly perilous post, with the result that its first thirty three occupants suffered martyrdom. In the first centuries of the Church to accept "the awful keys," as Chesterton called them, was tantamount to signing one's own death warrant.

Though information about them is scanty, I shall return to a brief discussion of Linus and a number of his successors and their reigns toward the end of this chapter. In the meantime I should like to paint for you a picture of this "ugly climate" we mentioned above. For vis-a-vis the mobilized might of an intolerant Rome, the true greatness and inspiring saintliness, the deep faith and burning zeal, the endless courage and unwavering determination of the early pontiffs is best illustrated.

After the great fire Christianity was outlawed. Tertullian the historian tells us that the simple terse edict of Nero was: *"Christiani non sint!"* ("Let there be no Christians!"). The maniacal ruler had hoped to exterminate the new cult, which he saw as a threat to the polytheistic state religion and consequently to the very foundations of mighty imperial Rome, with wholesale slaughter. The slaughter took various forms: decapitation, crucifixion, burning at the stake, being devoured by wild animals.

There is ample documentation available on this matter, too. The writer Tacitus, whose boyhood was passed in Rome during the time of Nero, states in his history textbook, *Annales:* "Christ, the author of that name (Christian), was executed in the reign of Tiberius by the procurator Pontius Pilate; but, repressed temporarily, the deadly superstition erupted again, not only throughout Judea, the source of this fanaticism, but even throughout the city (Rome), to which all atrocities and shamefulness flow and where they prosper." In addition to this testimony regarding the crucifixion of

Christ, Tacitus provides us with the pagan attitude toward Christianity. He calls the Christian faith "a depraved, excessive superstition," "the scourge of the human race."

His two fellow historians of the first century were of identical view. Pliny refers to Christianity as "a deadly superstition," while Suetonius' phrase is, "a novel and wicked superstition."

In volume XV of the *Annales*, Tacitus deals specifically with the various forms of execution: "Hoping to squash rumors that he was the arsonist, Nero wrongly blamed those fanatics commonly called Christians and had them punished in the most hideous ways. Many of these Christians, hated by all decent people for their decadent ways, were arrested. Some who confessed also provided enough information to convict vast multitudes not only for arson but for hating humanity. In their deaths they were made sport of, being pursued and devoured by ravenous dogs, nailed on crosses, burned alive. The emperor used his own gardens for these spectacles. There was a backlash of public sympathy for these Christians who deserved to be made an example of, however, for Nero's ferocity was so insatiable."

But, alas, Nero had badly miscalculated as did many of his successors. Rather than drown the infant religion, the blood of the martyrs drenched it in glory and nurtured its seed. The more martyrdom, Tertullian tells us, the more eagerness there was on the part of the non-Christians to find out what there was about Christianity that inspired the ultimate sacrifice. And they often liked what they found, for Christianity's promise rendered the old pagan worship empty of any substance and meaning. Great numbers of conversions were the result. With his barbaric attempts to crush it, the emperor was thus unwittingly, but very effectively, contributing to the propagation of the Church.

Of course, the real reasons for the spread of Christianity were the divine assistance promised it by Jesus ("Behold I am with you all days, even to the end of the world"), and the burning zeal of the clergy and the laity. Over the next three centuries, despite the bloodbaths known as the persecutions, Christianity was to flourish throughout the Mediterranean world: in Italy, from Asia Minor and Greece in the east to Spain in the west; from Egypt and North Africa in the south to Gaul at the northernmost frontier of the empire.

Gamaliel's evaluation was vindicated. Since the new religion was truly of God, there was nothing man could do to suppress it. And it has been vindicated in all the centuries since. Even occasional wicked popes have not been able to block the forward march of Christ's Church on earth.

Upon the death of Nero in 69 A.D., Rome was plunged into political chaos and the next twelve months would see four men ascend to the purple, the first three of whom would fall to assassins. The fourth, Vespasian, now had enough problems restoring some civil sanity and governmental stability without taking on the Christian issue. Consequently the persecutions eased. In his decade-long reign he focused his attention on the Jewish unrest in the province of Judea. His successor and son, Titus, spent his abbreviated reign, 79–81, also suppressing the Jews. But the uneasy peace the Christians had known was to be shattered under Titus' successor and brother, Domitian. This merciless despot fomented, among the pagan rabble, outbreak after outbreak of anti-Christian violence from 81 to 96 A.D.

After these outrages were stopped by the kindly old emperor, Nerva (96–98), the Christians lived, for a time, relatively free of harassment. In fact, many emperors in the course of the empire's remaining four centuries appeared to want no part of abusing Christ's followers. But at the same time while not wanting Christian blood on their hands some of these rulers would weakly yield to public pressures and political exigencies whenever the pagan cry was raised, for one reason or another, "Enforce the law! The Christians to the lions!"

Proof of one monarch's mixed emotions on the matter can be found in an exchange of letters, in the year 111, between Pliny, provincial governor of Bithynia in Asia Minor, and the emperor Trajan. The governor, seeking his master's counsel and a vote of confidence, seems to agonize in his letter at being on the spot with respect to enforcing unjust laws upon people guilty of nothing more than the practice of their religion:

> "It is customary for me, Lord" he begins, "to refer to you all matters about which I have any doubt. For who is better able to direct my uncertainty or instruct me in my ignorance? I have never been to trials of Christians. Thus I know little about how to proceed. I should like to know whether there is any distinction made on the basis of age or whether persons, however young, are dealt with in no way differently from their elders; whether pardon is granted for repentance or not; whether punishment is given for the name 'Christian' itself even if it be free from crimes or for the crimes generally associated with the name.
>
> "Meanwhile, this has been my procedure: when people are brought before me as Christians I ask them if they embrace Christianity. If they say, 'Yes,' I ask them a second and third time, threatening punishment. When they persist, I order them executed, for if nothing else they deserve to be punished on account of their intransigence. In the case of Roman citizens so charged I have them sent back to Rome for arraignment."

Pliny goes on to state that the whole messy situation has deteriorated into a witch hunt with anonymous charges and tips winding up on his desk. He continues:

> "As for those who denied any link with Christianity, I tested them further by having them call upon our gods with incense and wine and venerate your image and denounce Christ. They tell me that true Christians can be compelled to do none of these things. These I acquit.

Even those who admit to having once been Christians hasten to point out that their only guilt was gathering on appointed days at dawn to chant hymns to Christ, binding themselves by oath not to commit some crimes, but rather to refrain from acts such as theft and adultery and reneging on debts and betraying one another. Part of the ceremony included taking the most ordinary and harmless food. To be honest all I can find wrong with them is a stupid, immoderate superstition. . . . But I am optimistic that large numbers of them can be rehabilitated if an opportunity is given for repentance."

Pliny's discomfort is obvious in his attempts to soft-peddle the 'crime' of being a Christian, alluding to the liturgy as mere group-singing and the Eucharist as "the most ordinary and harmless food (bread and wine)." He will do his duty and enforce the anti-Christian statutes but he'd rather the whole problem would blow away. He hopes that Trajan will relieve him of this personal Gethsemane.

The emperor's distaste for and discomfort over punishing the Christians can be clearly seen in his low-key rescript: "You have followed the proper procedure, my dear Secundus (Trajan's affectionate name for his good friend Pliny, i.e., the Second; quite like our "Junior"), in examining the cases of those reported to you as Christians. For there can be no general rule which has, as it were, a consistent pattern."

The next lines are the key to Trajan's policy and reveal his reluctance to harass the Christian community further: "They must not be hunted down. If they should be turned in and found guilty, naturally they would have to be punished. But with this proviso, that a person who denies that he is a Christian and has made this clear in actual practice, i.e., by worshipping our gods, although suspect because of his past behavior, should obtain amnesty as the result of his repentance." (Trajan here empowers Pliny and all provincial governors to grant *venia*, i.e. pardon, to Christians who meet the pagan worship test.) "But anonymous charges certainly ought to have no validity whatever. For not only does it set a very bad precedent but also is not in accord with the spirit of our age," all of which is one grand euphemism for: "Enforce the law when the populace is watching your every move, but try to avoid being boxed into such a situation in the first place."

To his discredit, however, the emperor, when forced to a choice, appeared to opt for the *Scylla* of Christian blood over the *Charybdis* of civil unrest.

In like manner Trajan's heir to the throne, Hadrian, commiserated with one of his provincial governors in the latter's abhorrence of maltreatment of the Christians. Responding to Minucius Fundanus, successor to Serenus Granianus who had registered strong disapproval of any maltreatment, Hadrian wrote: "I received a letter from your very worthy predecessor. It is a letter much deserving of your attention to put an end to vexatious suits and to give no encouragement to informers to carry on their trade of malice. So, then, whenever your people have anything to say against the Christians let them prove it in public, so that the Christians can defend themselves in an open court of law. You are duty-bound to hear them in a judicial manner solely. For it is your responsibility, not the mob's, to judge the merits of any case. If, therefore, the informer shall prove that the Christians have violated the law, punish them strictly according to the dimension of the crime. And on the other hand, if you find the charge to be malicious and empty be sure to punish that then."

Antoninus Pius who came to the throne next and Marcus Aurelius right after him, both endorsed the Trajanic-Hadrianic policy as the best way to solve a dilemma of conscience. While Aurelius, a fundamentally decent man, was reigning, a ferocious pagan attack upon the faithful took place in the Roman province of Gaul. The year was 177. Some Christians were killed on the spot by the rioters. All the rest were hauled off to the provincial tribunal, charged with all manner of heinous crime. Instructions soon arrived from the distressed emperor back in Rome ordering the governor to throw out all other charges and try the Christians only by the Trajan rescript, i.e. condemn to death all those who unyieldingly profess the faith; exculpate those who acquiescently renounce it.

Not all future occupants of the throne of Rome, however, would have such qualms about abusing the Christians. With various degrees of intensity the persecutions would flare up now and again when pagan animosity and civil unrest rose to the breaking point. The Christians were despised for a number of reasons. They were held to be bigots, subversives and even cannibals (this last category stemmed from Nero's warped interpretation of Christ's admonition to his followers: "Unless you eat my flesh and drink my blood you shall not have life in you"). They were accused, too, of hurting the economy by weakening the state religion. Several small industries were predicated upon the practice of the pagan rites. Vendors of sacrificial lambs, dealers of fodder for the same animals, priests of Jupiter, all particularly abhorred the Christians and contributed vigorously to the anti-Christian mood in the Roman world.

This mood drove Christian worship literally underground. In World War II, much of London's population was spared nocturnal annihilation at the hands of Nazi bombardiers by the city's network of underground railtracks. At the height of the Nazi blitz the subways did double duty as bombshelters. At the height of all the persecutions, the Christians used their network of underground cemeteries, the catacombs, as clandestine places of worship. Deep in the bowels of the Roman countryside, the dampness of these corridors, with their walls lined from floor to ceiling with the niches of the dead, the faithful renewed the simple but sacred ritual of the Last Supper. The eerie darkness was broken only by the gentle flickering of their *luminaria* (tiny oil lamps), the profound silence only by their religious prayers and chants.

Though these cemeteries, as all others at the time, were protected against desecration and intrusion by the statute, *Violatio sepulcri,* several emperors broke the law and conducted raids upon worshipping groups. Documents still extant tell of Roman troops breaking in on the sacred rites, slaughtering prelates and priests, men and women, boys and girls. But because the network of galleries was so vast (containing the remains of hundreds of thousands of the faithful) and so labyrinthine (twisting four, five, and even six levels deep for hundreds of miles around the walls of Rome) the formal worship of Christ went on. Even some popes suffered martyrdom in the raids. We know from a letter by Cyprian, the saintly bishop of Carthage, that Pope Sixtus II "was put to death in the cemetery on the eighth day before the Ides of August (Aug. 6, 258) and with him four deacons." In October of that same year Cyprian himself, while celebrating Mass in the cemetery of Saint Callistus, was beheaded by government troops.

These "catacombs" (from the Greek *kata* meaning down, and *kymbas* meaning hollows, "down in the hollows"), as a result, took on an additional sacredness and a number of early popes elected to be buried there where they could "lie side by side with the martyrs of the faith" instead of on the Vatican hill where Peter and most of the other pontiffs still lie in rest. Tomb inscriptions written in Greek tell us that the following third-century popes, all saints, were entombed in one chamber in the underground cemetery of Saint Callistus: Pontian, Anterus, Fabian, Lucius I, Stephen I, Sixtus II, Dionysius, Felix I and Euthychian. In other crypts in the same cemetery were placed the bodies of Popes Caius I, Eusebius, and Melchiades.

Since so many popes, bishops and martyrs were buried in them, the catacombs, long centuries after the final persecutions ended, remained a focal point of Christian pilgrimage. Abandoned and pretty much forgotten during the Middle Ages, many of them have in the past two centuries been rediscovered and opened to the public and to pilgrimages again.

In any discussion of the Christian persecutions there is bound to be a listing of the worst ones. Under Nero, Domitian, Trajan (despite his ambivalence) and Marcus Aurelius (despite his, too) there were severe pogroms. In the early 200's Septimius Severus conducted an especially savage campaign against the practitioners of the growing cult. There are written accounts of armed soldiers breaking into homes where Christian prayer sessions or instructions were taking place, arresting all participants, hauling them off to arraignment in some kangaroo court. After a sham trial the accused were often murdered in one of the forms of execution cited previously.

Several other third-century emperors came down hard on the Christians. We know that under Maximinus in 235 Pope Pontian was exiled to the mines of Sardinia and died a violent death there. It was, according to the same reports, Pope Fabian who had his remains brought back to Rome and entombed in the Callistus cemetery. Decius from 249 to 251 abused the Christian community; Valerian, from 257 to 260.

In between some of the persecutions the Christians enjoyed brief respites of relative tranquility. For example, Valerian's son, Gallienus, in 268 suddenly put a stop to the outrages and granted amnesty to imprisoned Christians and even restored confiscated churches and cemeteries to the community. Christians at this time even gained some new privileges, e.g. eligibility to hold public office, dispensation from the pagan rituals. The last quarter of the third century was in fact comparatively quiet. Sadly however there was a gathering storm with the worst to come. Under Diocletian, the very devil himself, the Christians were to be brutalized beyond description from 300 to 305. Pope Marcellinus was decapitated and his body ordered to be left lying in the streets for a month to terrify the faithful. Christians' homes were destroyed, their cemeteries violated, their books burned, their bodies brutalized, and ultimately their lives taken. The Christians were being blamed for all of Rome's many problems. Pagan priests advised the butcher-emperor that Christian worship had so incensed the Olympic deities that Jupiter *et al* were, as a result, raining down their awesome wrath upon the city and the empire. But the long, dark night for Christianity was soon to give way to a new dawn which was to bring with it mixed blessings.

In the year 312 A.D. there was a fierce battle for the throne between Maxentius and Constantine. The latter, with his powerful legions, came sweeping down from the north on the ancient Via Cassia. Reaching the Mulvian Bridge which spans the Tiber on the eastern end of the city of Rome, Constantine had a vision of a fiery cross in the sky encircled with the words: *In hoc signo vinces* (In this sign you will conquer).

Confused, he nonetheless had his soldiers paint the symbol on their shields and helmets and ordered it to be the army's standard. The following day he crossed the bridge, routed Maxentius' forces, and seized the throne. He credited Christ with his victory and eventually embraced the new faith. Constantine thereafter returned all confiscated property to the Christian community and even ordered great basilicas to be raised over the tombs of the two apostles, Peter and Paul. He donated to the reigning pope, Miltiades, for use as a papal residence and Church headquarters, the property of the Laterani family on the southwestern end of the city. With few exceptions the Lateran was to be the papal residence for the next thousand years. On certain festive occasions the popes went over to celebrate rites in St. Peter's and would sometimes stay in the humble papal residence adjoining the basilica.

In 313 Constantine met in the northern city of Milan with his co-emperor Licinius and issued an edict granting total freedom of worship and full citizenship rights to Christians throughout the empire. This proclamation, known as the Edict of Milan, signaled that the long-animity of the Christians had culminated in a triumph of sorts for the Church and especially for the papacy.

Christianity even became the state religion. In the centuries to follow, Christ was to enjoy the veneration once reserved for Jupiter; Mary, the special status once afforded to the pagan goddess, Venus; the popes, the homage once afforded to the emperors. The blood of untold thousands of martyrs had proven to be the elixir of life for the Church. Reminders of Christianity's victory ornamented the city. Where once stood hundred feet high monumental columns bearing the images of Trajan and Marcus Aurelius were now statues of Peter and Paul. The renowned pagan temple, the Pantheon, which originally honored all the gods of paganism, was now a Christian shrine honoring all the martyrs of the Church.

I have tried thus far in this chapter to portray as vividly as I might the awful environment in which the early popes reigned. Though we know little of the circumstances of their elections to the papacy and not much more about their reigns, what scanty information there is available on the matter I should like at this point to pass along to you.

The first roster and biographies of the popes were compiled by Saint Irenaeus at the end of the second century. The *Liber Pontificalis* written in the sixth century became another important source of papal information.

We are rather certain that Linus, the second pontiff, reigned from 67 to 76, that he was martyred and that he was buried near Peter on Vatican hill. A tradition persists that Linus, following the admonition of St. Paul in his letter to the Corinthians (1 Cor. 4:2–16), initiated the regulation that women must wear a hat or some other head covering when attending the sacred rites.

Unlike Peter, Linus was not a Jew but an Italian from Tuscany.

Cletus, the third pope was a Roman who led the Church from 76 to 88. Martyred under Domitian, he too was laid to rest near the tomb of Peter.

About Clement I, 88–97, the fourth bishop of Rome, there is available considerable material. Scholars have long believed that he was a Jew because of the many scholarly allusions to the Old Testament that punctuate his epistles. We also know that he lived just a few hundred yards south of the Colosseum and that he used his residence for the celebration of the liturgy. Parts of his house still exist and serve as foundations for the basilica built in his honor during the Constantinian era, the ruins of which in turn support the beautiful church erected by Pope Pascal II in 1108 and which remains to our day in a marvelous state of preservation.

We know, too, that Clement was a close friend of both Peter and Paul and that he had been ordained a priest by Peter. In a letter to the diocese of Corinth, Clement firmly asserted his primacy. He stepped in to rule on a serious doctrinal dispute. One of the apostles, John, was still alive and living not too far from Corinth but evidently chose not to intervene and by thus bowing to the bishop of Rome lent still another example of apostolic support to the theory of Petrine succession. Clement is said to have suffered exile to the Crimea under Trajan and to have been martyred there by drowning. According to tradition his body was recovered by Saint Cyril, apostle of the Slavs, in the ninth century and translated back to Rome where it now reposes under the altar of the Basilica of St. Clement.

Clement's successor, Evaristus (97–105), was a Greek from Bethlehem who subdivided the dioceses into districts known as parishes. He, too, was martyred and lies buried near Peter.

Alexander I (105–115) made some additions to the prayers of the Mass. He is buried on the Via Nomentana near the site of his martyrdom by decapitation.

For the next decade (115–125) the Church was shepherded by Sixtus I whose liturgical contribution was the beautiful prayer, the *Sanctus* ("Holy, holy, holy, Lord God of Hosts, Heaven and earth are full of your glory, Hosanna in the highest!"). He also forbade the laity in those times to handle the sacred vessels used in the celebration of the Mass.

A Greek monk, Telesphorus, succeeded Sixtus from 125 to 136. The *Liber Pontificalis* states that he regulated the Lenten fast.

The ninth pontiff was Hyginus, son of a noted Athenian philosopher. Martyrdom ended his four-year reign (136–140).

Pius I (140–155) came to the chair of Peter from northern Italy. He is remembered for his excommunication of the Gnostic leader, Marcion, and great numbers of his followers. Pius, who established two of Rome's oldest parish churches, St. Pudentiana and St. Praxedes, was martyred and is buried on the Vatican.

May I recomend at this point, for the reader eager for more readable biographical material on these popes, two fine works both published by Van Nostrand Co., of New York: *Popes Through the Ages* by Joseph S. Brusher, S.J. and *The Papacy—A Brief History* by James A. Corbett.

In our next chapter we shall trace the growth of the papacy in the Middle Ages focusing on several individual pontiffs whom we feel did much to shape the institution as we know it today.

Ubi Petrus, Ibi Ecclesia!

CHAPTER III

THE MIDDLE AGES

After three hundred years of bloodshed, Christianity emerged scarred but triumphant over her imperial tormentors. In fact, by the last quarter of the fourth century her bitter foe, paganism, had been proscribed and Christianity established as the official State religion. Great houses of worship began to soar to the heavens across the landscape of the intramural city. A new age for the Church and for the papacy had begun.

Unfortunately, however, Constantine's generosity to and protection of the Church and the Supreme Pontiff came with some strings attached, for the emperor could not completely detach himself from the conventional, all-domineering role of the office of emperor. His imperial majesty was inclined to rule over everything, Church included, in the Roman world. This precedent of governmental control over Church affairs extended on into the fifth century resulting in the following contradiction. While the primacy of the bishop of the Rome diocese was fully recognized and defended by the hierarchy, the clergy, the laity, and the civil authorities, the emperor reserved the right to overrule the pontiff. Contemporaneous with this string of strong-willed emperors was a string of weak-willed popes, resulting in a period of what papal historians like to call *"Caesaropapism."*

This governmental meddling in Church matters was probably a necessary evil, since the popes of the time appeared unable to live with or without their imperial 'benefactors.' With the Roman world long since split into an eastern and western empire and the stronger of the emperors reigning from distant Constantinople, the Supreme Pontiff's freedom was constantly imperiled and menaced by northern European monarchs. What security the popes did enjoy then could be traced to Roman imperial patronage.

At times this arrangement would result in grave damage to what there was of papal prestige. For one example, some excommunicated heretics would circumvent papal authority and appeal directly to the emperor for reinstatement. For another, some who aspired to hierarchial posts would travel the same route. Caesaropapism ultimately impaired Church unity and reduced the occupant of the throne of Peter to a mere figurehead.

As the shadows of the fifth century lengthened, this state of affairs continued. Even after the last western emperor was overthrown in 476 by Odoacer (first barbarian ruler of Italy) the popes were still often manipulated in ecclesiastical and spiritual issues by the Byzantine emperors. To the everlasting credit of Odoacer it must be pointed out that he, though a follower of the Arian heresy, was far more humane and decent to the Holy Father, Pope St. Simplicius (468–483), than the last bunch of decadent, incompetent western emperors had been.

But even Odoacer's tolerance did not alter the fact that the papal elections of the time were usually chaotic travesties. Often the election results were challenged by dissident bishops, many times overturned by disapproving emperors. One Arian emperor, the Ostrogoth, Theodoric (493–526), rendered verdicts in several contested elections. As long as the western empire had lasted, popes had to be confirmed by the Roman rulers. After the fall of the west, the eastern emperors reserved the right to confirm.

This unfortunate environment notwithstanding, the popes had been making some organizational progress for the Church. Ever so gradually, but surely, the hierarchy was becoming more structured. The various political divisions of the empire had provided diocesan lines. Roman provinces consisted of municipalities, one of which was designated as the seat of the provincial government. A bishop of such a provincial capital was *ipso facto* archbishop with supremacy over the others. All the prestigious imperial cities were archbishoprics, viz. Rome, Constantinople, Antioch, Alexandria, Jerusalem and Carthage. Among these Rome still enjoyed primacy and was deferred to in particularly controversial or important issues. Back in 381 the Council of Constantinople had declared that the bishop of Constantinople shall have the prerogative of honor after the bishop of the Petrine diocese, i.e. Rome.

But as the eastern capital's prestige increased, Rome's decreased, both governmentally and ecclesiastically. At a council held in Chalcedon in the middle of the next century, eastern bishops legislated broader jurisdiction and extraordinary powers to the archbishop of the diocese of Constantinople. Alarmed at this trend and pointing out that political eminence or lack of same had no bearing on Rome's position as the repository of ultimate and supreme Church authority, Pope St. Leo I (440-461) vehemently repudiated the bishops' course of action. The Roman pontiff took pains to persuade the eastern prelates that it was Peter himself who decided that the Eternal City would be the *Sedes Ecclesiae*, and that this fact was immutable. The bishops, awed by the confidence and the certitude exuded by the Holy Father, soon after acquiesced.

It must be pointed out here, lest the reader be misled, that despite the burden of Caesaropapism, some popes even before Leo had asserted themselves rather strongly in certain important Church matters. It was Pope St. Sylvester I (314-335) who endorsed the verdicts of the Council of Nicea (325) in the Church's struggle against the dangerous and epidemic heresy known as Arianism. The Council fathers had issued a fiery denunciation of

Arius, a priest from Alexandria who insisted that Christ was not truly divine. From this assembly came the Nicene Creed ("... (Jesus) is God from God, Light from Light, true God from true God, begotten, not made, one in Being with the Father"). This was the first ecumenical, i.e. universal, council of the Church, not a mere synod or national conference. Thus all the doctrinal might and prestige the Church could summon (a worldwide meeting of the hierarchy with the total backing of the throne of Peter) was wielded in the defense of truth.

Pope Sylvester, a Roman, was also very instrumental in the structuring of the post-persecution Church. Under his guidance the building of St. Peter's and the Lateran basilica, St. John's, was carried out. He also saw to the erection of other splendid churches and in fact lies entombed beneath one of them on the Via Salaria.

Another strong fourth-century pontiff was Julius I (337-352). With the strife between the eastern and western hierarchies threatening to evolve into a full scale schism, Julius, profoundly concerned, had his delegates conduct a council at Sardica (343). As might be expected, the emperors, at this time two sons of Constantine, Constans in the west and Constantius in the east, involved themselves deeply in the controversy. Constans was strongly pro-orthodoxy while his dissident brother favored Arianism. Political intrigue and vicissitudes and threats notwithstanding, Julius went courageously ahead and overruled the eastern bishops' excommunication of the priest Athanasius. The latter was the inexorable defender and protector of orthodoxy and the Roman ideology and an immovable obstacle to the Arian cause. Once again a council had underscored the preeminence of Rome as the eternal see of Peter. Unfortunately, however, the council had fallen short of its principal goal of arresting the heresy, for the Arian disciples stiffened their resistance to this attempted *coup de grâce* and continued to spread their heretical views throughout the eastern world.

After Julius' exoneration of Athanasius, the bishop of Rome would forever more be looked to as the chief justice by clerics and prelates condemned in their own lands by fellow religious. Julius' reign also saw impressive growth in the Christian community of Rome, despite great political and ecclesiastical upheavals.

Emperor Constans lost his life in a rebellion. His brother Constantius then tried for a *rapprochement* between the Arian and Orthodox communities. To reconcile the eastern bishops with Peter's chair, Constantius asked Liberius to rescind Julius' ruling on Athanasius. Angered and frustrated by papal intransigence, he had Pope Liberius (352–366) exiled to Thrace. Eventually a compromise was reached—the facts of which are for the most part lost to us—and Liberius returned to Rome. Santa Maria Maggiore, one of the four great Roman basilicas, was erected under the direction of this long-suffering pope.

Another fourth-century pontiff, St. Damasus I (366–384), devoted much of his energy to propagating and promulgating the theory of Petrine succession, emphasizing Peter's mandate from the Lord himself. In the long rule of this Roman-born pope, the Church enjoyed a stretch of peace and harmony and progress. Then late in his reign new heresies erupted, one rejecting the divinity of the Holy Spirit. A writer of some distinction, Damasus is remembered for the eloquent epitaphs he had engraved on the tombs of the martyrs down in the catacombs. Here was indeed an intellectual giant and a saintly man who contributed enormously to the status of the papacy.

During this century, two colossal Church figures, both bishops, emerged who often towered over the popes themselves. Ambrose of the important diocese of Milan and Augustine of Hippo were blessed with abundant personal magnetism and charisma. Both had declared their support of the primacy of Rome. Both were acclaimed for their sanctity soon after their deaths.

The fifth century saw the various pontiffs advance a policy of greater centralization of supreme power in the Roman see. At this time also, the popes declared the right of every Christian to appeal to Rome for adjudication of any Church matter. And all around the Christian world papal legates and apostolic vicars were carrying out pontifical policies.

From early on in this century the Roman pontiffs were busy extinguishing the flames of heresy. In 401 Innocent I was elevated to the pontificate. This future saint, born in a village outside of Rome, spent a good part of his sixteen-year reign combatting the Pelagian heresy, which was epidemic in Jerusalem and Carthage. Innocent's condemnation of the heresy inspired Augustine's immortal phrase: *"Roma locuta est; causa finita est"*.

With political instability on the rise, with the weak-willed Honorius on the throne, with Alaric and his Visigoths storming the mighty walls of old Rome, the people turned more and more to the Holy Father for civil as well as spiritual leadership. This paved the way for succeeding popes to take on more and more secular duties.

In 440, imperial weakness thrust Pope St. Leo I, the Great, into the roll of defender of Rome against barbaric intrusions. Soon he was actually more influential in affairs of state than the emperor himself. And all the while he strongly resisted government meddling in Church matters. It was Leo who in 452 fearlessly advanced to the city gates to intercept Attila the Hun and successfully dissuade him from any further violence against Rome and Italy. A scant three years later, Leo boldly confronted the approaching Vandals led by the wily general Genseric. In the name of heaven he exorted them to spare the Eternal City. These northern vultures, however, encouraged by imperial incompetence, barged in and sacked the city. In keeping with their promise to the pope, though, they did not burn nor maim nor kill. Their sole interest was in material goods.

Leo had neither sought nor wanted the mantle of Peter. Upon his election he was plunged into despair over this "burden to shudder at." Apparently such shuddering has been shared by many of the bishops of Rome. Interestingly enough, the summer he died, Pope Paul VI touched on this very theme in an address at the papal residence in Castel Gandolfo outside Rome. There he told a throng of pilgrims that "the responsibilities of the papacy frighten me. The nature of the papacy evades our capacities to understand: 'Who is Peter?' 'Who is the pope?' I cannot answer. The question is greater than us and our ability to comprehend divine matters."

Despite Leo's Herculean efforts this continued to be a period of awful political unrest, with the Church itself in convulsion from heresies and internal division. One of Leo's successors, Pope Gelasius I (492–496), outraged by the meddling in ecclesiastical affairs of the eastern emperor, Anastasius, made clear his view on papal authority in an epistle to the throne, an excerpt of which we present here: "Please don't construe as arrogance what is a duty according to the divine plan. There are two powers, your august highness, which govern our planet: the holy authority of the supreme pontiffs and the power of the imperial thrones. And though you preside over man through your office, in matters divine even you must bow piously to those of us charged with the salvation of man."

Rome was a moribund city now but the papacy continued to advance in strength and influence even if it had to do so via the one step backward, two forward route. When Justinian seized hapless and helpless Italy in the middle 500's, the city of Rome was reduced to a veritable ghost town. The population, somewhere between one and two million at the height of imperial times, now stood at but a few thousand. Upon the death of Justinian, the Lombards swept down from the north and carved the boot-shaped peninsula into so many duchies. Meanwhile, the few hardy Roman citizens who had stood by their tragic city were left unprotected and ignored by the Byzantine, i.e. the eastern empire's, leaders. They thus looked to the only surviving institution, the Church, for help against their various enemies, particularly the ravenous Lombards. The pope was the one they turned to first.

For long stretches in the turbulent century, however, the Church actually played a comparatively minor role in the truly important affairs of the western world. The episcopates of many nations had aligned themselves closely with their sovereigns and made a point of declaring their detachment from Rome. This separatism was attacked and terminated under one of the true giants among the couple of hundred successors of Peter, Gregory the Great. This pontiff moved swiftly and decisively to end the autonomy of the various dioceses and to rehabilitate the prestige and influence of the Holy See. About this pope, born in Rome in 540, we know a great deal, which is attributable in no small measure to the fact that nearly 900 of his letters are still extant. In some of them we learn that throughout his boyhood Rome was under seige from first this barbaric army, then that one. We learn too of the unspeakable atrocities of those decades, how senators and plebeians alike were murdered in cold blood, how the cruel Lombards laid waste the city, leveled churches and monasteries, and ravaged the farms.

In one letter, Gregory relates the details of the Lombard massacre of forty Christians for their refusal to pay homage to the devil. This same age saw the Lombards conduct human sacrifices to their gods with Christian peasants as the victims. Through Gregory's writings we learn, too, of the famine and plagues that further devastated the populace of Rome and central Italy. Gregory had seen his parents, people of wealth and position, give up all their worldly goods and even each other to enter the religious life. The future pope's father, Gordianus, a Roman senator, devoted himself to working with the poor while his mother, Sylvia, spent the rest of her days as a cloister ascetic. She was in later times canonized and her feast is celebrated on the third of November.

After completion of his law studies Gregory entered public service and rose to the highest civil office in the city, that of prefect. The virtuous young man had hoped to help the beleaguered Roman people through public office. Eventually, though, he came to view his efforts there as futile and sought a higher commitment. He renounced the secular life, divested himself of his material goods, made his Caelian hill mansion into a monastery where he wished to spend the rest of his days helping by prayer and sacrifice the people whom he felt he failed to help significantly through political office.

Under Pope Pelagius II (579–590), Gregory was obliged to leave the monastic life and utilize his political skills and persuasive eloquence in the service of the papal diplomatic corps. For six years he labored in such vineyards as the imperial court in Constantinople. His absence was keenly felt by the people of Rome who dearly loved and leaned on him. In 586 Gregory rejoiced over his recall to Rome.

In the autumn rains of 589 the Italian countryside was gravely threatened. The city of Rome, cursed by a malarial Tiber River, lay in the grips of the resulting plague. Among the thousands of lives claimed by the plague was that of the Holy Father himself. In those days the choice of a new Roman bishop still resided with the clergy and people. With swiftness and unanimity they turned to the holy monk and longtime benefactor of the city, Gregory. Confirmation, however, of a newly chosen pontiff still was the exclusive right of the emperor, and to him Gregory fervently appealed that his election not be validated. Emperor Maurice wisely rejected the holy and humble man's entreaty whereupon Gregory reluctantly but courageously ascended the papal throne, determined to use to the fullest whatever power might accrue to him for the benefit of the masses, particularly the sick and the impoverished.

His was a glorious and memorable reign which saw the conversion of Arian Spain, the beginning of the conversion of England, the institution of the solemn liturgical song of the Church which bears his name, *Gregorian Chant,* and the easing of suffering among the Roman people including the long-tormented Jewish community.

As pope he began to sign his correspondence with the phrase, *"Servus Servorum Dei"* ("Servant of the Servants of God"), a practice retained to this very day by the pope. Gregory died in 604. In the midst of the great social and political upheavals of the sixth century, he had stood as a colossus in the protection and advancement of the Church. However, despite the papal influence and prestige sown by him throughout the west, the papacy was entering a period in eastern Christendom wherein it would become a nearly forgotten institution and force. And because of corrupt and inept Byzantine rulers, the popes would remain as defenders of Italy but they would also remain politically subserviant to powerful European emperors. Civilian meddling in ecclesiastical affairs went on and on, often to extremes. In 653 for example, Emperor Constans II had Pope St. Martin I arrested and exiled to the Crimea for an act of *lèse majesté.* All the poor pope had done was to overrule the emperor's erroneous view of the human and divine nature of Christ. Though he died a lonely outcast in a desolate outpost on the imperial frontier, Martin emerged posthumously triumphant. When scores of miracles were credited to him he was declared a saint by all segments of the Church.

Imperial dominance of Church business continued for another century but help was on the way. In the first half of the eighth century Rome and its neighbors in central Italy were plagued by the relentless assaults of the merciless Lombards from up north. Alarmed for the very life of the city, Pope Stephen III in 754 negotiated an uneasy peace with the fierce Lombard chieftain, Aistulfo. When it became clear that Aistulfo had little or no real intention of living up to the agreement, Stephen appealed through emissaries to other powerful rulers for help. Finding a sympathizer across the Alps in the person of Pepin, king of the Franks, the pontiff made a courageous, back-breaking journey over the mighty mountains to personally implore Pepin to come to his aid. Whereupon Pepin led a formidable force of Franks back over the snow-capped peaks into Italy and down to Rome where they routed the hated Lombards.

These developments turned things around for the papacy, at least for a time. For upon the defeat of Aistulfo's intruders, Pepin bestowed a large portion of central Italy upon the chair of Peter. This *Donation of Pepin*, as it was called, outraged the eastern emperor who, though unable to protect Italy because of his preoccupation with domestic woes, nevertheless did not want to lose his titular claim to the peninsula. Pepin seemed to care little about the distant emperor's feelings and reaffirmed the grant "for the love of Peter." Covering 17,000 square miles from Umbria to Lazio, with a population of three million, the territory destined to last eleven centuries soon became known as the Papal States. Stephen III, lover of the poor and true defender of the people, thus became the first of the pope-kings. (Later, in the thirteenth century, the city of Avignon and the surrounding area in southern France were added to the Papal States.) Succeeding Stephen was his brother, Pope St. Paul I (757–767), who had served Stephen as a papal diplomat. Paul emulated his brother predecessor's works of mercy with the poor, the sick, and the imprisoned and kept strong ties with the court of Pepin.

In 774 the Lombards renewed their treachery and had to be crushed by Charlemagne, son of Pepin. Throughout their existence the Papal States were to come under frequent assaults from first this northern belligerent, then that one. That is why in the mid-800's Pope Leo IV enclosed the Vatican territory with soaring walls, gaining for the Church's headquarters the nickname of "Leonine City." Declaring himself a protector of papal independence, Charlemagne backed up the land grant of his father. And with this protection came a new wave of Caesaropapism. In Charlemagne's view, the pope's *raison d'etre* was to pray and to preach. The "defender of St. Peter" would take care of all other Church matters, e.g. the appointing of bishops, the training of seminarians, the convoking of synods and councils. When Pope Leo III in November 800 came under a heavy barrage by anti-papists, a barrage which imperiled his very life, Charlemagne came back down to Rome to settle matters. The pope's tormentors were condemned and swiftly struck down.

Charlemagne, having decided to remain on in the Eternal City for the holy season of Christmas, was attending Mass in the great basilica of St. Peter when the Holy Father in a surprise move placed a crown on the head of his benefactor, proclaiming Charlemagne *Imperator Romanorum* (Emperor of the Romans). Though Charlemagne's domain already included all of central Europe (what we know today as France, Germany, Switzerland, Austria, Holland, Belgium, and even parts of Hungary, Yugoslavia, Romania, Poland, and of course, Italy) this was the first formal suggestion that he was more than a king, that he was indeed an emperor of a vast empire. The surprised ruler was obviously flattered, indeed overwhelmed, by the gesture and consequently deepened his resolve to protect the pope and his apostolic office.

As mixed as the blessing of Charlemagne's patronage was, it was far better than what was to follow for the popes pursuant to the death of the emperor in 814 and the rapid collapse of his empire thereafter. In 858 Pope St. Nicholas the Great (the third Roman pontiff to earn the honorary designation of "the Great") made it clear that he had no intention of perpetuating the Caesaropapist policies reinstituted under Charlemagne. This virtuous pope, a native son of Rome, who had served Popes Leo IV and Benedict II and had been overwhelmingly elected, courageously condemned Lothair, king of Lorraine for the latter's wish to shed his wife and take another. During his decade-long reign Nicholas also denounced and removed some German archbishops and in doing so angered the emperor, Louis II, who led his armies into Rome for the express purpose of intimidating the Holy Father only to back down as all of Pope Nicholas' antagonists always did.

But other than the reign of Pope Nicholas there were few bright spots for the papacy throughout the rest of the 800's, the 900's and early 1,000's. Without its former imperial patronage and protection, the papacy was to suffer a terrible setback, for the collapse of the Carolingian empire, while immediately followed by political and social chaos, paved the way for the feudal system. The very nature of feudalism, i.e. rule by powerful clans and feudal lords, reduced the popes to mere pawns of the various powerful factions. The papacy became a travesty with priests being poorly trained, bishoprics being purchased, candidates going to the highest bidders, papal elections being skillfully manipulated and carefully orchestrated in advance by the leading power brokers. This sad era was to see the the hierarchy more concerned with civil affairs and political intrigues than with purely ecclesiastical matters. With the periodic confusion of anti-popes (i.e. another prelate, sometimes two, claiming the throne of Peter over the duly elected pontiff), with corruption in the papal court, with decadence among some of the popes themselves, this was to be the low point, the most humiliating, debasing period in all of papal history.

One ruler from Ravenna, in 955, placed his young son on the throne as John XII. This libertine, after the death of his father and benefactor, turned to Otto I, king of Germany, for protection, all of which opened the floodgates to a period of domination of the papal office by German rulers. Germany at the same time was fast becoming the European military power. And when this Teutonic control of the leadership of the Church was replaced by that of the Roman nobility, namely of Theophylactus and his family, the temporal power of the popes was reduced to a shadow. In this black span of time some of the most unsuitable men came to the throne of Peter, while some pontiffs were assassinated for not fitting into the Theophylactus scheme of things.

Though this long dark night still had some time left a new and better day was slowly dawning. Ever so gradually there was evolving a new piety, a new sanctity, a new commitment to fundamental Christian values and practices, especially in the monasteries of Europe and more especially in the abbey of Cluny in the east of France.

After the scandalous reign of Benedict IX (1032–1044) which ended with his resignation, a fine priest, John Gratian, rector of the ancient and venerable church of St. John at the Latin Gate in Rome, assumed the mantle of Peter. However, having given, with the best of intentions, viz. to rid the Church of a sinful pastor, a considerable sum of money to the hedonistic Benedict to induce his abdication, John Gratian, as Gregory VI, left himself vulnerable to charges of having purchased the papacy.

Soon two other men were claiming the Petrine crown: Sylvester III, the anti-pope of Benedict IX's reign, and Benedict himself, who had quickly grown bored with retirement in the abbey at Grottaferrata. Adding to the woes of Gregory VI, who incidentally enjoyed an excellent reputation and the affection and esteem of the Roman people, was the fact that the German monarch, Henry III had made up his mind to depose the pontiff and replace him with one of his own choosing. The Holy Father stepped down in December of 1046 and was quickly exiled to Germany along with his chaplain and close advisor, the holy monk Hildebrand. After the death of the ex-pontiff a few months later, Hildebrand returned to the monastic life he loved at the abbey in Cluny, vowing never to return to Rome and the political vicissitudes of the papal court. (Later developments were to change his plans.) Thus two consecutive papal reigns were terminated, not by death, but by abdication.

With the ascent to the throne of Pope St. Leo IX, the reform movement born à century earlier in the monasteries of Europe was to grow and prosper. Having implored the brilliant and talented Hildebrand to forsake his monastic life in order to assist in sweeping papal reform programs, Leo, first in a number of truly great reform popes, convoked a council within two months of his election which inveighed against lay control of the papacy, simony (i.e. the selling of indulgences), clerical marriage and other abuses.

Leo's reign, while it did much to turn things around for a Church in dire need of reform, was also to be witness to one of the saddest hours in Christian history, the eastern schism. Michael Cerularius, the reigning patriarch of the diocese of Constantinople, was a prelate with exalted ambitions. His aim was to place his see on a level equal if not superior to that of Rome. Consequently he deliberately fomented confrontation and conflict with the pope. When Cerularius closed all the Latin rite churches in his diocese unless they adopted the Greek or eastern ritual, the pope sent as his legates, Cardinals Humbert and Frederick to mediate the problem. Having persuaded the inept emperor, ironically named Constantine, to back him, Cerularius denounced the legates and their bishop. The papal legates, invested with full authority by Leo who had meanwhile passed away back in Rome, proceeded to excommunicate the patriarch and all who supported him. The eastern Church had been easing away from Roman control for many centuries. This latest confrontation served merely to formalize the rift. While Cerularius had made a major issue over certain rituals of the Latin Church, e.g. using unleavened bread for the Eucharist, clerical celibacy and certain fasting practices, there never was any serious disagreement over doctrine. Social and cultural differences seemed to lie at the bottom of the trouble.

In subsequent papal reigns the Churches of the east and west further demonstrated their animosity toward each other. Under Nicholas II in 1059 the feud was to flare up again with even greater intensity. When the Roman pontiff refused to sanction the election of Photius, a Cerularius sympathizer, to the patriarchate of Constantinople, the angered Photius declared Nicholas excommunicated. Nicholas retaliated in kind and from then on one incident after another drove the Churches of the east and west further apart until eventually they were *de facto* two separate entities, with the east denying the primacy of the pope. The final break came when Rome added to the Apostles' Creed the Latin word *"filioque"* ("and from the Son") which expressed the claim that the Holy Spirit came not only from the Father but also from Christ, the Son. Constantinople condemned this as tampering with the Creed which had been so carefully drafted by the ecumenical council and declared the measure heretical. The sacking of Constantinople during the crusades, about which more will be said later in this chapter, served only to widen the breach, intensify the bitterness and just about destroy east-west Church relations and communications until this past decade.

Today, thanks largely to Pope Paul VI's ecumenical

spirit, his breadth of vision and unwavering determination we may in our lifetime be witnesses to the reunification of these two sister Churches. By mutually rescinding the excommunications and counter excommunications of 1059, Pope Paul and the then reigning patriarch, Athenagoras, on December 7, 1965, took a colossal step toward ending the 900-year-long estrangement. Less than two years later the pope made an historical visit to Athenagoras in Istanbul to escalate their efforts toward reconciliation. This was truly the spirit of Vatican Council II in action.

During the Holy Year of 1975 there was more high drama involving the two Churches. At a solemn ceremony in the Sistine Chapel, the pope and a delegation from the patriarchate of Constantinople led by the metropolitan, Meliton, commemorated the momentous event of a decade earlier. Near the end of the ceremony the Holy Father quite unexpectedly approached the metropolitan and knelt to kiss his feet. Just as dramatic was Meliton's placing of a bouquet at the tomb of Pope Leo IX at whose authorization the papal delegation had originally excommunicated the Orthodox leaders.

Despite the violent storm that broke during his reign (1059–1061), Pope Nicholas II must be credited with some major steps toward the restoration of papal dignity and prestige. His most important measure of reform was the promulgation in 1059 of the new papal election guidelines. According to the decree the election of the pope was to be taken from the hands of emperors, kings, and aristocrats and put into the hands of the cardinal-bishops of the Church. This declaration of papal independence was bitterly opposed by the German powers, so long accustomed to control over the chair of Peter and its occupants. But Nicholas had taken the precaution of lining up support, military if necessary, of other nations, especially the Normans, to ensure his independence. Before his death in the city of Florence in July of 1061, Pope Nicholas further advanced the career of the beloved and highly regarded monk, Hildebrand, by naming this great advocate of reform as archdeacon of the Roman church. Nicholas was succeeded by Anselm, bishop of Lucca, who took the name Alexander II. Under this pontiff, too, the reform movement continued to receive considerable impetus.

Finally on June 30, 1073 Hildebrand was consecrated bishop of Rome, taking the name Pope Gregory VII. One of the greatest successors of Peter, Gregory at once set out to free the Church completely from political interference and intrigue. Kings and emperors had insisted that the appointees to the episcopate must be cleared through them. This fearless pontiff emphasized that bishops were principally spiritual rulers and as such were exclusively under his dominion. When the powerful German king, Henry IV, whose predecessor Henry III had made things so miserable for Pope Gregory VI, continued to throw his weight around in matters ecclesiastical, Gregory VII retaliated by excommunicating him. Gregory's show of papal resolve and muscle turned things around for the Church and the see of Peter. In 1085 the twelfth year of his reign, Pope Gregory VII died in the town of Salerno, south of Rome. Seven and a half centuries later, in 1728, Pope Benedict XIII acknowledged Hildebrand's holy life and dedicated service to the Church in an impressive canonization ceremony in St. Peter's.

Gregory's extraordinary reign was followed by the brief but holy one of the Benedictine monk, Desiderius, abbot of the monastery of Monte Cassino. Having for months declined the cardinals' selection of him as pope, Desiderius at last consented to serve, under the name Victor III. But suffering from poor health and broken in spirit by a persistent anti-pope, the corrupt Guibert of Ravenna, Victor passed away at his beloved monastery in September of 1087.

With the election of Urban II early in 1088 the string of good popes was extended. Born in the Champagne region of France, Otto of Lagery became a monk at Cluny. Under another monk-pope, Gregory VII, Otto had labored in the area of Church reform. As Pope Urban, while continuing his battle against internal abuses and the struggle with Henry IV, he became more concerned with the growing Turkish threat to the eastern empire and the developing Moslem domination of the Holy Land with its great Christian shrines. It had been Gregory VII's intention to organize a military campaign to rescue the holy places from "non-believers." This was eventually carried out under Urban II at a conference of bishops in Clermont, France in 1096. The papal call to arms was heeded by 50,000 Christians who gathered at Constantinople in Turkey. It was hoped that this "First Crusade," as it came to be known, would be a unifying force between the estranged Churches of east and west. It resulted rather in the retaking of Jerusalem and its Christian sites, including the holy sepulcher of Christ, and the spilling of much innocent blood.

Subsequent crusades, set in motion either by popes or kings, were militarily less successful. In fact, the fourth crusade, which marched on Constantinople, so antagonized the Byzantines who quickly denounced the reigning pope, Innocent III, that the breach between the Roman and Orthodox Churches instead of being closed was actually widened. There were to be eight crusades in all, lasting from 1096 to 1291. The last few did result in something of a *rapprochement* between the eastern and western worlds, reflected in expanded mutual trade. None in any way, though, enhanced the credibility of the Christian message of love and peace.

The reign of Innocent III (1198–1216) brought the papacy into the thirteenth century. This good and effective pope did much for the Church by further regulating the papal elections, by vigorously attacking the Albigensian heresy, and by reconciling the dissident Armenians and Maronites to Catholic unity. With an eye toward further reform, the intellectual Innocent convoked the Church's twelfth ecumenical council, the Fourth Lateran Council as it was called.

Francis of Assisi made the trek to Rome for an audience with Innocent III seeking the pontiff's sanction for a new monastic order. Pope Innocent gave his consent and blessing not only to St. Francis but also to St. Dominic and St. John of Matha who had approached him with similar requests. Innocent was to be immediately followed in the new century by two papal titans, Honorius III and Gregory IX.

When Cencio Savelli, a native son of Rome, came to the papacy as Honorius III he was eminently prepared, having served in key positions in the pontificates of Pope Celestine III and Innocent III. This fine scholar, expert canon lawyer, and consummate pragmatist was an apostle of peace through his role as confidant and ally of European noblemen, princes and kings. Like his predecessor, he also fostered the monastic orders throughout his eleven year reign. Honorius' love for the people was well known. Once when local grain merchants had burdened the people of Rome with outrageous prices, Honorius moved to secure cheaper grain from Sicily. A crusade, the fifth, was conducted during his reign under the leadership of King Andrew of Hungary. It proved to be a dismal failure.

On March 19, 1227, Ugolino De Conti, bishop of Ostia, was elected by his fellow cardinals. Though already an old man, De Conti, as Gregory IX, was to enjoy a long (14 years) and fruitful reign. As a young priest with an excellent education De Conti had served in the papal diplomatic corps. He had been on close personal terms with St. Francis, St. Clare and St. Anthony. He was a strange amalgam of liberalism and conservatism. He advocated academic freedom at the time when Aristotle was about to be purged from the curriculum of Christian academies. And at the same time, completely intolerant of heretics, he endorsed the law of the German emperor,

Frederick, calling for death by fire for convicted heretics. In conjunction with his bitter struggle against heresy Gregory launched the ill-famed Inquisition. Paramount among his goals was reconciliation with the Orthodox. Though he did bring about the return of the Syrian Monophysites to the Roman Church, all the rest of Gregory's efforts in this matter proved futile. In the twilight of his reign the old pope codified canon law.

The papacy entered the fourteenth century still under the cloud of residual Caesaropapism. Conflict arose between Pope Boniface (Benedict Caetani) and Philip IV of France over taxes on clergy and church property. When the feud heated up, Boniface had to be rescued by his Italian papal forces in order to avoid standing trial before a Gallic court. The harried pontiff died soon after this and, with his passing, the institution of the papacy was to enter into another period of decline in influence, prestige and power.

History is the record of the rise and decline of nations and institutions. At this point in time France was claiming center stage in the European political arena. This transalpine nation was becoming—in fact had already become—profoundly influential in Church affairs.

Following the half-year reign of Blessed Benedict XI the papal residence shifted from the Tiber to the Rhone. The papacy, which had just climbed to unprecendented peaks of power after a millennium-long struggle with the imperial and feudal systems, had come upon a new type of antagonist, the national state, which came into existence in the late medieval period. For nearly a year after the learned Benedict's death the factions in the ranks of the cardinals were unable to agree on a successor. Emerging finally as a compromise candidate was Bertrand de Got, archbishop of Bordeaux, who became Pope Clement V. With Italy in political, social and economic chaos, with Rome particularly turbulent and as a result dangerous even for the Holy Father himself, Clement had no desire to cross the Alps. Therefore, he sought a suitable site in France for the papal throne. His choice was the picturesque little town of Avignon on the banks of the Rhone. Here in this papal enclave in the Provence region of southeastern France (the old Provincia Romana of Caesar's Gaul) the papacy was to remain for nearly seventy years. Petrarch the poet and classical scholar was fond of referring to this period as the papacy's "Babylonian Captivity." The Church thinkers of the time were deeply disturbed by this transference of papal power. But in a more analytical, dispassionate view, it was a practical measure calculated to achieve freedom of action and safety of person for the "holder of the keys to the kingdom."

All seven pontiffs during the Avignon era were Frenchmen as were three-fourths of the cardinals created by them. And despite the fact that these popes came to be looked upon by their contemporaries as little more than chaplains of the French court they were, except for Clement, far from subservient to the throne.

Clement (1305–1314) and his six successors, to a man, insisted that the Avignon residency was a very temporary arrangement and that the pope's return to Rome and the original see of Peter was imminent. But the "imminence" was to drag on for seven decades. Clement's death left the "shoes of the fisherman" unfilled for two years while the factions in the cardinalate wrangled over the choice of a successor. In August 1316, after a long stormy conclave, the local bishop of Avignon, Jacques d'Euse, became Pope John XXII (1316–1334), a good administrator, and almost laughably inept theologian.

Because of their close ties with France, the papacy and the Church suffered in their relations with other influential European nations such as England and Spain. All this while back in Rome the Church was represented by a committee of cardinals whom the Romans resented. The flock was embittered because the pope was still technically their bishop and since the transfer to Avignon the needs of the diocese of Rome received scant if any attention.

Ascending to the papacy after John were Benedict XII (1334-1342), Clement VI (1342-1352), Innocent VI (1352-1362), Blessed Urban V (1362-1370), and the last of the Avignon popes, the pontiff destined to bring the chair of Peter back to its original site, Gregory XI (Pierre Roger de Beaufort) who ruled from 1370-1378.

Petrarch and other eminent personages of the day argued vainly for a return to Rome, but it was due largely to the persuasive and relentless efforts of an unschooled but dynamic Dominican nun, St. Catherine of Siena, that Gregory shifted the papal headquarters back to the left bank of the Tiber. When this Tuscan nun's letters (dictated since she could not write) went unheeded, she went to Avignon, skipped the fine points of protocol, to remonstrate with Pope Urban V, warning him that the longer he kept the papacy out of Rome the more nails he was driving into the coffin of the Church. Impressed, perhaps alarmed even, Urban did visit Rome but found it in worse turmoil than ever—crime, civil war, plagues—and hurried back to the pastoral tranquility of Provence.

Catherine continued her fiery campaign and, via the simple but eloquent letter that follows, convinced Gregory XI to come home to Rome despite the great pressures on him from the French government, the French people and the predominantly French college of cardinals. You will note in the letter, which Gregory is reported to have read in "awe and amazement," Catherine's three-point program for the pope: residency in the Eternal City, Church reform and the restoration of political and social calm in Italy:

"Most holy and dear sweet Father in Christ sweet Jesus:

I your unworthy daughter Catherine, servant and slave of the servants of Jesus Christ, write to you in His Precious Blood. With fervor have I longed to see in you the fullness of divine grace for then you might be the means, through divine grace, of pacifying all the world. And so I implore you, my father, to use the instrument of your power and goodness with zeal and with ardent desire for the peace and honor of God and the salvation of souls. And should you ask me: "With the world so ravaged, how shall I attain peace?" I shall reply, on behalf of the crucified Christ, that it befits you to achieve three principal goals through your power.

Do you uproot in the garden of Holy Church the malodorous flowers, full of impurity and greed, swollen with pride, that is, the bad priests and rulers who poison and rot that garden.

But reflect, sweet father, that you could not do this easily unless you accomplished the other two things which must precede the fulfilment of the first, that is, your return to Rome and the uplifting of the standard of the most Holy Cross. Let not your holy desire fail on account of any scandal or rebellion of cities which you might see or hear; nay let the flame of holy desire be all the more kindled to wish to do all this swiftly. Do not delay, then, your coming. Do not believe the devil, who sees his own loss and so tries harder to rob you of your possessions in order that you may lose your love and charity and that your coming be hindered. I urge you, father, in Christ Jesus, to come swiftly like a gentle lamb. Respond to the Holy Spirit who summons you. I tell you, come, come, come, and do not wait for time, for surely time shall not wait for you.

Answer God, who calls you to hold and possess the seat of the glorious shepherd, St. Peter, whose vicar you have been."

January 17, 1377 witnessed the solemn re-entry of the papacy into the city of Peter in the person of Pope Gregory XI. The Avignon papacy was over. Under Gregory's successor, Pope Urban VI (Bartolomeo Prignano of Bari), however, the Church in 1378 was thrown into still another convulsion. Upset by Urban's tactlessness in executing reform measures, the cardinals voted to invalidate his election and replace him with Clement VII. Urban stood his ground. Clement moved back to Avignon, supported by France, Scotland and Spain while Urban was backed by Italy and eastern Europe. This so-called "Papal Schism" resulted in a series of anti-popes, a sorry state of affairs indeed, severely damaging to papal prestige and honor. It was not resolved until Martin V accepted the keys in 1417. In time, Church leaders came to recognize the Roman popes during that period as the legitimate and duly elected heirs of Peter's chair and the Avignon claimants as anti-popes.

This chapter has spanned eleven hundred years which saw both papal splendor and shame, great sanctity and sin, a long, long era which bore witness to the human and divine natures (like Christ's) of the Church and Christ's commitment to remain with the Church all days. Neither the gates of hell nor occasional unworthy occupants in Peter's chair could destroy the institution. The papacy's incredible resilience enabled it to come back from catastrophe again and again and served to point up its divine aspect. The relatively few scoundrels elected— even Jesus had one Judas Iscariot in his hand-picked twelve—served only to underscore its human side.

But the sun of the Renaissance was now quickly rising over Europe, a new epoch in world history in which the papacy was also to play a prominent role. This is the role I hope to discuss with you in the coming chapter.

Viva il Papa!

CHAPTER IV

THE RENAISSANCE AND BAROQUE ERAS

With Europe, and especially Italy, beginning to be adorned with works of art and treated to literary gems in quality and quantity far in excess of any previous period of human history, there came to the pontificate one Thomas Parentucelli as Pope Nicholas V. Born on the 15th of November, 1397, in the Liguria region of Italy, ordained a priest a quarter of a century later, and elected pope in 1447, Nicholas was a true child of this shining period and the first of the so-called 'Renaissance popes.' An enthusiastic humanist and a devotee of all forms of culture, Nicholas aimed to make Rome not only the spiritual capital of the Christian world but also the intellectual and artistic capital of Europe via a new St. Peter's, great libraries, museums and art galleries. Sometimes accused, often unjustly and exaggeratedly so, of worldliness, the kind and gentle pope gave great attention and energy to the renewal of the spiritual health of the diocese of Rome.

Later Renaissance popes, such as the disgraceful and decadent Alexander VI, would give the papacy a black eye. The other eye would be blackened by the awesome and awful Spanish Inquisition. The 16th century pontiffs would suffer under the weight of Luther and the Protestant Reformation he would precipitate, when half of Europe would repudiate papal claims to spiritual authority and church leadership. As with troubles of earlier centuries much of this crisis was provoked by the papacy itself which had long recognized the need for reform but too long delayed any significant changes.

But for now the papacy under Nicholas was enjoying a period of esteem and importance. The Jubilee Year of 1450 was hailed by the Holy Father as a celebration of the restoration of Church unity and the renewal of the authority of the see of Peter.

Two great political problems, however, were to consume a disproportionate measure of the pope's time and energies. For one, Constantinople, the headquarters of the estranged but still beloved eastern Church, was falling to the Moslem Turks. In 1453 the city finally fell and with it vanished the last vestiges of the ancient Roman empire. And when Nicholas V endeavored to reconcile the eastern Church's hierarchy and clergy to the papacy he was thwarted by the centuries-old anti-Rome bitterness. For another there were renewed threats to the integrity of the Papal States by various Italian princes. This political and geographical power base, while injurious to the spiritual image of the papacy, did significantly contribute to ecclesiastical freedom and papal power. And Nicholas' immediate successors would continue to be troubled by these same issues. Callistus (1455-1458), Pius II (1458-1464) and Paul II (1464-1471) all tried without success to organize a crusade to recapture Constantinople and in so doing bring the Byzantine, or eastern, Church back into unity with Rome.

With what time and energy were left to him, Pope Nicholas V managed some outstanding achievements. Under him Valla the writer, Fra Angelico the painter, and Alberti the architect were all put to work artistically glorifying the seat of Christendom. During his pontificate the renowned Vatican Library was inaugurated and stocked with priceless ancient tomes. The tireless pope also commissioned the translation, by the preeminent scholars of the time, of the Greek works into the more commonly known Latin, to foster and facilitate scholarship. He also encouraged a hunt through Italy's old monasteries for more manuscripts of Cicero, Sallust, Seneca, Pliny and other classical writers.

While under later popes the greatest scholars and writers, artists and builders of Italy and Europe (giants such as Bramante, Giotto, Michelangelo, Raphael, Sangallo and Maderno) were imported to Rome to toil in the artistic surroundings of the papacy, the credit for instituting this papal maecenate must forever fall to Nicholas. Indeed there is owed to this outstanding pontiff a lofty place of honor in the world's halls of learning and patronage. Plagued by poor health for the final five years of his life, Parentucelli, with his eyes gazing upon the crucifix, passed away, in the Vatican on his birthday in 1455. His remains lie in the grottoes beneath St. Peter's in a small tomb fittingly inscribed with Latin verses by a successor, Pope Pius II.

The glow surrounding the papacy was to be short-lived, unfortunately, for under Sixtus IV (1471–1484) things would take another sorry turn. At this point in time the moral state of the cardinalate was at an unprecedented low. Many of the college's members were unworthy of the rank. Several had mistresses, some were alcoholics, others gambling addicts, not a few were devoted to luxury, while a number of them saw nothing wrong with selling indulgences and using the proceeds to bolster their thinning coffers. Still others were more interested in being landowners than serving the Church, finding more gratification from involvement in political factions, shady deals, blatant bribery, and flagrant nepotism. They had their cronies move into Rome and live off the material wealth of the Church they professed to serve. This sorry state of affairs was ameliorated not at all when Cardinal della Rovere was elected pope with the name, Sixtus IV. For as pope, Sixtus continued to be an ardent practitioner of nepotism, placing his relatives in key positions whence they could and did plunder the Church's treasury.

Nonetheless, Sixtus did achieve some good in his reign and even gained a measure of historical immortality via the construction, in 1473, of his private chapel just to the right of St. Peter's. This chapel, called "Sistine" for its builder, would in turn be immortalized by the titan of the Renaissance, Michelangelo. From 1508 to 1512, the Florentine genius labored, supine, to paint the Old Testament across the length and breadth of the Sistine chapel ceiling.

Sixtus and his immediate successors seemed bent on absolute political as well as spiritual power, on riches, on self-aggrandizement. They continued to patronize the arts, but for selfish reasons, not in the spirit of their recent predecessors. New papal elections came to be manipulated by the most influential cardinals to ensure their further entrenchment. This produced a few more unworthy occupants for Peter's chair, such as Innocent VIII (1484-1492) and the infamous Borgia family pope, Alexander VI. With their sacriligious and unpardonable behavior, the hierarchy was angering and scandalizing the laity and actually paving the way for the approaching upheaval, the worst ever to afflict the Church, the Protestant Reformation.

Cardinal Rodrigo Borgia as Pope Alexander VI (1492-1503) was to disgrace the office of Peter perhaps worse than any other of the relative handful of bad popes had done. Over the course of forty years, this wealthy man had connived his way to the papacy. During the election of his immediate predecessor, Innocent VIII, he had openly tried to buy the office with money, land and promises of high office. The Spanish-born Alexander came to the throne with something less than a priestly image. For starters he was the father of a half-dozen illegitimate children. Some of these he made dukes. One, Cesare, his third son, was named a cardinal and placed in command of the papal armies. Alexander's only daughter, Lucretia, went through three marriages. The first was annuled, the second brought to a violent end by the murder of the husband by his brother-in-law, Cesare. Lucretia's brother wanted the victim's property and did not feel any qualms about taking such a route to it.

Thanks to "His Holiness" whatever Cesare wanted, Cesare got. This very paradigm of decadence served Machiavelli as a model for the latter's protagonist, "The Prince." The unscrupulous pontiff was also linked with a murder, having been strangely suspected of arranging the death by poison of his bitter foe, Cardinal Orsini. There were more variations to come on the sorry Borgia theme. All the Borgias in every city and backroads village in Spain, it seemed, were imported to the papal city and put in sinecures where they could live off the coffers of the Church. The college of cardinals suddenly had an unusual number of Spanish members.

This moral laxity in high places, meanwhile, was infuriating the Italian religious reformer, Girolamo Savonarola, a Dominican priest, who in 1497, with his fiery eloquence, openly denounced the behavior of Pope Alexander VI and the entire papal court from his base in the city of Florence. Leo IV's massive Vatican walls reverberated with the shockwaves of Savonarola's barrage. Alexander retaliated with a decree of excommunication, but the zealous Dominican, undaunted, continued with and, in fact, intensified his philippics. Strange to say, but the Florentines who had been all along increasingly supportive of Savonarola's stand began to desert him in droves when the zealot disobeyed the corupt pontiff's injunction to stop preaching. It was for Savonarola (as the French said about Napoleon after the battle of Leipzig) *la commencement de la fin.* For disobedience toward the chair of Peter, regardless of the woeful state of it, was something the Florentines were not prepared to support. Matters reached a point of high tension in Florence with rioting in its narrow streets and Savonarola was arrested by the authorities for disturbing the peace. A kangaroo court found the tragic reformer guilty and sentenced him to death by hanging. His remains were burned and his ashes scattered upon the lazy Arno. His crusade died with him.

Alexander's ignominious reign was to last another six

years. One evening he and his son, Cesare, went to dine at a cardinal's villa risking the contaminated air of a Roman August. On the 13th of that month, in the year 1503, the libertine vicar succumbed to malaria. Critics of the papacy then, and ever since, would use Alexander as an argument against the institution when in actuality he is exhibit "A" in its defense. Surely an office which could survive an Alexander VI must be under the guidance and care of forces higher than even Borgia was able to affect. Cesare tried to manipulate the conclave following his father's death but was unable to and he and all the other parasitical Borgias were on their way out.

On September 22, the cardinals of the Church elected the good and decent, but elderly, Francesco Piccolomini who chose the name Pius III. While the new and ailing pontiff aimed at broad and swift reforms, our Lord, whose vicar on earth he was, had other plans. Pius was summoned home to meet his Master on October 18, concluding a reign of but twenty seven days. Rome lost another bishop. Again the cardinals went into conclave and this time raised to the pontificate fifty-year-old Giuliano Della Rovere, the bitter foe of Alexander VI. Here was indeed a vigorous ecclesiastical and political, *especially* political, leader: a man of action, a foxy diplomat, a fearless warrior. Having adopted the name Julius II, the new pope waited no time at all to swing into action. To protect himself and his court from, among other things, the eternal hoodlum element of Rome, Julius founded the popular and colorful Swiss guard. In his patronage of the arts Julius was without peer. Under his mandate the gifted architect, Bramante, began work on the building of the new, i.e. the current, St. Peter's. (On April 18, 1506 the foundation stone of the new shrine of Christendom was laid. One hundred twenty years and twenty pontiffs later, the basilica was consecrated by Urban VIII. Contributions from every Christian land had come into the Vatican for the basilica's construction.) It was Julius who summoned Michelangelo to Rome to design a papal tomb and who then reassigned the "giant of the Renaissance" to ornamenting the Sistine ceiling. Young Raphael of Urbino heeded the Holy Father's call to come and fresco the walls of the Vatican palaces. In short, Pope Julius had managed to shift the seat of the Renaissance from Tuscany to Rome. All these art projects were, however, prodding Martin Luther further down the road to revolt.

Chronic ill health notwithstanding, Julius was possessed of astonishing energy and extraordinary single-mindedness and brought both of these factors to bear on the restoration of the Papal States, on the revival of the worldly dominion of the papacy and on the renewal of the prestige and independence of the Holy See, all of which had been left in shambles by the Borgia crowd. Aiming at a program of sweeping reform for the Church, Pope Julius convoked the Fifth Lateran Council which, while falling somewhat short of its goals did manage to produce some corrective and constructive measures. And thanks to the tireless pontiff, the Eternal City itself underwent at this time a remarkable transformation. Many new churches were erected, new streets and squares laid out, the bed of the Tiber diverted to reduce the menace of flooding, the Vatican museum and library enriched. On the 21st of February, 1513, after an extended illness, Pope Julius II slipped into eternal rest. Recognizing and appreciating his tremendous toils on their behalf, the people of Rome deeply mourned their bishop's passing.

Giovanni de Medici of the famous Florentine clan and a true product of the Italian Renaissance was to be the next bearer of the keys. Luxury had traditionally been the Medici way of life, and, as Pope Leo X, Giovanni was to be an eager practitioner of it. This long-entrenched noble family was accustomed to buying just about anything it coveted. For all practical purposes the Medicis had purchased the city on the Arno and were aiming now at the purchase of the Church. To some degree they succeeded, when one considers that the clan eventually produced three popes and a host of cardinals.

It must be admitted by his critics that Leo was a man devoted to peace and that he made commendable efforts toward its achievement. In like manner, however, it must be confessed by his defenders that he sullied the vicarship of Christ with his addiction to private luxury and public extravagance.

Materialistic, humanistic, pecuniary, Leo would sell indulgences and engage in other shady fiscal practices to finance his great, self-aggrandizing building projects. Under Leo and his predecessor the Renaissance achieved full bloom and splendor. Rome became a veritable showpiece of architecture, painting, and sculpture. But all the while they were thrilling the world with their artistic achievements, the popes were simultaneously scandalizing it by the extent they would go to toward realizing these achievements. And the sunny glow from all this splendor was to prove nothing more than the calm before the terrible storm gathering in northern Europe, the first lightning bolt of which would be hurled by the disenchanted German Augustinian priest, Martin Luther. When Pope Leo, in 1517, anxious to expedite the construction of the new St. Peter's, then stalled by lack of funds, resorted to granting indulgences in exchange for contributions, the long-simmering, volcanic Luther erupted. Indignant over the tactics in Rome, he publicly denounced Leo and his court in a list of ninety five theses which he tacked to the doors of the church at Wittenberg. Support from multitudes among the country's laity and from great numbers among its clergy and hierarchy was swift and fervent. The German princes gleefully endorsed Luther's proposal that they take over all church property and declare jurisdiction over all affairs of the Church in Germany. Though excommunicated and condemned by Leo X, the persuasive preacher had succeeded in reviving the germ of Caesaropapism in his homeland, setting the state up as the ultimate authority over matters spiritual, moral and doctrinal. In addition to enormous areas of Germany, the Scandinavian lands all embraced Lutheranism, and within the next two decades the Church of Rome lost much of her constituencies in Switzerland, Holland, and Scotland to Calvinism, and in England to the Church of England founded by King Henry VIII.

The lion's share of the blame for this latest and catastrophic sundering of the Christian Church must fall squarely on the collective shoulders of the occupants of Peter's chair during that period. For by their shameful personal behavior, their love of luxury, their hunger for political power, their "end justifies the means" policies, and their blindness to the deep and widespread resentment and animosity all this was engendering, they were actually pushing the first critical boulders of the avalanche that would slide from the summit of Rome. They were the co-architects in a way, along with the Luthers, the Calvins and the Henrys, of the Protestant Reformation. But the trauma of this latest splintering of Christianity was to be the shock needed to bring about extensive and genuine reforms within both the Church and the papacy.

It can be rather accurately charged that Leo X's reign was one of artistic brilliance and spiritual bankruptcy. And speaking of bankruptcy, upon the death of Leo X in 1521 the papacy was left in financial chaos. But help was coming. The brief reign (1522–1523) of Adrian VI was spent in a valiant effort to clean things up. At least it was a good beginning. Adrian's death allowed for another Medici to fill the shoes of the fisherman. Unlike his profligate cousin, Pope Clement VII (1523–1534) was a responsible and virtuous individual, though a bit too timid for the exigencies of the times. He did, however, stand up to Henry VIII in the monarch's request to have his perfectly valid marriage dissolved to clear the way to a new lustful union with the charming Anne Boleyn. Unfortunately for the Church, Henry answered the pope's denial of his request by forcing the Church in

England to sever its ties with Rome.

Alessandro Farnese of the noble Roman family was, as Paul III, the first in a succession of outstanding reform popes. In 1545, eleven years into his fifteen-year reign, Paul called the Council of Trent, a major milestone in the Church's long history. At this great assembly the Church fathers addressed themselves bluntly and painfully to the recent record of hierarchical abuses. With the help of the Christian saints and scholars of the time, the Church defined her position on all the fiery issues of the time, put an end to nepotism, restored a truly religious air to the Roman see, rehabilitated the college of cardinals to ensure that it would provide a reservoir of men, qualified for and worthy of the keys of Peter. Under Paul III's successors, particularly under Paul IV, Pius IV, and St. Pius V, the Church's counter-reformation would receive tremendous impetus. A great number of religious orders were born which helped to revive true clerical piety and dignity and restore lay respect for the priesthood.

Other results of Trent were a catechism of authoritative Catholic teaching, a standardized missal, and a regulated breviary (the special office of daily prayers said by priests everywhere). The Council had three sessions of approximately two years duration each over the span from 1545 to 1563. Three popes oversaw the Council's work: Paul III, Julius III, and Pius IV.

A man who had served Paul III and later Pius IV at Trent was the cardinals' choice in May, 1572. Cardinal Ugo Boncompagni, a native of Bologna, chose to be called Gregory XIII and in his thirteen year pontificate he distinguished himself and aided the Church in many ways. By his virtuous life he edified both the clergy and laity. Particularly committed to implementing and advancing the reforms of the Council, Gregory founded more than twenty seminaries to ensure the quality training of good priests. In Rome he built a new seminary for the Jesuits which still bears his name, the Gregorian University. It enjoys universal prestige to this day. The good pope was also very energetic in missionary programs and gave to civilization a revised calendar, the one in use today known as the Gregorian calendar.

Gregory was succeeded by the even more energetic Sixtus V in 1585. Besides beautifying Rome with squares and fountains and obelisks, Sixtus left an indelible influence in organizational matters. So efficient was his reorganization of the curia, in effect the pope's cabinet, that his system is, for the most part, still employed in our age by John Paul II. Thanks to Pope Sixtus V the college of cardinals was increased to a membership of seventy, a figure that stood until the recent reign of John XXIII when it was escalated to more than a hundred. And thanks, too, to Pope Sixtus V's stern measures, the Papal States, so long plagued by crime, were made safer for the citizens, and the papacy's financial condition much improved. On his death bed Pope Sixtus ordered huge sums of money withdrawn from the papal treasury in the ancient Castel Sant' Angelo on the bank of the Tiber and distributed to the poor.

So the counter-reformation continued as the Church continued to be blessed with good supreme pontiffs. Although the movement had failed to reverse the recent losses and bring back the dissidents to the flock of Peter, it was accomplishing the rescue of the papacy and the Church from the maladies of its recent past and the rekindling of the once flickering and fading allegiance to the Roman see of millions across the European continent.

Still, religious wars rocked the continent on and off for more than a hundred years after Luther's bombshell at Wittenberg and the popes were never to regain their former influence over the civil affairs of Europe. All this while, however, they maintained and would maintain for another three centuries, authority over the civil affairs of the city of Rome and the Papal States.

For the rest of the sixteenth century the pontiffs remained zealous in their push for reforms, improving the internal health of the Church, remedying abuses, restructuring the religious orders, nominating only worthy candidates for the cardinalate and the Italian bishopric.

Across the centuries, one European nation or another rose to dominate continental matters for a stretch. When Cardinal Ippolito Aldobrandini was elected as Pope Clement VIII he felt Rome was little more than extraterritorial Madrid, for at that point Spain was holding sway over her European sister nations. By effecting stronger relations with another great contemporary power, France (Spain's most bitter foe), Clement successfully halted Spanish influence over papal affairs and in so doing fortified the independence of the Holy See.

Soon after, Christianity began making strides in the Orient, and through Persia, West Africa and America. As the curtain dropped on the 1500's Pope Clement was busy creating a special office for the supervision of missionary activity.

In the year 1600, Clement proclaimed a great Jubilee, or Holy Year, in Rome and was encouraged by the response. More than three million pilgrims journeyed to the Eternal City to pray at the holy final resting places of the apostles and martyrs. This, combined with the fact that great numbers of Christians, even in places considered strongholds of Protestantism, were returning to the Roman fold was interpreted as a strong sign of the counter reformation's success.

Early on, the seventeenth century was witness to continued Church-State struggles, exemplified by Paul V's scathing indictment of Venice. The northern Italian state incurred the wrath of Paul (of the Roman Borghese clan) with its meddling in local Church affairs and its harassment of the Venetian clergy.

It was at this time too that Galileo was called before the Inquisition on two occasions for his defense of the Copernican system. He submitted and was placed under house arrest by the Church. A great debate arose which perdures in some sectors to this very day regarding what some conceive to be an incompatability between faith and science. This has not been the Church's stand. Even back then Pope Urban VIII eventually granted Galileo a pension and his apostolic blessing on the scientist's work.

Let us here consider briefly some of the more distinguished seventeenth century pontiffs and the highlights of their reigns.

Gregory XV (1621-1623), a member of the noble Ludovisi family, was zealous in restoring Catholicity and devoted to the revival of the Church in Germany where he gained some success, especially along the Rhine. He founded the Sacred Congregation for the Spread of the Faith in 1622. This vital Church agency (now known as the Sacred Congregation for the Evangelization of Peoples) stands today as Gregory's greatest monument. The arts enjoyed his enthusiastic patronage also.

The long reign (1623-1644) of Maffeo Barberini as Pope Urban VIII was marked by the expansion of the Congregation for the Spread of the Faith *(Propaganda Fide)*. And proof of the Barberini patronage of the arts was left all over the Eternal City through fountains, palaces, museums and sculptures, many of them the creations of the Baroque genius, Bernini.

Such an ambitious building program was not without its loud critics, however. From the Colosseum and other imperial structures, Urban took great quantities of marble for the fabric of some of his palaces and churches. Even the revered Pantheon was not exempt. Workmen were instructed to strip the bronze from the temple's dome to furnish material for Bernini's *baldachino* or canopy over the main altar in St. Peter's. This pilferage of the ancient stones gave rise to the wry pun: "What the barbarians didn't do (to old Rome) the Barberini did."

All the criticism aside, Urban did accomplish much spiritually and did provide Rome—and as a result, the whole Christian world—with beautiful and inspiring churches and works of art. To the Barberini pope the Church is also indebted for the suppression of the Jansenist heresy, and the beautiful form of worship known as the Forty Hours' Devotion.

Innocent X (1644–1655) succeeded Urban. A son of the Roman Pamphili family, this pope showed great zeal in maintaining the doctrinal integrity and purity of the Church.

During the reign of Alexander VII (1655–1667) Jansenism flared up again and he continued the battle against it. The Jansenists held that man was totally depraved, was predestined from all eternity to heaven or hell and was subject to limited grace and little or no free will. Alexander was another enthusiastic patron of the arts and the one who commissioned Bernini to build the *Scala Regia* in the Vatican. In fact it is Alexander VII of all the supreme pontiffs who is the first to welcome the pilgrims to Vatican City. It is his name (Alexander VII, P.M.) that is engraved on the facade end of what is perhaps Bernini's greatest architectural triumph, the breathtakingly beautiful colonnades that embrace the expanse of St. Peter's Square. (P.M. is the abbreviation for *Pontifex Maximus*, i.e. Supreme Pontiff, and it is found, attached to a pope's name, on every papal-commissioned fountain, monument, church and museum in and around Rome.)

Seventeenth century matters were brought to a close by two Innocents, XI and XII. Saintly and austere Innocent XI (1676–1689) enacted a number of effective reforms, improved the fiscal situation of the Church and resisted France's Louis XIV's efforts to control French bishoprics.

Following the brief reign (1689–1691) of the good and vigorous Alexander VIII, Cardinal Antonio Pignatelli was elected Pope Innocent XII. He took the Church just barely into the new century (he died September 27, 1700) and in his nine years remained wonderfully benevolent to the poor, officially ended nepotism in the papal court with his Bull (Edict) of 1692, and greatly improved the legal system of the Papal States.

What lay ahead in the rest of the century was a period of great difficulty for the papacy. There was lay and clerical revolt against authority. Civil powers encroached increasingly on the ecclesiastical domain. Terrible political tempests lashed Europe. Naturally the popes found themselves involved, at times unwittingly, but more often than not quite wittingly.

Perhaps the policy of Emperor Joseph II (1741-1790) of Austria best illustrates the shabby treatment of the Church by the temporal rulers of the time. Joseph considered the Church little more than another agency of the state, subject to control in every matter. Church finances were administered by the state; episcopal appointments and clerical training were likewise supervised by the state.

In France the Jesuits, staunchest defenders of the supremacy of the popes in Church matters in every land, were attacked and, by official decree of Louis XV, suppressed. The same order of priests was expelled from Spain.

With huge chunks of Europe protestantized, the popes in this era of absolute monarchs were persuaded to keep the good will of all the Catholic rulers and engage their support in preventing further losses. This resulted in papal concessions to the monarchs' demands for increased control over the Church in their respective lands.

Though suffering much humiliation at the hands of the various European tyrants, the eighteenth century pontiffs were, to a man, excellent vicars of Christ, deeply virtuous and totally devoted to the Church and to their people. Clement XI (1700-1721), Innocent XIII (1721-1724), and Benedict XIII (1724-1730), all the while the various royal houses, for example the Hapsburgs, continued to encroach on ecclesiastical jurisdiction, courageously resisted them and went on fighting those errors which would first here and then there crop up, particularly the heresy of Jansenism.

So good and holy was Pope Benedict XIV (1740–1758) that upon his death he was mourned even in the Protestant world. Horace Walpole, the noted English Protestant praised Benedict "for restoring the lustre of the tiara (the papal ceremonial crown) by his extraordinary virtues and sanctity."

Marking the final quarter of the century was, with the exception of that of Peter himself, the longest papal reign in history up to that point, that of Pius VI (1775–1799). Handsome Gianangelo Braschi, scion of a prominent Roman family, occupied himself with the struggle against a great menace to the Church, Freemasonry, and to rebutting the inflammatory and revolutionary philosophical ideas emanating from the banks of the Seine and the Rhine. Through it all, the pope found sufficient reserve energy and time to oversee wondrous engineering and building programs.

A by-product of the general social unrest of the times to effect the Church directly was the French Revolution. This upheaval was the source of great anxiety and personal suffering for Pius VI. In reprisal for some earlier anti-French measures from the see of Peter, Napoleon Bonaparte attacked the nearly defenseless and helpless Papal States. Priceless Vatican works of art and literature were shipped to Paris for the purpose of purchasing peace. The conqueror remained unsatisfied, compelling the pontiff to pay further indemnity in the form of cash and countless precious paintings, carvings and manuscripts. Never a race to lose their sense of humor, the Italians, upon this occasion concocted the following dialogue: Signor "A": *"Tutti i francesi sono ladri."* ("All the French are robbers.") To which Signor "B" responds: *"Non tutti, ma buona parte."* ("Not all, but a good part: 'Bonaparte'.")

In addition to these outlandish demands, Napoleon ordered what remained of the papal army disbanded and took the papal territory from the Holy Father's jurisdiction. But Bonaparte's rape of southern Europe was still not over and in the Holy City the aging and ailing Roman bishop was placed under arrest by French enforcers and transported, in captivity, north to Tuscany, and after about a month, across the Alps to Valence in France. The ordeal took its toll on the pope's spirit and frame and on August 22, 1799 he passed away with these words on his lips: "Forgive them, Lord."

Thus the papacy ended its eighteenth century in humiliating exile. Again there were gleeful declarations by the enemies of the Holy See that the institution was definitely dead, that the turbulent yet glorious pontifical story was concluded, that the eighteen-hundred-year dynasty of Peter was terminated with the dismal circumstances of his 247th successor, that Pius VI would be Pius the Last.

CHAPTER V

THE TURBULENT NINETEENTH CENTURY

As the 1800's dawned, a large number of the cardinals were residing in the region of Venice. This was at the time under Austrian control, with the result that the emperor, Francis II, attempted to write the script for the conclave following the death of Pius VI. But the cardinals would not be bullied and on their own picked the gifted Benedictine monk, Barnaba Chiaramonti who chose to be called Pope Pius VII. Like his long-suffering predecessor, this wonderfully holy and courageous man of God was to suffer long and terribly in the name of the faith. Like Pius VI, he too would be hauled off as a captive to France. Despite all the woes heaped upon him, Pius VII had one of the longest (1800–1823) reigns in history. From the earliest age he seemed destined to lead his beloved Church someday. His rise in the priesthood was meteoric and in 1785, at the age of forty five, Chiaramonti became a prince of the Church. Napoleon was duly impressed by the young cardinal's spunk when, in 1797, Chiaramonti remained in his diocese, Imola, despite its takeover by Bonaparte's soldiers. From his pulpit on Christmas day of that same year he praised democracy and denounced dictatorship. Still the pontiff was not above the political sport of give and take if it would promote harmony and ultimately serve the Church. For this reason he journeyed to Paris in 1804 to oblige Napoleon's wish that the pontiff crown him emperor in a special ceremony in the cathedral of Notre Dame.

But the pope's give-and-take spirit had its limits. In 1809 Pius VII resisted Napoleon's pressures to have the pontiff support France's policies against England and as a result the Papal States were officially confiscated and annexed as French territory by the angered emperor. Unintimidated, Pius VII promptly excommunicated Napoleon, fully aware of the awful consequences that would surely follow. And follow they did forthwith. In the wee hours of July 6 the ailing pope was visited by the emperor's gendarmes, given but minutes to gather his belongings and then hustled through the northern countryside, and from there over the mountains to Savone in France. Common people throughout Italy were indignant over Napoleon's shameful treatment of the vicar of Christ and openly demonstrated their esteem and affection for him as he passed through their villages and towns.

After French military disasters in Russia and Leipzig, and with Napoleon's empire on the brink of ruin, the pontiff was freed to return to his see in Rome. On the twenty-seventh day of May in 1814, he arrived back in Rome. By his fortitude throughout his most recent ordeal and by several subsequent actions, Pius gained for the papacy increased prestige and autonomy.

The Congress of Vienna, a general political conference, was summoned to settle the chaotic affairs of Europe after the first abdication of Napoleon I on April 12, 1814. Bonaparte's dreams of conquest were broken by crushing defeats at the hands of the allied forces of Russia, Prussia, England, Sweden and Austria. Instead of a palace in Paris, Napoleon was lucky to escape with his life and a sentence of exile to a humble dwelling on the tiny island of Elba. With Cardinal Consalvi as the pope's personal representative at the Congress, the Church recovered the Papal States.

As his victors were still deliberating in Vienna, Napoleon was prepping for another, and last, hurrah. Rather pathetically the "little Caesar" mustered a handful of followers and landed in France on the first of March in 1815 for another go at world conquest. And for an instant it looked like he would pull it off. France rallied around its former emperor. King Louis XVIII fled. Napoleon's dream of conquest was renewed but it was to be short-lived. Waterloo in the south of Belgium was the scene of the last of the Napoleonic wars. For the second time, on June 22, 1815, Bonaparte abdicated, surrendering to a British warship in the vain hope of securing asylum in England. Instead of gaining all the creature comforts and the gaiety of London, Napoleon wound up again in lonely exile.

From 1815 to 1821 he would try to fill his last days writing his memoirs on the forsaken shores of the island of St. Helena. His final months were passed in yet another futile, agonizing battle. This time the enemy was cancer.

Back in Rome, Pope Pius VII remained enthroned. To Pius' credit he was as magnanimous in triumph as he had been fearless under attack. He did not now, nor did he ever, bear any bitterness toward Napoleon. On the contrary, he interceded with the British to go easy on the Corsican and upon the latter's death took great pains to shelter the shattered Bonaparte family. Having steered the papacy and the Church through another dark hour, the old pope died peacefully on August 20, 1823.

Gregory XVI (1831–1846) guided the Church to the middle of the nineteenth century. Much of his reign was taken up by a crusade against tyrannies in eastern Europe and Spain. Not interested in pyrrhic victories for the Holy See, however, Gregory employed his considerable political talents and a realistic approach in dealing with the various *de facto* governments and consequently achieved some major diplomatic concessions for the Church.

One week after Gregory's death, on June 16, 1846, the cardinals cast their ballots in favor of the easy-going, popular, well-known liberal, Giovanni Cardinal Mastai-Ferretti. Of the many long and stormy pontificates in history, Pius IX's would be, as we shall see, the longest and the stormiest since perhaps the first reign, that of St. Peter himself.

Giovanni, having outgrown his boyhood epilepsy, embarked upon his training for the priesthood and in the spring of 1823 he was ordained a priest in Rome by His Holiness himself, Pope Pius VII. And just as his ordination was a departure from the routine so, too, would be his entire priesthood and pontificate. By virtue of his assignment, early in his priestly career, as assistant to the apostolic delegate to Chile, he would become the first pope to have seen the new world. 1827 was another milestone for Father Mastai-Ferretti when he was consecrated by Pope Leo XII as archbishop of Spoleto. Beloved by his flock, the hardworking, deeply spiritual prelate was named a prince of the Church in 1840 by Pope Gregory XVI. By this time he had already developed a reputation as a great liberal, a thinking man much ahead of his time. And as Pope Pius IX he wasted little time in living up to that reputation. Early in his reign he could point to a number of effective reforms within the Papal States. A measure which especially achieved great popularity for him was his declaration of a general amnesty for all political prisoners within his domain. As a consequence of this dictum, a wildly adoring crowd of the faithful one day blocked the papal carriage from passage near the Vatican. Pius watched in amazement as his admirers detached the horses and pulled the vehicle by hand through the historic streets of Rome.

Many accomplishments highlighted his early reign. For instance, he managed to get a foot of the Roman Church back in the door of the Holy Land by reestablishing a Latin patriarchate in Jerusalem (1847), which ever since the great schism had only enjoyed an Orthodox hierarchy. His efforts also resulted in a limited concordat with Russia which allowed for the appointment of Catholic bishops. But there was gathering all this while a violent storm which would prove calamitous for the Church and its pontificate. The storm would be known as the Italian Unification Movement. In the Italian language it had the simple but noble name of *Il Risorgimento*. Initially, Pius IX was an enthusiastic advocate of the idea that the various states on the boot-shaped peninsula unify, the better to protect their mutual interests against the economic and military powers beyond the Alps. However, when it became clear to him that the unification crusade was thrusting Italy toward all out war with Catholic Austria, long a meddler in peninsular affairs, Pius in 1848 disavowed it. Whereupon events moved swiftly and inexorably for the pope, the Church, Italy, Europe. Leaders of the resurgence branded him a traitor and a liar. Rome was snatched from the papal territory and declared a republic. The papal prime minister, Pellegrino Rossi was assassinated by the revolutionaries. The pope's imposing palace across town on the Quirinal hill was bombed and the tiny army of the Swiss guard disarmed.

Toward the end of November in 1848, Pius, crestfallen at the turn of events, imposed exile on himself and journeyed to Gaeta of the State of Naples. (This was the last transfer for any reason of the papal residence from Rome. Pius XII came close to a transfer, however, when, in the early 1940's, Hitler seriously contemplated kidnapping him.) From his exile the disheartened pope implored the great European powers—Austria, France, Spain and Naples—to intervene. The French responded. (In 387 B.C. the Roman commander Marcus Manlius had repelled an attack on Rome by Gallic troops. Twenty three centuries later, on July 2, 1849 A.D. to be precise, another Gallic army would not be denied.) French troops poured into the Eternal City on that sultry summer day, quickly restored order, and soon after escorted Pope Pius IX from Gaeta back to his episcopal seat.

But the machinery of the national movement, stalled for a time by the events in Rome, was shifted into high gear again. Pius, weary and worried over what would happen to the Church, the people, the papacy, remained intransigent in his opposition. There were many who felt that he was altogether overly influenced in all this by his widely hated secretary of state, the Machiavellian Cardinal Antonelli. Assassination plots were forged against both but were never carried out.

1860 was witness to an incursion, by Victor Emmanuel II of the State of Piedmont and his troops, into the northern tip of the Papal States. And upon this occasion Emmanuel assumed the title: "King of Italy." For his actions the king was promptly excommunicated by Pius IX. But papal sovereignty over that stretch of territory from Rome to Ravenna was drawing, this time irrevocably so, to a close. An anti-clerical mood was becoming epidemic throughout Italy fomented by Cavour, Mazzini, Garibaldi and others in the forefront of the *Risorgimento*. Once again Europe was in turmoil with France fighting a losing war against Germany. Italian unification leaders declared their intention to seize the last holdout, Rome.

By 1870 the French troops had been recalled from Rome compelling the pope to make this ironic decision: to ask Austria for help against his fellow Italians. When Austria declined to help, the future was clear. On the 20th of September in 1870, Italian troops stormed the *Porta Pia*. Seeing the futility of it all, the Holy Father gave the order for his valiant troops to concede. As the white flag was raised the chanting, deliriously joyful *Risorgimento* warriors marched over the ancient stones of the streets of Rome. Throughout the rest of that fateful autumn developments broke fast. Principal among them was the abolition of the *Patrimonium Petri* and the secular authority of the pope. All that was left to the Church territorially was the tiny 108-acre enclave, the walled-in city within a walled-in city, the Vatican. Behind the soaring Leonine walls, warmed to a honey-colored glow by thousands of Roman sunrises, the beleagured Pius permanently retreated, bitterly and sadly styling himself: "The Prisoner in the Vatican." He would not exit until carried out in death.

The new government of Italy made many efforts at establishing harmonious relationships with their "prisoner," not so much out of a sense of magnanimity as a fear of a sympathy backlash among the people. But all overtures toward detente were impeded by the pope's resentful rejections of all concessions and indemnities offered by his conquerors and by the rabid hatred of the Church by left wing radicals, Freemasons, and other political groups. Pius officially stated his position on the issue in his then infamous, now famous, encyclical, *Non Possumus* (We can not!). Despite the turn of events against him, Pius did not forsake the virtue of forgiveness, and early in 1878 received the dying king, Victor Emmanuel II, back into communion with the Church. Any hopes by the advocates of detente that this was a sign of the softening of Pius' antipathy were quickly dashed by Papa Mastai-Ferretti's refusal to recognize Umberto I as king.

On February 7, one month after Emmanuel's passing, the eighty-six-year-old pontiff died, weary, distraught, embittered, misunderstood, a victim of merciless circumstances. Still revered and loved by some elements of his people, he was scorned most vehemently, and most paradoxically, by his former ideologues, the liberals. As the *Risorgimento* pushed ahead, Pius shed completely and forever his once liberal philosophy. In retrospect it can now be seen that what shattered and angered Pius so, viz. the removal of the papacy from all secular governmental matters, actually was to elevate the spiritual and intellectual status and esteem of the institution and perhaps ensure its survival.

The greatest event of the Pius IX pontificate was certainly the Vatican Council, the twentieth such ecumenical council in the Church's history. Convened in 1869 when the pall of imminent seizure of the Papal States by Italian troops hung over the Church, it had to be adjourned *sine die* when the Italians took Rome. In its brief tenure it was important chiefly for its enunciation of the doctrine of papal infallibility, according to which the pope, when speaking on matters of faith and morals *ex cathedra* ("from the chair," i.e. in his official capacity as head of the Church and vicar of Christ on earth), cannot err. This universally held conviction on the part of the Church for many centuries meant that Pius IX's earlier declaration in 1854 that Mary, the mother of Jesus, had been conceived without original sin was a dogma to be believed by all the faithful.

Through the Council and by way of many other measures of his, Pius had reenforced the primacy of the pope, and had greatly centralized the power of the papacy over the world Church. Under his reign, missionary activity all over the globe received great impetus, Catholic hierarchies in several Protestant countries were reestablished. Sts. Francis de Sales and Alphonsus Ligouri were raised to the status of Fathers of the Church. Catherine of Siena was made patron saint of Rome and the still influential semi-official Vatican newspaper, *L'Osservatore Romano*, was founded.

Quanta Cura, another of the pope's powerful encyclicals, was issued in 1864 and was a bitter invective against the revolutionary excesses of the day, including the eroding influence of liberalism on religious integrity. Appended to the encyclical was a *Syllabus of Errors*, a list of eighty propositions from previous papal pronouncements condemning the excesses more specifically.

Out of their original context these propositions were vulnerable to distortions and were in fact often maliciously misinterpreted. For example, the last of these, which in spirit denounced those who would deny the Church a role in modern society, was translated as papal opposition to progress and modern society. While Pius' intransigence in the face of the mighty tide of change in Italy hurt his image with contemporary liberal historians, no objective observer could charge him with a unilateral opposition to progress and modern society. But the *Syllabus* became another weapon in the hands of Pius' foes and they wielded it vigorously, and often, to discredit him further in the eyes of the populace.

Pius' passing precipitated a new rash of predictions and fears that the Holy See was finished, and even if it should somehow miraculously survive, its voice would be so meaningless as to be worthless. But again the prophets of such papal demise were proven wrong. For Gioacchino Cardinal Pecci, the cardinal camerlengo (chamberlain) charged with verifying the pontiff's death, would be just the man to lead the Church boldly into its twentieth century.

PART II

The Pontiffs of Our Century

CHAPTER VI

POPE LEO XIII

Funeral arrangements also fell to Pecci. Custom called for the body to lie in state for public veneration in the Sistine chapel. However, Pecci feared that when the crowds gathered in the relatively small Sistine, the Italian government might send in its troops on the pretext of helping to maintain order, and once gotten them inside the Vatican for whatever reason, might never withdraw them. So that the government would not fabricate reasons for meddling, the camerlengo decided to have Pius repose in state before the high altar in the immense basilica of St. Peter. But even in death, and in spite of Pecci's efforts Pius was still not free from the animosity of his enemies nor even from attempted bodily assault. Over the years, Pius had expressed many times a desire to be entombed in his favorite church, the historic basilica of St. Lawrence Outside the Walls, a little beyond the Eternal City on the consular Via Tiburtina. On the day of the funeral, the papal cortege wended its mournful way down from the Vatican, around Castel Sant' Angelo and was proceeding over the bridge when a gang of Church-hating thugs attempted to wrest the casket from the Palatine guard and toss it into the swollen Tiber. For a few harrowing moments it seemed the attack would succeed, but the papal escort rescued Pius' remains and the procession continued on its way.

Normally, the post of chamberlain is not a stepping stone to Peter's chair, but in the conclave, organized by Pecci himself, the red-robed cardinals, assembled beneath the frescoes of the Sistine ceiling, looked to him for leadership in their turbulent times. Pecci decided upon the name Leo XIII.

Tall, slight of frame, ascetic, with white hair and piercing eyes, Leo presented a regal figure indeed. Though already quite old (68), the newly crowned pope spared no time in revealing the dynamic manner that was to mark his pontificate. And surely no one who witnessed the coronation ceremony ever dreamed that it was the beginning of a twenty-five year reign.

Born in Carpineto on March 2, 1810, young Gioacchino was educated at the well-known and highly regarded Jesuit College in enchanting Viterbo. His rise in the priesthood was rapid. Pope Gregory XVI selected the gifted scholar for service in the papal diplomatic corps. Having shown extraordinary ability in his early assignments, Pecci was named nuncio (ambassador) to Belgium in 1843, and two years later, bishop of the important diocese of Perugia. Pius IX gave him the red hat in 1853. As Cardinal Pecci he drew much attention for his eloquent and hard-hitting sermons on the social evils of the day. This crusade he continued via his encyclicals as pope. *Rerum Novarum* published in 1891, perhaps his most famous encyclical, took the Church's message to the factories and farms and slums and had a great impact on labor practices. Leo was liberal, progressive, providential. But his reign was not without trouble and tension. Initially, those who hoped for an easing of the friction between the Vatican and the State took much encouragement from Pecci's conciliatory manner. In fact, Pope Leo urged Catholics to bend a little, to adapt to their various forms of government in the interest of peace. He advised against the clergy participating in politics and with his very effective, experienced diplomatic ways, he struck a peaceful balance, was able to cool anti-Catholic sentiment in various European lands, and for all the world seemed to be steering the Church and the Italian government slowly but surely toward an amicable relationship. And he did this despite the fact that early in the 1880's the still festering anti-papal revolutionary mood of Rome caused Leo to give some thought to leaving the Eternal City

for a less electrified atmosphere, perhaps in Austria.

In 1886, though, when Leo met with government leaders and demanded full restoration of his sovereignty, he once again incurred the wrath of the opposition. Thus the Roman Question went on begging for a solution. His diplomatic efforts with other individual states did, however, bear the fruit of reestablished official ties between them and the Vatican.

As Supreme Pontiff, Leo was also deeply committed to the improvement of religious instruction which he insisted be Aquinas-oriented. In addition to his expertise on the life and works of St. Thomas, he was also a poet of considerable talent in both ancient Latin and Homeric Greek. He spent much of his meager leisure time, right up to his death-bed, reading the likes of Virgil, Horace, Tacitus and Cicero. To foster learning he opened the Vatican library and archives to scholars and historians on whom he imposed but one stipulation, "to get at the truth and tell it in its entirety."

In retrospect, Leo XIII's reign can also be marked by his nomination of John Henry Newman for the cardinalate. Pecci used to call the future saint, *"Il mio cardiale."*

Indefatigable, Leo punished himself with incredibly long work days and monastic personal discipline. His table was frugal. Breakfast was a cup of *espresso* and part of a roll. Two in the afternoon was the hour for the main meal of the day which consisted of soup, a bit of meat, a portion of vegetables and a piece of fruit. For his beverage, he took a small glass of wine (usually French). His only recreation was a daily afternoon walk or ride in the luxuriant Vatican gardens. In the heat of the Roman summers this was deferred until the evening.

And while he demanded from all those who worked under him a similar commitment to hard work in the vineyards of the Lord, he still enjoyed their affection and esteem. People marveled at Leo's tender habit of holding the hand of anyone who came to speak to him.

Just when it seemed Pope Leo XIII would reign forever, the great man fell victim to pneumonia and pleurisy. Though he fought this battle as tenaciously and courageously as he had fought all others in his long, illustrious, and holy life, he did not prevail. Pope Leo XIII, scholarly pope and friend of the working man, skilled diplomat and renowned teacher of religious truths, architect of ideas and giant among the hundreds of successors to Peter, succumbed to his ailments in his little Vatican apartment overlooking the *Piazza San Pietro* on the evening of July 20, 1903. He was 93. As the western sun cast its orange glow over the city, Rome's church bells tolled the sad message of the loss of its beloved bishop.

Originally Leo's remains were entombed alongside many of his predecessors in the grottoes beneath St. Peter's, but in 1924 they were removed to the Lateran basilica, St. John's, where they lie across from the tomb of another giant of the papacy, Innocent III.

CHAPTER VII

POPE PIUS X

Early in his reign Pope Leo XIII had been particularly impressed by the holiness and brilliance of a young monsignor, Giuseppe Sarto, from Riese in northern Italy. When first the Holy Father named him bishop of the diocese of Mantua, Sarto sought to decline the appointment partly out of natural humility and partly out of his desire to continue the behind-the-scenes work he loved. Two months later, in November of 1884, Sarto visited the pope and made an in-person request that Leo rescind the appointment. The pontiff smiled compassionately but answered with a firm, irrevocable, "No!" When the new bishop departed, Pope Leo confided to aides that the people of Mantua were getting a saint for a spiritual shepherd. (And indeed, on May 29, 1954 Giuseppe Sarto, Leo's successor as Pius X, was canonized a saint in St. Peter's by Pope Pius XII.)

Leo advanced Sarto's priestly career further by choosing him for the college of cardinals in 1893 and at the same time assigning him as patriarch of Venice, one of the most esteemed positions in the Church. (Pope John XXIII, as Angelo Cardinal Roncalli, and Pope John Paul I as Albino Cardinal Luciani, both served in the same post just prior to their elections to the papacy.) From his earliest days as cardinal, Sarto was considered by many, Leo included, as highly *papabile* (an Italian neologism meaning an outstanding prospect for the papacy).

As night fell over the Tiber on August 4, 1903 the Romans at their favorite coffee bars, sidewalk cafes and local trattorie toasted the election that morning of the new fisherman. And as the hubbub swirled about in the old, picturesque streets six stories below, the new pope, Pius X, stood at the window of his small apartment and nudged open a shutter to look out over the rooftops of his beautiful diocese. (How sad it was that this gregarious, people-loving man felt obliged to maintain Pius IX's "Prisoner of the Vatican" policy. Like his two predecessors, he refused to leave the little enclave throughout his reign, though he longed to go out into the streets and piazzas of his diocese to meet his flock.) His reverie was interrupted by a knock on the door. It was the popular and handsome young monsignor with the musical name, Raphael Merry del Val, who had brought with him the first documents to be signed by the new pope, letters to all the world's heads of state officially announcing the pontiff's election. Merry del Val was completing his final assignment as secretary of the conclave and took the opportunity to ask the Holy Father's permission to leave the Vatican the next day to return to his home.

Recognizing a rare talent in him, the Holy Father implored the monsignor "not to abandon me." A few short months later, the pope startled the world by naming the thirty-eight-year-old Merry del Val both a cardinal and the Vatican secretary of state. Pius, in explaining his choice to some of the cardinals, stated: "Merry del Val is my choice for one reason, that he is a linguist. Moreover, having been born in England, educated in Belgium, being of Spanish nationality, and partly of Irish descent, living for so long in Italy, son of a diplomat and one himself, he is admirably conversant with problems of every nation. He is able to brief me each day with an extraordinary perception on affairs around the globe."

In addition to their working alliance, a deep and beautiful bond of friendship quickly grew between the two men. And Merry del Val, as Pius predicted he would, was to prove a marvelous asset to his beloved pontiff. He was considered the first truly great papal secretary of state and the preeminent *papabile* in the college of cardinals.

Pius, who prayed almost frantically throughout the conclave that the cardinals might not choose him, once elected, poured his total and astounding energy and sanctity into the staggering task confronting him. Two days later, August 6, at eleven in the morning he received in formal audience the entire foreign diplomatic corps. Sarto, who had grown up in the country and whose greatest ambition in the seminary was to be a good priest in some quiet village parish, could not and would not hide his peasant upbringing, but nonetheless won the reverence and affection of the ambassadors and ministers with his humility, his purity, his intelligence, his piety and his wit. This last quality, which he maintained and consciously worked at (he loved to hear and to tell hilarious stories) to the end of his days, particularly endeared him to all who met him. He used his mealtime as his only source of recreation and insisted of those who shared his table that they not engage in solemn talk at that time. Whenever someone broke this understanding the pope immediately sentenced the offender to tell a funny story.

Pope St. Pius X lived and worked by his personal motto: *Instaurare omnia in Christo* (to renew everything in Christo). After the intransigence of Pius IX toward the Roman Question and the somewhat less rigid stance of Leo XIII, everyone waited anxiously to learn what Pius X's position would be. While his reign did not see the resolution of the problem, it did steer a middle course that left the door open for much hope and optimism and helped to lay the groundwork that resulted in the concordat of two pontificates later.

Papa Sarto never divested himself, nor did he desire to, of his humble ways. It was his express wish that "the new cross that God has given me to bear," as he referred to the burdens of the papacy, not alter the purity and simplicity of the lives of his family. Hoping to gain the pontiff's favor, or at least his appreciation, some bigwigs in government and industry sought to provide Pius' brother Angelo with a better job. The pope insisted that Angelo stay on at his post in the village post office. Rosa, Maria and Anna, his sisters, had from his first pastorate lived with him and looked after his domestic needs. It was assumed that these three would move into the Vatican after his election. To avoid the slightest semblance of favoritism the Holy Father secured an apartment for them about half way between the Vatican and the Tiber, in the crowded Roman quarter called "Il Borgo."

By his simple goodness, quiet wisdom, burning zeal and unshakable courage he had an invigorating influence on the Church and a placating effect on some of its bitter foes. Catholics today who angrily oppose the current direction of the Church as "secularization" might like to know that Pius back then had an abhorrence for the spirit of modernism in the Church and articulated his vehement opposition to "secularization" in his 1907 encyclical, *Pascendi*. It must be here understood that by "modernism" Pius X was not referring to man's technological advances, for those he wholly endorsed and encouraged. Rather the term, as he used it, meant the revision and accomodation of the dogmas of faith to the fads of the day. Because of the Holy Father's relentless attacks on modernism a dangerous Church trend in that direction was effectively slowed.

Noted for his affection for the common people (and theirs for him), Pius X was one of the most loved popes ever to occupy the throne of Peter. (He was in the habit of carrying a little cash in the wide sleeve cuff of his white soutane and whenever someone obviously in financial need appeared before him he would inconspicuously reach in for a fistful and slip it into the poor person's hand.) By his direction, Church music, which he thought was not as solemn and inspiring as it could be, was reformed. The papal court was reorganized, as were the

seminaries. The priest's breviary was revised. The mind-boggling task of updating and codifying all of canon law was undertaken. Already known for his constant exhortation to Catholics everywhere to receive Holy Communion frequently, he came to be called the pope of the Eucharist when he lowered the age for receiving the Sacrament to the age of reason (approximately seven years old), so that everyone could receive that many more times in his or her lifetime.

One day at an audience, a British lady introduced her four-year-old son to His Holiness. In a brief conversation with the lad, the pope found an unusual maturity and intelligence, especially with regard to Holy Communion. Pius advised the mother to bring her little one to him the following day. "I'll personally give him Holy Communion," the pontiff insisted.

Spring of 1912 saw hundreds of French children under the supervision of their nuns and priests journey over the Alps to Rome so that they might personally thank the Holy Father for giving them, at such a tender age, the privilege of receiving the Eucharist. All of this was consistent with the pontiff's deep love for children. He was happiest in their midst. It was for them that he established the Confraternity of Christian Doctrine (CCD) and encouraged lay involvement in Catholic Action groups everywhere.

Tragically, though, this inherently happy and optimistic man of God was to spend his final years and months in a state of increasing melancholy and worry. With his handsome face crowned by that full shock of white hair, his square jaw, clear complexion, smiling eyes, and erect frame belying his woefully burdened spirit, Pius deplored the collision course being pursued by the contemporary world powers. He foresaw the holocaust we call World War I and fretted over his inability to do anything about its coming. He agonized at each report from France that the clergy was suffering increased harassment, and from Germany where the Church was under a merciless barrage of threats and intimidation, and from remote Mexico where bishops were dragged from their chanceries to suffer humiliation and worse, bodily harm, and even from the seminaries of Rome where theological students from every nation were being summoned home to do their part in the coming war.

All his life Giuseppe Sarto took pride in having dominion over his emotions. But the frustration and anguish pent up inside of him spilled over for all to see in his final days. On August 1, 1914, Germany declared war on Russia, and two days later on France. On the next morning Britain declared war on Germany. The savagery of World War I had begun. During those days the pope was beseiged with requests to bless the cause of first this nation, then that one. He fumed. When the Austrian delegate to the Holy See came for an audience in full military garb and asked for an apostolic blessing upon the Austrian armies, the pope erupted. "I bless peace, not war," he bellowed at the stunned ambassador. The audience was over.

A bronchial infection which the once robust pope would have managed without effort was now too much for him. With the European War, soon to become a World War, raging about him, the future saint slipped away at about one in the morning, August 20, 1914, in the embrace of his devoted friend and secretary of state, Raphael Merry del Val.

CHAPTER VIII

POPE BENEDICT XV

With the battlefield expanding rapidly, the cardinals buried one pope and then went into conclave to create another, seeking among themselves a diplomat *extraordinaire* who might have just the formula for easing global tensions. They found one in little, laconic, likable Giacomo della Chiesa (a name which translates propitiously to James of the Church). Though he faced a frightening task, della Chiesa accepted his election under the name of Benedict XV. A product of a superb education, including the Gregorian University of Rome, Giacomo as a young priest profoundly impressed his superiors in his every assignment. At age twenty five he had become a doctor of sacred theology. Soon after he entered the papal diplomatic service and rose swiftly through the ranks. Cardinal Rampolla, Leo XIII's secretary of state, was so taken with young della Chiesa's brilliance that he had made him under-secretary and sought his counsel in every decision. Convinced that he would be an outstanding administrator as well, Pope Pius X in 1907 selected him first for the archbishopric of Bologna and then in 1914 for the cardinalate.

As the Supreme Pontiff of the Church and spiritual father of Catholics of every nation della Chiesa felt obliged and wholeheartedly endeavored to maintain a position of neutrality. In the third year of the awful war, 1917, Pope Benedict sought the role of mediator between the powers. That same year he sent Eugenio Pacelli, the "man born to be pope," as the papal nuncio to Germany.

From his nunciature in Munich the brainy Pacelli, who would be tapped to steer the Church through the next World War two decades later as Pope Pius XII, conducted important talks with the German chancellor and kaiser, especially on the topic of Belgium independence. Tragically, though, the Holy Father's hopes of bringing all the belligerents to the conference table were dashed. Recognizing his powerlessness to halt the war he put his full energies behind a campaign to at least reduce the suffering. For one example he enjoyed considerable success in prodding the combatants into an exchange of disabled prisoners. For another, he was instrumental in helping, financially and otherwise, the war's civilian victims in all the nations involved.

Woodrow Wilson's dream of a League of Nations had a devoted friend in Benedict. Having given all his personal moral support and all the prestige of his holy office to the idea, the long-suffering pontiff was understandably crushed when it failed.

Though the war, its prelude, and its aftermath took up a large measure of Pope Benedict's time and attention and efforts for most of his reign, he was still able to accomplish many things to advance the cause of the gospel and of the Church throughout the world. Even with the war still raging, the tireless pontiff oversaw the final stages of the work on the revised code of canon law. Typical of him, though, was his reluctance to accept any of the credit and his eagerness to attribute the success of the project to its initiator, his predecessor, Pius X. He wrote a dozen encyclicals, the greatest of which were *Ad Beatissimi* (November 1, 1914) in which he outlined some concrete plan for restoring peace, and *Pacem Dei Munus* (May 20, 1920) in which he appealed for the preservation of the newly acquired peace.

Another document which does not enjoy encyclical status is his address entitled *Des le debut* (August 1, 1917) to all the belligerent peoples and their leaders. Benedict's inherent goodness, love for God's children,

personal agony over the horrible war, compassion and understanding for all parties involved all come through in his touching and tender words:

> "... Since the beginning of Our Pontificate, in the midst of horrors of the terrible war which has burst upon Europe, We have considered three things among others:
>
> To maintain an absolute impartiality towards all belligerents, as becomes him who is the Common Father, and who loves all his children with an equal affection;
>
> To endeavor continually to do the utmost good to all without distinction of persons, nationality or religion in accordance not only with the universal law of charity, but also with the supreme spiritual duty laid upon Us by Christ;
>
> And finally, as is demanded by Our pacific mission to omit nothing, as far as in Our power lies, to contribute to hasten the end of this calamity by trying to bring the peoples and their leaders to more moderate resolutions in the discussion of means that will secure a just and lasting peace."

Under "Papa Benedetto" as his Roman flock called him, the estrangement between the Church and Italy was guided further toward its ultimate solution thanks to the conciliatory spirit of the pope's communications with the State. In his speeches and writings he would refer to his homeland as "beloved Italy" and to the Italian ruler as "his majesty, the king of Italy" instead of "the duke of Savoy."

In the sixth year of the reign of Benedict XV, Joan of Arc was raised to sainthood.

With the little time left to him on earth this wonderful priest, this true *Alter Christus* and outstanding pope worked with incredible vigor to foster a new *Pax Romana*, a genuine and lasting peace. He had lived his life true to his name, "of the Church," from his days as a seven-year-old lad playing priest, "saying Mass" in vestments made by his grandmother on an altar fashioned by his grandfather, to his historic pontificate helping to save the world from itself.

In the early days of 1922 His Holiness, exhausted from

all the awful burdens, had little resistance to offer against an attack of influenza. The flu had an easy time of advancing to pneumonia. Still he insisted on keeping his public appearances. On the morning of January 12, Benedict celebrated Mass in the chilly basilica and distributed the Eucharist to a hundred communicants. Later that day, the incessant cough that was ripping his poor chest took a grave toll on what little was left of his energy. Nine days later every cardinal residing in Rome was summoned to the bedside of the dying fisherman. (In the group, but alone with his memories, was the man all of Rome thought would surely someday be pope, but whose time had now passed, Cardinal Merry del Val, secretary of state and *alter ego* of St. Pius X.)

Late that afternoon Benedict became delirious with violent fever but rallied slightly at about ten that night. Reflexively he inquired the time and when told became frantic. Throwing back the covers he struggled to get up, crying prophetically, "There's plenty of time until six o'clock and much for me to do!"

But the course was almost run. As the night wore on, the pontiff's life ebbed away. The following morning the daily Vatican bulletin on the Holy Father's condition, though expected, stunned Rome: "The Supreme Pontiff, Benedict XV, on the 22nd of January at the hour of six, with great holiness fell asleep in the Lord."

In his last moments of lucidity he called out in a voice strong enough to be heard clearly in the adjoining rooms and corridors: *"Offriamo volentieri la vita per la pace del mondo."* ("We gladly offer our life for the peace of the world.")

Late in the morning of the final day of the conclave following Benedict's death, word was passed throughout the throng of Romans waiting excitedly in St. Peter's square that the scholarly archbishop of Milan, Achille Cardinal Ratti, was their new bishop and *ipso facto* the Church's new Supreme Pontiff. For his papal name Ratti chose Pius XI.

It was but four years earlier that this same man, as Monsignor Ratti, was quite happy and contented in the important post which suited his intellectual gifts and in which he assumed he would finish out his priestly life, that of the director of the Vatican library.

CHAPTER IX

POPE PIUS XI

Born May 31, 1857 in Desio near Lake Como to the wife of an affluent manufacturer, Ratti early on impressed his teachers with his first-rate, brilliant, and encyclopedic mind. Because of his serious manner and his contemplative nature he came to be known as, "the young old man" among his teachers. Achille took seminary training at the Lombard College at Rome, an institution laden with prestige and traditionally reserved for the gifted and promising, a sort of ecclesiastical West Point where future officers of the Church's army matriculated. On a sunny but chilly Roman December 20th in 1879, the cerebral Achille Ratti, with the owl-like countenance, was ordained a priest. Then on the following morning in the church of San Carlo on the Via del Corso in Rome, before row after row of family and cousins, *compari* and *amici* who had made the happy trek together by train from Desio, Father Ratti celebrated his first Mass. His last Mass would be celebrated in the same city six decades later, not under the name of Father Ratti but rather of Pope Pius XI. Between those two Masses this man, one of the greatest human beings of our century, would spend a magnificent priesthood and a beautiful private life.

Though bookish all his life, Achille had an athletic side too. This model of spirituality also endorsed the Spartan philosophy of "a healthy mind in a healthy body." From early boyhood, mountain climbing held a special fascination for him and he continued the activity through his school days and seminary years and even far into his priestly career. "There are few recreations more wholesome for body and mind," he used to say.

Ratti was also a gifted writer with a most charming and readable style. His delightful little book, "Memoirs of a Mountaineer," recalls his bouts with a number of Alpine peaks. And it is evident that his approach to these endeavors and his preparations for them were a fine blend of his mountaineering skills and his painstaking, scholarly methodology. On July 29, 1889 young *Don Ratti* (*Don* is the Italian term for addressing a priest), another priest and two guides were the first Italians to conquer Monte Rosa on the Swiss-Italian border, a most treacherous ascent to a peak of 15,400 feet. Ratti's account of the deed is simply eloquent:

"Solemn silence dominated all about. In the endless velvety blue sky the stars shone brightly. All around us the enormous masses and their immense shadows extended and intermingled on the white expanses of ice and snow."

Father Ratti goes on to describe the group's rest period after a dozen hours or so of climbing:

"As we reposed in the snow we thrilled to the background, a huge massive wall of solid ice whose brow protruded out over our heads and provided a canopy of crystal. Surely it was not the most comfortable resting place. Still it was rather safe for anyone with a measure of self-confidence. Anyone sitting down found his feet dangling in space. One dare not take a step in any direction nor fall asleep. But then who could ever sleep in the face of such breathtaking scenery? The cold was so intense that our coffee, our food, indeed even our wine was frozen solid. Yet we sat there each absorbed, lost, in his own deep thoughts. The deafening silence was only occasionally interrupted, and then by great avalanches breaking loose below us. While we could hear the awesome cascade we could not view it. From our resting point we saw the dawn break in all its fiery splendor, lighting up a thousand white slopes with a medley of pastel tints. Soon it was time to move onward and upward to our goal, Dufour Peak."

Achille's penchant for academic challenge had earned him doctorates in canon law, theology, and philosophy. The exceptionally erudite young cleric was summoned to the Apostolic Palace in the Vatican to receive the personal commendation and encouragement of His Holiness, Pope Leo XIII. At the age of twenty five, Father Ratti was given a teaching post at the seminary in Milan and there was held in esteem and affection by the young aspirants. Seven years later he was invited to join the staff of one of the world's most prestigious libraries, the *Biblioteca Ambrosiana* in Milan. And so for the next three decades Ratti was engaged in library work, a task most compatible with his love of scholarship, his reverence for books. From all points of the globe came scholars to study and research at the *Ambrosiana* and virtually all sought the counsel and assistance of the future pontiff. As he viewed it, the principal role of the librarian was to help out in all the intellectual activity that was going on around him. Accordingly, whenever someone requested his guidance, Ratti obliged him, quickly and gladly, putting aside whatever private study he was pursuing.

Remarkably, the energetic priest still found room in his schedule for other sacerdotal functions. For instance, he served as chaplain for an order of nuns in Milan, taught religion classes for children in the city's slums, and because of his fluent German was able to serve as chaplain for the German community there. Early in 1914, Ratti journeyed to Oxford where at the renowned university he delivered a two hour address, in Latin, on the 400th anniversary of the birth of Roger Bacon. (At the time Latin was still the international language of scholars.) Later that same year he was appointed by Pope Pius X to the position of prefect of the Vatican library. This was the most thrilling milestone of his priesthood—thus far, that is—and he truly loved the work and relished the challenge.

Then in the spring of 1918, with no advance notice, he was selected by Benedict XV to be the apostolic envoy to Warsaw, a post created in answer to the Polish bishops' request. The prelates felt that the physical presence of a Vatican representative would remind the troubled people of Poland that at least their ties with the Church of Rome had not been altered by the political upheavals engulfing them.

Though reluctant to leave his first love, the library, once he accepted the new assignment Ratti brought to it the same zeal and total commitment he had given his every previous mission. His residence in Warsaw remained always open to all who might desire to see him for whatever reason. When Trotsky's Red Army advanced on the Polish capital, many foreign diplomats rushed to evacuate but not the one from the Vatican. For this demonstration of loyalty and courage Ratti won the hearts and admiration of the people and was raised to the ranks of papal nuncio. Poles everywhere rejoiced that the pope would consider their beleaguered country worthy enough and important enough for such a high level of diplomatic relations and they jammed the old cathedral to witness the nuncio's consecration as archbishop by Bishop, later, Cardinal, Kakowski. Trusted completely by both the Germans and the Poles, Ratti was to stay on long enough to play a vital role in the post war settlements. After a virtual lifetime spent in the calm of the library, the remarkable scholar had been tossed into the maelstrom of international politics and had done another customary *summa cum laude* job.

Back in Rome the Holy Father was planning the next phase of Ratti's career. 1912 would see him recalled from Warsaw to Rome where he was given the red hat of the cardinalate by an admiring and grateful pontiff and then shipped off to take charge of the very important diocese of Milan.

But before assuming his new duties he went on a pilgrimage of spiritual renewal, first to Lourdes and then for a month of meditation and prayerful solitude at the ancient Benedictine monastery high upon Monte Cassino. His entry into his new see was a memorable one. From his flock he received a tumultuous welcome. An airplane showered flowers upon his entourage, bands and soldiers

paraded to the *Duomo* (as the Milanese call their cathedral) where some forty thousand applauding citizens filled the piazza out front to overflowing.

Crowds of young people shouted: *Viva Il Cardinale della gioventu!* ("Long live the Cardinal of the youth!"), to which he quickly rejoined: *"Vivano i giovani amici del Cardinale!"* ("Long live the young friends of the Cardinal!").

In his moving first public address he clearly revealed that he intended to be truly the people's cardinal. "The house of your shepherd will be ever open and accessible to you. However young, however poor, however humble you may be, never for a moment feel that my steps are so high that you cannot easily climb them to come and see me."

Barely had Cardinal Ratti established his episcopal residence in the industrial city, five months to be exact, when the announcement of Pope Benedict's death on January 22, 1922 saddened the Catholic world. Soon the cardinal found himself packing for a train ride unaware that he was on his way to a rendezvous with destiny. He paid little or no mind to the many references to him in the press as one of the leading *papabili*. On February 6, he entered the conclave with fifty-two other members of the sacred college. Once again the Michelangelo-frescoed Sistine chapel was the polling place. After the traditional solemn rites the balloting began and a decision was swiftly reached. Cardinal Laurenti, the noble and pious director of the Propagation of the Faith was his colleagues' choice. But then something mindboggling occurred. Cardinal Laurenti declined the election and in a quavering voice implored the college to "choose for this most exalted office someone stronger and better able to sustain the heavy burden."

The incredulous cardinals began soon to ballot again and after several votes decided in favor of Achille Ambrogio Damiano Ratti. This time the elected one accepted, taking for his pontifical name Pius XI.

Then something else startling took place. Pope Pius XI wished to end, at long last, the awful animosity between the Church and the Italian State which was now entering its fifth decade. Seeking to initiate "that peace for which humanity is longing" and not wishing to be the next "Prisoner of the Vatican," the new Pius, against the counsel of some conservative cardinals, proceeded through the halls of the Vatican to the balcony of St. Peter's where he would impart his first apostolic blessing.

Down in the jammed square the multitude, now aware of the election of a new pope but unaware of who he was and what he was about to do, surged toward the basilica. For it was inside St. Peter's that each new pope for the last forty years had made his first appearance. When blocked at the basilica doors by the Vatican gendarmes and the Swiss guards and informed of the impending papal appearance on the outside balcony, the tide frantically reversed itself to be able to witness this moment of history.

At the first glimpse of their new bishop in his white papal cassock the Romans went wild with joy. And their government leaders went wild with hopeful anticipation that the long period of tension which they had often sought in vain to end was indeed about to come to a close. They read in Pius' gestures the message that he could live with the abolition of the old Papal States and the creation of the tiny city-state of the Vatican. Just as anxious as Pius XI was to put aside the long festering bitterness was Benito Mussolini, former right-wing journalist, now Fascist party leader, soon to be absolute ruler of all of Italy. Not for the humaneness of it all was Mussolini so terribly interested but rather for the political advantage he hoped would come from a concordat.

Laying the groundwork for a solution to the touchy issue consumed a great deal of behind-the-scenes energy on the part of the new pope. After four years of exchanging "feelers" the Church and State commenced informal negotiations in the late summer of 1926, with

Signor Barone, an Italian privy councillor, representing the government and Marquis Pacelli, brother of Eugenio Cardinal Pacelli who would follow Ratti to the chair of Peter as Pope Pius XII, stating the Vatican's case. After more than a hundred conferences, often lasting from ten in the morning to seven at night, on this lower diplomatic level over a span of two and a half years, an understanding was reached and, in January of 1919, meetings were arranged on a higher level. Involved now was a veritable army of jurists, specialists, protocolists, rhetoricians on both sides. The papal secretary of state, Cardinal Gasparri, was now articulating for the pope while Mussolini himself was the king's spokesman.

At noon on February 11, 1929, Cardinal Gasparri received Mussolini in the Lateran Palace. In the presence of their respective entourages the two men signed the agreement which would be known as the Lateran Treaty.

On the following day the pope observed the seventh anniversary of his coronation in the festively decorated basilica. As he entered the great church he was exuberantly cheered by eighty thousand of his spiritual sons and daughters. Among the honored guests were high-ranking Italian government and military dignitaries and important personages from other nations. After Mass he stepped out on the central balcony to bless the quarter of a million cheering people in the square. That night the happy Romans gathered below the pope's window to applaud and serenade him with the *Te Deum* and other hymns and then walked en masse to the royal residence to pay homage to the king and queen.

Foremost among the many provisions of the Lateran Treaty was the creation of a sovereign and independent new state, a 108-acre enclave in transpontine Rome called Vatican City, and a guarantee of the pope's inviolability by the Italian State. In many respects the State had done the papacy a favor by confiscating the territory of the Papal States. For the pontiffs ever since, relieved of the time and energy-consuming burden of civil rule, have been able to devote all of their attention and vigor to the spiritual aspects of their office and to become known to the world for their exemplary sanctity.

Also provided by the Lateran pact were some extra-territorial Vatican properties in and around Rome: the three other patriarchal basilicas (i.e. in addition to St. Peter's), St. Mary Major, St. John Lateran and St. Paul's Outside the Walls along with the real estate on which they stand plus some other buildings in the Eternal City and the papal summer estate in the town of Castel Gandolfo in the Alban hills.

In addition, the Italian government granted financial compensation, Catholicism was established as the official state religion, the Church was obliged to offer prayers for Italy and her people, and religious education programs were instituted in the schools. Other passages in the agreement which must have pleased the Church leaders were the requirement of a religious ceremony for a marriage to be valid, the prohibition of divorce and the promise of no government meddling in ecclesiastical affairs.

The uneasy tranquility achieved by the settlement was soon shattered, however, by Mussolini's assaults on the clergy and on Church property in reprisal for admonitions from the pulpits about the inherent evils and dangers of fascism. Anti-papal demonstrations were conducted in the streets and squares of Rome; copies of the Vatican daily, *L'Osservatore Romano*, were burned under the pope's windows; a bishop's residence was set aflame; Mussolini's thugs disrupted meetings of Catholic youth organizations and pummeled the participants. And all the while the police managed to see nothing. Instead they charged the young people's clubs that were part of the Catholic Action movement with disturbing the peace and creating the unrest. But there would be no backing down by the inheritor of St. Peter's mantle. On the contrary, Pius strengthened the wording of his personal warnings and obloquies and encouraged his bishops and priests to do likewise. And in 1931 the Holy Father formalized in a papal encyclical his denunciation of fascism as a system which sought to obliterate God from the fabric of society. In the fascist view the child's first duty was to the state, body and soul. Everything else, family, Church, social life, was in a very distant second place. Pius XI saw fascism as a movement which would in time ". . . absorb, swallow and annihilate the individual and the family. This would be an absurd contradiction to the normal order of things, for the family existed before the state." He charged that fascism, with its exaltation of the state and the submission to it of the individual, was founded largely in the discredited paganism of old Rome.

Because of the ugly emotional climate, however, the pontiff chose an unusual way to release the document. Fearing attempts by the Italian government to censor or crush the encyclical which was entitled, *Non Abbiamo Bisogno*, His Holiness summoned the young cherub-faced, congenial highly-regarded American monsignor, then attached to the Vatican secretariat, Francis J. Spellman (the future cardinal archbishop of New York). Spellman's mission was to smuggle copies of the encyclical past the gauntlet of the fascist police, up through northern Italy, over the Alps into France, there to release to the world in the French capital of Paris the spirited pontifical words of protest.

When the world-wide reception of the document was warm and sympathetic, Mussolini, ever the expedient politician, withdrew from open warfare with the Church and made overtures toward harmonious relations with the Vatican indicating that the fascists would cease and desist their attacks on the clergy, the CYO (Catholic Youth Organization), the Church and her property.

In twenty nine other encyclicals (the largest number ever written by one pope), Pius XI, the consummate scholar, continued to illuminate the problems and evils of the day and to propose concrete courses of action by which to combat them. Tireless in his crusade for justice, peace, and the dignity of the human being, Pius issued more statements denouncing atheistic communism and others criticizing nationalism, racism and anti-Semitism. Forty years after Leo XIII's plea on the same subject, Pius XI wrote the encyclical, *Quadragesimo Anno* (1931), criticizing the exploitation of the worker by laissez-faire capitalism and at the same time urging social and industrial reform. It can be said that the key *motif* of his pontificate was his determination to impress upon the world the gravity of the dangers of both communism and fascism. Papal denunciations of atheistic communism, not only in Russia, but also in Spain and Mexico were particularly bitter and frequent, climaxing in the 1937 encyclical, *Divini Redemptoris.*

Besides these encyclicals and the treaty and concordat negotiated with the Italian state, Pius' reign is also notable for a whole series of concordats (Church-State pacts, carrying the force of law, concerning matters of mutual concern with the particular understanding that the State recognize the special, inviolable status of the Church in its midst). One such accord was reached with the new dictator in Germany, Adolf Hitler, in 1933. *Der Feuhrer* wasted no time in violating it, however. His persecution of the Church in the country of the Rhine was savage and was promptly and loudly condemned in official papal utterances and documents and especially so in the powerful encyclical of 1937, *Mit brennender Sorge,* addressed to the bishops of Germany. And, like *Non Abbiamo Bisogno,* this, too, Pius smuggled out of Italy.

Throughout his pontificate it was also his desire that the laity enjoy a greater share in all things religious and that more cordial relations be fostered with the Eastern and various Protestant Churches. Playing vital supporting roles in virtually all of Pius' endeavors were Cardinals Pietro Gasparri, architect of the Lateran pact, and Eugenio Pacelli. It is Pacelli, as the fascinating and enigmatic Pope Pius XII, about whom we will next be chatting at some length. As secretary of state for the last nine years of the reign of Pius XI, Cardinal Pacelli was in large measure the inspiration of his master's policies.

Pope Pius XI was a stern, confident individual who had for the better part of two decades steered the bark of Peter through violently stormy seas. But as the clouds of the most violent storm (World War II) in human history were thickening, Papa Ratti's tour of duty was drawing to a close.

Late in 1936 the eighty-one-year-old pope had taken ill and the world was informed that he was dying. But the "death watch" taken up by the press in the Eternal City was aborted by the pontiff's resolve to recover and to finish the course. To the astonishment of all, including his physicians, Pope Pius XI celebrated Easter Mass 1937 on the papal altar beneath Bernini's *baldacchino* in St. Peter's and by then had resumed his previous hectic schedule. He had "much to do," he told his close aides. "The pope cannot be ill," he told his doctors. "The pope is in the hands of God who will call him from his labors in His own good time. We shall continue to work until called." And so he went on with his holy work, but he did so under awful bodily suffering, in his own words, "the most atrocious pain." He continued his personal, courageous, relentless war against the "twin political devils of the twentieth century, communism and Nazism."

After two and a half years of living and working with pain as a constant companion, Pius XI, in February, 1939 began to slip away. In the early morning hours of February 10 he was given the last rites of the Church by the papal sacristan, Monsignor Alfonso Camillo de Romanis. An hour and a half later, at 5:31 a.m., Pius XI died. His passing was attributed to cardiac asthma aggravated by a cold. Eugenio Pacelli, the cardinal chamberlain, certified the pontiff's death.

Rome was once again the focus of world attention as the cardinals gathered for the election of a new pope. Newspapers were filled with speculation. Heading everyone's list was the distinguished son of Rome, Eugenio Cardinal Pacelli. This was a sure sign to most that Pacelli would never be elected since an old adage claimed, "He who goes into the conclave a pope, comes out a cardinal" (the heavy favorite never wins). Still the prevailing opinion was that the next pope would be Pacelli.

The voting began on March 2 in the Sistine chapel. Two ballots were taken in the morning, neither resulting in the forty two (of sixty two) votes needed for election. However, it was later learned, there was a strong trend from the beginning toward Cardinal Pacelli. After lunch a third ballot was taken which resulted in his election as Pope Pius XII, a great and holy man whom many still living fondly remember today.

CHAPTER X

POPE PIUS XII

Behind the Church of Santa Maria in Vallicella (more commonly called the *Chiesa Nuova* or New Church), in a typical old quarter of the Eternal City is Via degli Orsini. In number 34, a stately but old apartment building, on the second day of March in 1876, Donna Virginia Graziosi Pacelli, wife of Filippo Pacelli, gave birth to her third child, a boy. The other two children, Francesco and Elisabetta, played happily down in the courtyard as the future pontiff entered the world. Today a marble slab to the left of the entrance reads: "In this house was born on March 2, 1876, Eugenio Pacelli, elected Pope Pius XII on March 2, 1939."

Yes, that's right. Pius was elected pope on his sixty-third birthday, his electors unknowingly fulfilling an old prophecy. Two days after his birth, Eugenio was taken to the church to be baptized by his granduncle, Monsignor Giuseppe Pacelli. After the ceremony, a close friend of the family, Monsignor Iacobacci, held the tiny new member of the Church in his arms and in a serious tone made a statement which in time would prove not only astoundingly prophetic but also amazingly accurate; "Sixty three years from today the people in St. Peter's and all Rome will loudly praise this *bambino*."

Throughout his seminary days and priestly career others predicted the throne of Peter for young Pacelli. An Oblate priest, Joseph Lemius, one of Eugenio's professors remarked: "I am filled with admiration for him. Watch his career closely. He may well be pope someday." Evaristo Carusi, Eugenio's professor in Roman law made a similar forecast.

At the consistory on December 16, 1937 when Pius XI gave the red hat to five new cardinals, including Pacelli, the Holy Father remarked that he would soon be called into eternity, and then added, in Latin, this prediction: "In your midst stands one whom you do not know." That evening Pius confided to one of his closest associates that with those words he had pointed to Pacelli as the next pope. Ultimately the prophecy of Pacelli's ascendancy to the chair of Peter was still being made right up to the final hours before his actual election. On his way into the conclave on the evening of March 1, 1939, Pacelli stumbled and fell to the pavement. He was helped to his feet by the aged Jean Cardinal Verdier of Paris who smilingly but prophetically punned in Latin: *"Vicarius Christi in terra!"* ("The Vicar of Christ on earth"; *"terra"* also means "ground").

Donna Virginia Pacelli was known and admired throughout the neighborhood for her piety and for her devotion to Mary. Several times daily she would lead her children in prayer before their living room shrine to the Blessed Mother. For the rest of his days Eugenio would also be deeply devoted to Mary.

Filippo, Eugenio's dad, belonged to the so-called "Black Nobility" whose members throughout the period of the Roman Question courageously stood by the Church and defended the rights and honor of the pope and refused allegiance to Garibaldi's Italy. And he educated his children to be faithful sons and daughters of the Holy Father. This was in keeping with a long standing family tradition, for many generations of Pacellis had served the Holy See in high posts.

Frail little Eugenio began school at age four, going first to the *Scuola Materna* (nursery school or kindergarten) and then to the *Scuola Elementare,* both run by Sister Prudence and Sister Gertrude of the Congregation of Divine Providence in the *Rione Ponte* section of the city. In 1939 a bust of Pius XII was unveiled at the entrance of the school and the pope sent a personal letter of thanks declaring: "I owe the first principles of my Christian piety to my mother and after that to the reverend sisters of the Congregation of Divine Providence."

Eugenio later attended a private school in the Piazza di Santa Lucia near the renowned and beautiful Jesuit church of *Gesu'*. Before and after school while waiting for his big brother Francesco, the brainy and devout Eugenio would go into the *Gesu'* to pray before the famous painting of the *Madonna della Strada* in one of the side chapels on the left.

At age ten Eugenio received his First Holy Communion. At the luncheon following the Mass a family friend, Cardinal Parocchi, asked the new communicant which Saint Eugenio was his patron saint. The serious lad proudly and quickly replied, "Pope Eugenio, of course!" The cardinal was deeply impressed at the boy's reverence for the papal office. A short time later, Eugenio became an altar boy at the *Chiesa Nuova*, serving Mass there early each morning and assisting at benediction, novena and vesper services several evenings each week. How he loved to be around the church, priests, nuns, incense, statues, icons, vestments! How he thrilled to the Latin language and the Gregorian chant! His mother always knew where to find him.

He brought the same academic commitment to his *Lyceum* (high school) studies that had distinguished his early school years. At the *Lyceum Ennio Quirino Visconti*, one classmate described him as "a boy with great destiny; a tireless scholar; friendly in his dealings with everyone, though somewhat reserved; tall, thin, glasses, very intelligent but well-balanced; a genius in Greek and Latin and gifted in modern languages as well. Very pious." Here, too, a tablet was unveiled after his election stating: "Eugenio Pacelli studied here in this Lyceum from 1891 to 1894. He who now as Pope Pius XII illumines the entire world shone here as a young rising star."

Fortunately for Eugenio the family owned a small farmhouse in the northern countryside just outside the village of Onano near Viterbo. Here he summered with his family and replenished his frail health by relaxing and reading in the warm sun of the *campagna*. He also enjoyed collecting coins and stamps. Eugenio tried to build up his meager frame by swimming, canoeing and horseback riding. He was an excellent equestrian.

Often the contemplative Eugenio chose to go off on long solitary walks in the hilly countryside among the wheatfields and vineyards of his friendly neighbors. On these long hikes he would read his prayer book, finger his rosary beads, and in the solitude ponder what to do with his life. Should he be a lawyer, a professor of classical languages, a physician? All these professions held a strong appeal for the gifted youth. But none compared in appeal with the priesthood.

Upon completion of his Lyceum studies in the summer of 1894, Eugenio went to a retreat house on the Via Nomentana beyond the Porta Pia. This was near a favorite spot of his, the Church of St. Agnes with her ancient catacombs below. Young Pacelli had an abiding interest in archeology and would come out here frequently to wander in the subterranean cemeteries of the early Christians, pray at length before the tomb of Agnes (he had a special devotion to this young virgin martyr), and then wander some more, studying the ancient epitaphs along the way. After four days in a small monastic cell he had decided that God was calling him to the priesthood and further decided to follow that call.

"Mi farò prete!" ("I'm going to be a priest!") he joyfully proclaimed upon arriving home. While his father had some reservations, Eugenio couldn't have made his mamma any happier. Toward the end of October that same year, enthusiastically recommended by his pastor as a "boy first rate in every respect," Eugenio was accepted into the prestigious seminary, the Roman College called more commonly the *Capranica* for its founder, Domenico

Cardinal Capranica. Established in 1457, the Capranica can be found down in the old Campus Martius very near the Pantheon in Rome.

Within a very short time Pacelli had distinguished himself as one of the best students in his class at the Capranica and indeed in the whole college. Consumed by a desire to learn, Eugenio would use even his recreation time in learning modern languages. His fantastic, photographic memory enabled him to remember whole lectures word for word. His academic achievements never turned his head and he remained always well-liked, admired and fun to be with.

Along with some classmates Pacelli also took courses at another great seminary, the *Gregoriano* or Gregorian University. This hectic program of studies was not without its price tag however. In 1895 Eugenio's health began to suffer seriously from the rigors of his seminary studies. Already thin and becoming thinner, Eugenio developed a hacking, relentless cough which alarmed his parents. The family doctor warned that the boy was on the brink of tuberculosis and blamed it on the dankness of the old building, the meager diet and the demanding schedule.

Signor Pacelli decided to use his influence at the Vatican and got permission from Pope Leo XIII himself for the youth to live at home, where he could benefit from his mother's care and cooking, and continue at the seminary as an extern. This was a rare, if not unprecedented, dispensation. Eugenio was saddened and discouraged by all of this and for a while, but only for a while, considered giving up his studies for the priesthood to pursue a career in law.

After spending that summer at Onano, Eugenio found himself considerably strengthened physically and decided to continue. In the fall he returned to the Gregorian. So scholarly was he that no one school could sufficiently challenge him and on November 11, Eugenio registered in the *Sapienza*, the school of philosophy and letters, for intense studies in history, philosophy, Latin and Greek. At the same time he enrolled in a course in theology at the papal anthenaeum of St. Apollinaris, located just a few steps from his home. Due to his matchless intellect and unswerving industry, he soon obtained the academic degrees of baccalaureate and licentiate *summa cum laude* and was ready to receive Holy Orders.

Frail health still plagued Eugenio, however, and prevented his participation with his classmates in the ordination ceremonies at the fourth century basilica of St. John Lateran. Instead, he was ordained on Easter Sunday, April 2, 1899 by Francesco Paola Cassetta, auxiliary bishop of Rome, in the bishop's private chapel. The next morning in the presence of relatives and friends, the newly ordained priest celebrated his first Mass in the venerable basilica of St. Mary Major on the summit of the Esquiline hill. Vincenzo Cardinal Vannutelli, the archpriest of the basilica, delivered the homily. For the Mass, Pacelli had chosen the Pauline chapel, which Pope Paul V of the Roman Borghese clan had built, because of its painting of Mary above the altar. Tradition of dubious origin says that it is the oldest painting of Mary in the world and that it was painted by St. Luke the evangelist. It was Father Pacelli's wish to dedicate his priesthood to Mary and entrust it to her protection and guidance.

Soon after, he was assigned as a curate to the *Chiesa Nuova*, the very church where he had served as an altar boy, the parish where he had grown up and where everyone still loved him and was very proud of him. In addition to his parish duties, Eugenio took on graduate studies at the Apollinaris. He already possessed one doctorate, in theology, and was now seeking another, in canon and civil law.

His first love in the parish was working with children, teaching them catechism, preparing them for First Communion. But his curate days were to be few. Pacelli's outstanding work in the parish plus his excellent record in the seminary did not go unnoticed by Pope Leo, who had a program of training exceptional young clerics for the papal diplomatic service. One day, Monsignor Gasparri, a man who was going places in the Vatican (the future secretary of state and at that time secretary of the Congregation of Extraordinary Ecclesiastical Affairs), called on Father Pacelli with an offer of a position in the Vatican Foreign Office. Pacelli, who wanted nothing more than "to work among the people of my parish," was stunned and at first resisted. Then, mindful of his promise of obedience, he willingly accepted the new assignment.

For the next decade and a half, Pacelli served as a quiet but highly competent and highly regarded *minutante* (research aide) in the office of the Congregation of Ecclesiastical Affairs, and in the library, helping with the massive project inaugurated by Pius X, the codification of canon law. At thirty eight years of age, Pacelli, who started his Vatican service under Pius, was now working for Benedict XV. When the immense task of codification was completed, Pacelli and Gasparri were singled out for special lofty praise.

In the frantic, early days of the First World War, Gasparri, now a cardinal, and Pacelli took on additional duties in the offices of the secretary of state. Their responsibilities included maintaining a liaison with the hierarchies on both sides of the conflict, answering appeals for aid from pastors all over Europe whose churches and parishes had been devastated, organizing a relief program for the innocent victims of the war. Pacelli worked long days, sometimes twenty hours, seven days a week, often forgetting to eat. But he was being schooled on the highest level in world affairs, training that would serve him pricelessly during his own pontificate.

When Cardinal Gasparri soon after became secretary of state, Pacelli was advanced to the post Gasparri vacated, that of secretary of the Congregation of Ecclesiastical Affairs. Thus the boy "born to be pope," the lad who had grown up practically within the shadows of the Vatican walls, had taken one more step toward the papal crown so often predicted for him.

As the war continued to turn Europe into a wasteland, Pacelli's career was to take a sudden and dramatic turn. One summer morning in 1917 the slender, bespectacled, intense forty-one year old Eugenio was working at his desk undistracted by the warm Mediterranean breeze coming through the open shutters, riffling the papers and the plants. Just before noon he received a message that he was to report at once to the office of the Holy Father. With the sash of his long black cassock flapping vigorously, the future pontiff strode briskly through the corridors of the Apostolic Palace until he reached the apartment of the Holy Father.

Upon entering, he found Pope Benedict conversing with Cardinal Gasparri, the man who had originally invited Father Pacelli to abandon his *primo amore*, parish work, and come to join the somewhat byzantine bureaucracy of the Vatican. Benedict was sitting behind his desk, his high, fair forehead crowned with a full shock of jet black hair, made blacker by its contrast to the white satin *zucchetto* or little skull cap worn by the pope, his penetrating eyes shining out from beneath bushy brows. Never one to waste words, *Papa Benedetto* fixed his gaze upon the summoned one and said in his thin, deliberate voice: "Francis Cardinal von Bettinger, archbishop of Munich, the papal nuncio, is dead. You are to succeed him." In an instant the priestly lifestyle of Eugenio Pacelli was transformed from the irenic routine of a Vatican congregation into the turbulent and perilous duties of a wartime diplomatic post.

Before leaving for his quarters in Munich just one week later, Pacelli was consecrated a bishop by the pope himself in a special ceremony in the Sistine chapel and was at the same time elevated to the rank of archbishop.

Particularly upset over the new assignment was the

nuncio's elderly mother. Throughout his years in the Vatican, Pacelli had been able, several times a week, to bicycle or even walk over to spend some pleasant hours with Mamma Pacelli, enjoy her pasta dishes, take her home remedies for every sniffle or sore throat. Now she worried over what would become of her little Eugenio's fragile health. After a touching farewell to his family and friends, the nuncio was on his way, armed with a diplomatic passport, through the Italian and German lines to the nunciature at Munich. Upon arrival he plunged, in his customary manner, quickly and whole-heartedly into the critical mission.

Before long he had ingratiated the citizens of Munich with his gentle ways and amazed and delighted them with his near native fluency in the German language, displaying an incredible command of even the subtlest idioms. In time he even took to the pulpit preaching and lecturing in German. Possessed of rare oratorical gifts, Pacelli would hold his listeners in thrall with the high pitched resonance of his melodious voice, with the scholarly content of his sermons, and with his fiery eyes which seemed to look straight past the temporal world and deep into eternity.

Upon the newly appointed nuncio's shoulders fell the responsibility of trying to end the war by way of negoti-ation. His was the task of selling the pope's peace plan to the belligerents. While he found the kaiser willing to talk and listen, Pacelli failed in his objective thanks largely to self-serving diplomats from all sides. He had learned a valuable lesson and quickly grew in stature as a diplomat himself. All the disappointment notwith-standing, Pacelli with his presentation of Benedict's pro-posal had unknowingly prepared the way for Woodrow Wilson's settlement plan a year later, a fourteen-point proposal, seven points of which had been in the original papal outline.

Whenever the workload in the nunciature permitted, Pacelli would go out into the streets to mingle with the people. A familiar sight in the medieval streets of Munich was the reed-thin prelate, gold pectoral cross gleaming in the sun, bent over ministering to the dying, comforting the wounded, feeding the starving.

Just a few weeks after the armistice, in December 1918, Pacelli mounted the pulpit of the cathedral to speak out in strong language against the post war menace of bolshevism now sweeping through the battered Deutschland. Communist zealots hoping to capitalize on the despair of the vanquished German people were everywhere trying to sell them the communist bill of goods. Pacelli was determined to neutralize the propaganda. Some days later a small group of German communist terriorists broke into the nunciature bent on reprisal against the courageous Roman prelate. Hearing the commotion in the vestibule, the stately nuncio, dressed in the colorful and impressive robes of his office, cooly and confidently descended the elegant staircase to meet his would-be assassins. Though they immediately leveled their revolvers at him, Pacelli never flinched. "Why have you come here armed?" he asked indignantly. "This is a house of peace, not a den of murderers!" Fearlessly he pointed out the folly of their intentions: "You are on extra-territorial soil. It is never wise to kill a diplomat." He then proceeded in a sympathetic way to counsel the terrorists. One by one they put their pistols away and, red-faced, withdrew. A little while later they returned, unarmed, to apologize and ask forgiveness. When word of the incident spread, the archbishop was held in even greater awe than before, by friend and foe alike. "He fears absolutely nothing and no one," they whispered to one another.

One afternoon later that same month, the nuncio received at his Munich residence an old friend who had helped him so much in his library research for the codification of Church law, Achille Cardinal Ratti, former curator of the Vatican library, now on a diplomatic mission through Poland and Germany on behalf of Pope

Benedict XV. As the two men talked of diplomatic matters and then over a glass of Rhine wine, and later a cup of *espresso*, reminisced about their days in Rome, they could not possibly have dreamed that each was looking at a future pope. But in the drawing room of the nunciature that winter afternoon sat the next two leaders of the Roman Catholic Church, Pius XI and Pius XII.

In the post war period the nunciature in Munich continued to be a busy place and Pacelli applied himself assiduously to each new lesson in peacetime diplomacy. Then in January of 1922 there took place in Rome a sequence of events that would have far reaching consequences on his future.

On the twenty-second day of that same rainy month, the elderly Giacomo della Chiesa, Pope Benedict XV, the "Good Samaritan of humanity" succumbed to influenza. And from the ensuing conclave Ratti emerged as Pius XI. Cardinal Gasparri was retained as secretary of state, a move with few precedents in papal history. Thus Pacelli's two dear, best friends and benefactors were now in the top two offices of the Church. And they both would keep a close watch on the efforts of the nuncio to Germany and his work toward a concordat with that government which would ensure freedom of religious worship and education to members of the Church in their own land. He eventually achieved this goal with the predominantly Catholic Bavarian region of Germany.

Pacelli can be accurately described as the first of the modern papal diplomats, for he thought nothing of using the airplane in his mission, flying frequently to various German cities and other nations in the cause of peace not only for the Church but for all the world. In the course of his labors, he acquired an incomparable polish, courtliness, sophistication.

The year 1925 came and with it a new assignment for Eugenio Pacelli. In accordance with the wishes of the Holy Father, he was transferred to the nunciature in Berlin where he ultimately succeeded in securing a favorable concordat from Protestant Prussia to go with the one from Bavaria.

For the next four years he served in Berlin where with his abundant charisma, his endless personal magnetism, his superb, flowing German and his intriguing personal appearance he became the idol of the citizenry. An advocate of punctuality and personal discipline, he had to admire the German's reverence for and practice of these virtues. Convinced that he would be more effective in his role by getting into the cultural mainstream of life in the country, he early on sought to Germanize himself somewhat. He put together a largely German staff, selected a German nun for his housekeeper, a German priest as his top aide, and another for his confessor. (The nun, Sister Pasqualina, was to remain in Pacelli's service to the very moment of his death at Castel Gandolfo in October of 1958.)

As the year 1929 was winding down he was summoned back to his beloved hometown on the Tiber. If ever he had any doubts about the Germans' feelings for him they were about to be dispelled. Saddened at the news that their good friend Pacelli had been recalled to Rome, that he was going home for good, tens of thousands of Berliners, tears streaming down their cheeks, lined the route from the nunciature to the railroad station on the clear but chilly night of his departure. Many held torches to light the way as he passed. Visibly moved, Pacelli stood all the way in the open carriage provided by the local authorities, blessing again and again the people he had come to love. (It was this attachment that his attackers after World War II used as "evidence" of his sympathy for Nazism.)

Pacelli was returning to a Rome different from the one he left a dozen years earlier, to Romans still jubilant over the long-awaited settlement of the feud between their State and their Church. On December 29, 1929, Pacelli inched closer still to the papacy when in an imposing ceremony he received the red hat of the cardinalate from a grateful Pius XI.

At once the aging Gasparri began to groom his favorite protege for the vital office of secretary of state. Then in February of 1930 Gasparri stepped down and proudly watched his personal choice replace him. The new Vatican policy maker faced a world where the goliaths of unemployment, hunger and despair were cultivating the spread and growth of ideologies inimical and perilous to the spread of the gospel. But never before was one so eminently prepared for the office. Cardinal Pacelli, at this point a youthful fifty four, knew the world and its problems probably better than anyone else.

True to his family name, the secretary of state was a dedicated pacifist. But this did not deter him from locking horns on several occasions with *Il Duce*, Benito Mussolini, the fascist ruler. Knowing that Mussolini had gained control over the media in Rome, Pacelli suggested the plan, in 1937, to have Monsignor Francis Spellman fly the encyclical, *Mit brennender Sorge,* over the Alps into Paris, there to release it to the world press. Had it been given to the press in Rome it most surely would have been turned over to the fascist leaders to be edited, censored, distorted and probably suppressed. Pacelli and Pius XI by this single measure were in effect putting Mussolini on notice that the Vatican could not, would not be gagged. (For his efforts in the matter, Spellman was soon made auxiliary bishop of Boston.)

Again it was Pacelli who had Marconi himself install the powerful Vatican broadcasting station whose soaring steel tower became a symbol of hope for freedom and justice and the dispenser of Christ's message around the world. The voice of the Vicar of Christ could now reach his children almost anywhere on the globe.

As secretary of state, Pacelli dueled with the fascist chief over other issues, too, especially over Mussolini's harassment and attempted suppression of the organization called Catholic Action and its affiliated youth societies. Vatican observers considered Pacelli Pius XI's *alter ego,* and many times the Holy Father supported the idea saying, "Cardinal Pacelli speaks with my voice and my thoughts."

Undertaking far-reaching journeys for his commander-in-chief, Pacelli became a sort of roving ambassador. 1934 found him in South America for the Eucharistic Congress in Buenos Aires. His objective here was to strengthen Vatican ties with a populace nominally but not truly Catholic. One year later he was off to Bernadette's Lourdes in the south of France to foster pilgrimages to the famous grotto. Upon his return, Pacelli was appointed papal chamberlain. On the busy agenda for 1936 was a 16,000 mile tour of the United States for an in-depth study of the American Church and its strengths and problems. At his side constantly on the six-week sojourn was an old friend from pre-war Rome, auxiliary Bishop Spellman of Boston who would soon be cardinal archbishop of New York.

Representing the pope once again, Pacelli flew to France in 1937 to consecrate the basilica of St. Theresa, the Little Flower, at Lisieux. St. Theresa had been recently beatified and canonized by Pius XI. During this trip he found the opportunity to indulge an old passion, preaching, stopping off in Paris to deliver a highly acclaimed sermon from the pulpit in Notre Dame. But it wouldn't be very long before Nazi troops would be strolling the tree-lined boulevards, taking their enjoyment at all the chic sidewalk cafes. An awful storm was coming and Pius XI and his friend could not stop it. It would be a long, dark night for this lovely City of Lights—and for the world.

At the Eucharistic Congress in Budapest the following year, Pacelli celebrated an outdoor Mass attended by thirteen cardinals, two hundred and fifty bishops and tens of thousands of the faithful. Sadly, this was to be one of the last times Hungarians would be able to express openly their religious fervor.

That same year the German Fuehrer condescended to

visit his future puppet, Benito, in the Italian capital. Achille Ratti and Eugenio Pacelli, the two great apostles of peace, made no effort to veil their feelings for Adolf Hitler, who had let it be known that he had hoped to pay a courtesy call on the Vatican Head of State and to view the Sistine chapel and the Vatican museum. Prior to the Fuehrer's arrival, His Holiness and his 'other self' departed for the papal summer villa at Castel Gandolfo in the *Castelli Romani,* and let it be known they would not be available. As for the Sistine and the museum, they were "closed indefinitely for repairs."

While the European situation worsened through early 1939, the Holy Father's health did likewise. This distressed Cardinal Pacelli deeply and he repeatedly urged the ailing pontiff to slow down. To which the latter always indignantly replied, "The world would be far better off with a dead pope than with one who cannot work full time." Pius XI passed away on February 10, 1939.

Late in the afternoon of March 2nd, with the *Piazza San Pietro* overflowing with Romans and pilgrims and tourists and foreign correspondents waiting with wild anticipation the cardinals' decision, Caccia Cardinal Dominioni stepped to the lectern and its microphones on the central balcony of the basilica. After waiting a few moments for silence, he cleared his throat and boomed the Latin message out over the public address system: *"Nuntio vobis magnum gaudium! Habemus Papam!"* ("I announce to you a great joy! We have a pope!") The excited crowd raised a long and deafening roar. After a long pause, Dominioni continued: "The most eminent and reverend Lord Eugenio . . . ." He was overwhelmed by another vocal eruption as the crowd wildly and joyfully finished the name: "Pacelli! Pacelli! Pacelli!" Reluctantly they quieted down to let the cardinal say what they already knew, ". . . Cardinal of the Holy Roman Church, Pacelli!" Now Dominioni's voice, too, was charged with emotion as he cried out over the thundering multitude one last piece of information, ". . . who has taken the name of Pius XII."

By now the delightful din had crescendoed to the point where it could be clearly heard throughout the Trastevere district, in the Piazza Risorgimento, along and even across the Tiber. Moments later it rose still higher as the ascetic, regal figure of Papa Pacelli, Rome's very own, appeared on the balcony. He looked and acted every inch a pontiff. "From the time he was a young man," Cardinal Dougherty of Philadelphia, one of the electors, observed, "he was spoken of as the future hope of the Church. He has a remarkable combination of the highest qualities of body and mind. He is tall, ascetic. His is a Roman face, a face such as one finds on old coins and statues dug up throughout the old Empire. He has a most charming manner. His disposition is gentleness personified."

Pius XII, who would come to be known by several honorary terms such as the Angelic Shepherd and the Pope of Peace, began his reign in a world-wide atmosphere of tension, with the savagery the world knows as World War II just around the bend. During the six months before the storm finally broke, Pius made every possible diplomatic effort to get the conflicting powers together at the conference table where he hoped they might mediate and adjust their differences. "It is more glorious to kill war through words than to kill men through iron and to obtain peace through peace rather than through war," he pleaded. But in vain. Though no one ever worked longer and harder for the cause of peace, Pius XII could not avert the impending carnage. His was merely a voice crying in the wilderness since Germany and Russia were not in the least disposed to genuine peace talks, having already secretly worked out a plan to slice up Poland and the Baltic countries.

Nonetheless he kept on trying and throughout the summer of '39 the Vatican was a beehive of diplomatic activity. In the end, when he came to the bitter and heartbreaking realization that his war against war was irrevocably lost, Pius made one final, touching, eloquent plea: "We who are armed with nothing but the sword of truth speak to you in the name of God. Justice is advanced with reason, not with arms. Conquest and empires not founded on justice receive not the blessing of God. Nothing is lost by peace. Everything is lost by war!" The hierarchies of the Anglican, Orthodox and Protestant Churches praised and supported the pope's peace efforts but no one could stop the awful machinery of war set in motion by ruthless individuals and satanic forces.

The inevitable came to pass. In the early morning hours of September 11, Luigi Cardinal Maglione, Vatican secretary of state, telephoned the pontiff. After answering in his customary, disarmingly unassuming manner, "*E qui Pacelli*" ("Pacelli here"), the Holy Father heard the sad news that Germany had invaded Poland. For the next half dozen years Pius XII was to rise each morning to look out upon a different world from the one he knew as an altar boy at *Chiesa Nuova*, a world in flames. Having lost then the hope of defusing the war, he followed the example of Benedict XV in the first World War by organizing relief programs for the victims. To keep people from dying of exposure and starvation and illness, the Vatican would ship clothing, food and medicines to the needy areas. For the duration of the war and then long after it, Vatican aid was to reach into Belgium, Holland, Norway, Denmark, France, Yugoslavia and Greece. Pius' deep compassion for the suffering also resulted in the creation of the Vatican Information Service whose principal duty was to help families locate missing relatives.

Though the pope had tried every tack he could think of to keep Italy out of the war, imploring Mussolini again and again to remain neutral, the fascist chief soon chose to throw in his lot with the Nazis. This would eventually bring the war to the threshold of the Vatican.

Despite papal pleas to keep Rome an "Open City," i.e. to leave her out of the conflict because of her historic sanctity and her unique status as the seat of Christendom, as the burial place of the apostles and martyrs, as the world's greatest repository of irreplaceable art, the Allied Forces rejected such an idea on the grounds that Rome, with her railroad system and airfields and ammunition depots, was being used to supply the enemy.

At about eleven in the morning of July 19, 1943 a hundred American bombers flew over the Tiburtine section of Rome and in their wake left a great deal of destruction to life and property. Among the victims was the venerable and beautiful sixth century basilica of St. Lawrence Outside-the-Walls which suffered extensive damage. The noise and the tremors were heard and felt all across the city and Pius who was talking to a small group in his study high upon Vatican hill rushed to his window and, transfixed in grief, watched the ugly smoke clouds rising over Tiburtina. Concerned at once about innocent victims, the Holy Father telephoned Monsignor Giovanni Battista Montini (later Pope Paul VI), secretary of Ordinary Ecclesiastical Affairs, and told him to go to the Vatican bank and draw a large sum of money, take the first car he saw in the courtyard and drive to the scene.

When the pope himself arrived at the site, terrified men, women, and children ran toward the tall white figure, their *Santo Padre*, to whom they now looked for comfort and strength in their dark hour. *Papa Pacelli*, their fellow Roman, walked among them comforting the injured and dying, his white soutane stained with blood where his spiritual sons and daughters had touched and grasped his garment as children so often do when scared. One lady thrust her infant into the Holy Father's arms. Tears welled in his eyes when he quickly realized the baby was dead. And those same eyes brimmed again when he was informed that a few bombs had struck the section of Campo Verano, Rome's largest cemetery, and had destroyed the Pacelli family plot where the pontiff's parents had been interred. But there were still works of mercy to be done, and Pius, with Montini ever at his side, began to distribute the money from the Vatican bank until it was all gone. Then, before he departed, he climbed up on the rubble of the basilica of St. Lawrence to say soothing and encouraging words to his flock and to lead them in prayer. On his return trip to the Vatican, Pius sobbed all the way. Back in his study he dashed off a bitter letter of protest to President Roosevelt in which he described graphically the horror he had just viewed.

The internal crisis long simmering in Italy now came to a boil. Mussolini was asked by King Victor Emmanuel, on July 25, to come to the royal summer residence, the Villa Savoia, and after a dramatic colloquy the *Duce* was placed under arrest. News of Mussolini's demise was received joyfully by most of the people. There was not the slightest sign of a fascist backlash. This was eloquent testimony to the ultimate bankruptcy of Mussolini's movement.

Less than a month after the first air assault on the Eternal City, on August 13 precisely, Allied planes struck again, in an effort calculated to "shake the Italian will to resist." This time the bombs fell in the Lateran district near the most venerable of all cathedrals, St. John's. Again the pope was one of the first on the scene. Again his cassock was stained with blood as he returned silent and melancholy to his tiny country beyond the Tiber.

Later that same nightmarish summer, after the Italian army had surrendered, Nazi troops goosestepped into Rome and ringed the Vatican "to protect the Holy Father and the Eternal City."

On November 5, at around eight in the evening, a German plane dropped four small bombs on the Vatican itself. It was the hope of the Nazis that the pope, now recognizing the Badoglio administration as the official government of Italy, would be intimidated, and secondly that the public would suspect the Allied Forces as the villains in this air raid also. Many windows in the enclave, including some high up in the cupola of St. Peter's, were blown out. When word of the treachery raced through Rome the next morning, many thousands of Romans converged in St. Peter's square to gather beneath the pope's window. There for several hours they cheered their pontiff's courage and poured out their love for him. The German high command in the city offered to enter the Vatican and "investigate the whole matter." Pius coolly declined the offer. While vowing to respect the integrity of the Vatican the German leadership also urged Pius to let them escort him to a neutral country in the interest of his "personal safety." This "generous" offer was also coolly rejected. Rome's bishop had no desire, nor intention, of neglecting his own diocese. Hitler began to contemplate the idea of hauling Pius XII off to captivity in Germany.

Weeks later, when a full report of the investigation of the incident reached his hands, Pope Pius XII publicly denounced the culprits in strong language. While unwilling to have his words result in still worse blood baths for others, he was not in the least afraid of reprisals against himself. It can be safely said that Eugenio Pacelli was never lacking in courage, nor in open contempt for tyranny. This is evident from his whole life. Following is an excerpt of his statement on the Vatican bombing which, while not mentioning them by name, is abundantly clear in its between-the-lines inculpation of the Nazis:

> "Such an attack, deliberately planned with as little honor and screened with as little success behind the anonymity of the pilot, on a territory sacred to all Christians, sanctified by the blood of the apostle Peter, the world center for masterpieces of art and culture, and guaranteed by a solemn treaty, is a symptom hard to explain away of the depth of spiritual disorientation and moral decadence of conscience to which some erring minds have sunk!"

On March 29, 1944, a few days after the brutal massacre of more than three hundred Italian political prisoners

in the Ardeatine caves just beyond the walls of Rome
(a reprisal for an attack on a Nazi regiment by the anti-
fascist Italian underground movement, *La Resistenza*),
the Germans "generously" declared Rome an "Open City."
President Roosevelt responded with a promise that U. S.
forces would spare cultural and religious monuments in
the coming spring offensive but labeled Nazi military
exploitation of Rome as "an affront to all religions."
Promises from heads of state, however, were empty
words in the opinion of the Roman people. Their one real
hope, to hear them tell it, was Papa Pacelli, "our only
and best Ack-Ack."

At this point the campaign of persecution against the
Jewish minority in Rome, which had been launched with
the Nazis' arrival, was accelerated. In September of 1943,
the chief rabbi of Rome, Eugenio Zolli, had been summoned to Nazi headquarters and informed that he would
have to deliver to German authorities, by noon of the
following day, one million lire in cash and a hundred
pounds of gold, and that failure to do so would result in
the dispersal of the Jewish community in Rome. "Dispersal" was the Nazi euphemism for executions, impri-
sonments and atrocities. In vain the poor Jewish people
tried to raise the ransom. Rabbi Eugenio appealed to
Pope Eugenio who instructed the Vatican treasurer to
raise whatever gold was necessary even if it meant melt-
ing down sacred vessels. In his moving memoir, *Before
the Dawn*, published in 1954, Rabbi Zolli gives this
account of the matter:

> "By this time the German police were going out every
> night in search of Jews. Owing to the loss of our records, the
> fact that no count could be made of the numbers of Jews who
> had come to Rome from other places and were caught, and the
> secrecy with which much of the S.S.'s program was conducted,
> no reliable statistics are available as to the number of Jews
> who perished during the occupation of the city. Thousands
> were deported and killed, hundreds died in Roman prisons. We
> were helpless, never knowing where disaster would strike next.

My nights were semi-vigils. 'Lord,' I prayed, 'let me die with the others when and how You wish, but not as the German's wish! Have mercy on all men, upon all Your children!'

"For nine months the Wehrmacht continued to defend itself from its enemies, while keeping Rome in its grasp, but the Hebrews could not defend themselves against the S.S. Early in the occupation, before the S.S. had received any authorization to attack the Jews, one of their commanders, on his own authority, began the assault upon the treasury of the community with the demand, 'Fifty kilograms of gold within twenty-four hours; otherwise, three hundred hostages will be taken.'

"A plenary session of the council was called. I sent word that my presence would not be in the least helpful, since the discussion would be exclusively of financial matters. If I could do something—anything at all—they could count on me. I would do it regardless of danger. Meanwhile I sent my gold chain and five thousand lire. I provided my daughter with the opportunity of going in a car, for greater security and to save time, to collect gold rings without stones. She did so, and succeeded in a remarkable manner, and was thanked.

"At seven next morning Dr. Pierantoni came to my room. The community had succeeded in gathering together only around thirty-five kilograms of gold. Would I, he asked, go to the Vatican and try to obtain a loan of fifteen kilograms of gold? 'Right away,' I replied.

"Dr. Pierantoni arrived with a car. 'I am dressed like a beggar,' I remarked. 'We shall go in by one of the back doors,' he replied. 'The Vatican is always guarded by the Gestapo. A friendly person will be waiting for you, and so that you can avoid showing personal documents stamped 'Hebrew Race,' you will be presented as an engineer, called to examine some walls that are being constructed.'

" 'The art of examining walls has always interested me,' I answered.

"The builders greeted me; I let them talk; I gave my approval to the construction problem presented to me. Very comic! Then we walked and walked till we came to the office of the head of the treasury, then to that of the secretary of state.

"The Vatican had already spent millions in aiding fugitive Jews to reach safety. I said, 'The New Testament does not abandon the Old. Please help me. As for repayment, I myself shall stand as surety, and since I am poor, the Hebrews of the world will contribute to pay the debt.'

"Both the treasurer and the monsignori were moved. The treasurer disappeared and after a few minutes returned. He had gone to the Holy Father. 'Come back shortly before one o'clock. The offices will be deserted, but two or three employees will be here waiting for you and will give you the package. You may leave a receipt in the form of a simple note. There will be no difficulty.'

" 'Please give my thanks to His Holiness,' I said. I went back to the house of Pierantoni."

But all of this was merely buying time. One month later the dreaded Gestapo launched another assault on the tormented community, this time confiscating all art objects found in Jewish homes and deporting many adult males. German Ambassador von Weizsacker replied to the pope's vehement protestations that the Gestapo took no orders from the embassy and therefore he was powerless to do anything about the matter.

Appalled by the Nazi pogroms across Europe and in his own city, the pope did not discourage the steady flow of those seeking asylum across the various Vatican border check-points. In fact he fostered the flow by directing Rome's nuns, priests, monks and Catholic laity to open the doors of their convents, churches, monasteries and homes to their Jewish brethren. Even the ancient catacombs were pressed into service as secret shelters. Before long the Vatican, the papal villa in Castel Gandolfo, and nearly two hundred Catholic institutions in and around Rome housed thousands of Jewish fugitives including Rabbi Zolli. As the tension in the city grew more unbearable, the pope flexed what little Vatican muscle there was. St. Peter's doors were ordered closed. Pius took away the ceremonial halberds of his Swiss guard and replaced them with machine guns. Yet while the pontiff's intervention in favor of the persecuted Jews was particularly powerful, there were some critics who demanded he be more militant. Better than anyone else,

however, Pius XII was agonizingly aware that in this
situation he had to walk a scary tightrope. There was
very real danger that papal interference could antagon-
ize Hitler into intensifying his anti-Semitic bloodbath.
To an ineffective and possibly a counter-productive
grandstand play of standing on his balcony and loudly
condemning Hitler to all the globe, scoring ideological
and moral points while risking far greater carnage, Pius
preferred a less sensational strategy, but one which
seemed to promise better results toward the pure goal
of saving as many lives as possible. One must not
simplistically overlook the unfortunate reality that while
the pope had morality on his side, he had no military
resources to back him up and that a mere papal anath-
ema would not dissuade Hitler from his genocidal aims.
"Laws are silent in the face of weapons," Cicero observed twenty-one centuries ago, and an Italian proverb
echoes his conclusion, "Against force reason is worthless." *L'Osservatore Romano,* the Vatican daily, sharply
rebuked the Nazi regime, describing the pogroms as
heinous, indefensible, un-Christian and inhuman, and
ridiculed the theory that Jews born in Italy were "not
true Italians because of their race."

As the Nazis glowered at all this pro-Jewish activity,
not always covert, and tightened their grip on the city,
Pius XII became increasingly apprehensive that the
Roman citizenry would rebel. Again and again he
appealed to the people to refrain from such activity
which was surely not only to end in futility but also
to result in internecine reprisals.

For the remainder of the period of German occupation the Vatican continued to exert whatever pressure
it could, for whatever good it might achieve, on both the
German embassy officials and military leaders in the
city to stop the occupational forces' repressive policies
and bestiality. Fortunately, the occupation did not have
long to go. By mid-1944 both the Third Reich, which
would "last a thousand years," and its infamous archi-

tect, had just about come apart at the proverbial seams.

In the waning hours of the 4th of June, Allied troops, under cover of darkness, at last penetrated the ancient Aurelian fortifications and entered the Eternal City. Sunday, June 5th, dawned radiantly on the cupolas and monuments of old Rome and, as the good news was passed along, that unique Roman spirit sapped by the occupation began to blossom again. Smiles and *"Buon giorno's"* abounded. Cafe owners offered free *espresso* and *Frascati* as the day matured. Toward late morning whole families joined other whole families in a massive, joyous march up to the City on a hill to thank and to honor their very own *Papa Pacelli* for bringing them through Armageddon. Rome was reacquiring that special glow and that matchless gaiety for which she has always been admired, loved and envied by the rest of the world.

In the weeks to follow, the Holy Father was to grant audiences daily to large groups of American servicemen of every religious persuasion. Some were awed by his natural charisma, others fascinated by his looks, all held in thrall by his high-pitched, fatherly voice, many moved to tears of joy at being in the presence of Christ's vicar on earth.

Most of the audiences were general ones in the basilica of St. Peter, but occasionally Pius would receive smaller groups of the men in audience in the various antechambers of the Apostolic Palace. These gatherings were considerably less ceremonial and the pope delighted in exchanging a few light words with each sailor or soldier in the room. He astounded them all with the sweeping range of his mind and his *au courant* knowledge of sports, music, the stage and screen, as well as of far loftier subjects. On some occasions, not out of disrespect but rather out of spontaneous joy and love, the pope's visitors would depart from protocol. Pius' bony features burst into a boyish grin one day when at the conclusion of a small audience an overjoyed lieutenant called out, "Okay! Let's really hear it for His Holiness," and then led his surprised but willing men in a rendition of *For He's a Jolly Good Fellow*.

U. S. Brigadier General Edgar Hume told of how one day, soon after the liberation of the Eternal City, he happened to be in the Vatican when a delegation of several hundred Jews arrived to thank the Holy Father for his gallant fight and generous measures on behalf of the persecuted Jewish people of Rome. Some of the community, including the former chief rabbi, Zolli, were moved even to the point of becoming Christians.

A week before I wrote this chapter I went to the Jewish quarter along the lower bank of the Tiber and to the Synagogue, clipboard and pencil in hand for some personal recollections. Several of the officials at the temple spoke of a "great indebtedness to *Papa Pio*." One old man told me that were it not for the pope, he and every other male in his family would have been eliminated by the Nazis. "Savior of the world," was the way one Jewish lady, now bent low with the years, chose to describe Pius XII. Several members of her family had sought and been granted asylum out in the papal villa at Castel Gandolfo.

With the end of the war now in view, Pius prepared for a peacetime papacy in which he would devote much of his time and energy to closing the gaps between the belligerents, proposing foundations for the structure of a lasting world peace, expanding Vatican programs, restoring spiritual values to a world left hardened, embittered, and cynical by war.

Pius was destined to suffer continued anguish, however, in the post war era when he had to witness the persecution of the Church in more than a dozen countries which would in a short time fall under the tyrannical thumb of communism. He would to his death remain an implacable foe of this dangerous ideology and often wield in the struggle against it the once dreaded weapon of excommunication as he did in the cases of those responsible for the trials of Cardinals Mindzenty and Stepinac.

Still during the remaining thirteen years of his pontificate, Pope Pius XII found the time and vitality for vigorous ecclesiastical activity. In the strictly religious sphere he will be remembered for, among many other monumental accomplishments, the Holy Year of 1950, the Marian Year of 1954, and the proclamation on November 1, 1950 of the dogma of the assumption into heaven of the body of the Blessed Virgin Mary.

In many ways Pius XII prepared the way for his successor's great general council, Vatican II. Under Pacelli there were innovations, revisions, reforms in the liturgy, in the Eucharistic rite, in biblical studies, in the training of priests, in the organization of religious orders, in the Church calendar and in the college of cardinals. Among the thirty three saints canonized by this great pope was Mother Frances Xavier Cabrini, the first citizen of the United States to be raised to the altars of the Catholic Church.

A prolific writer, Pius issued forty one encyclicals on a wide range of themes. In the eight languages with which he was fluent (Italian, German, English, Spanish, Portuguese, French, Greek and Latin) he spoke out on virtually every topic under God's sun. He took a lively interest in the academic world and in every contemporary scientific and cultural issue. He loved to visit the astronomical observatory that the Vatican maintains in Castel Gandolfo and to pick the brains of the scholars there.

A profoundly spiritual man, Pius lived monastically, taking his meals in solitude, often sleeping on the floor, rising early and retiring late so that he might spend several hours each day on his knees in solemn prayer. One night in December, 1954, having prayed himself into a state of ecstasy, it is reported, he had an apparition of his Divine Master. The light in his eyes, about which all who met him marveled, was to burn even brighter thereafter.

Long and laborious days—eighteen hours, sometimes longer—continued to be the norm for Pacelli right up to his final weeks. Of all his labors, he enjoyed most the audiences which would afford him personal contact with his flock. The simple parish priest in him never faded. He received the mighty and the humble, the young and the old, the devout and the atheistic. Groups of all sorts sought an audience with him. Doctors, factory workers, scholars, journalists, farmers, teachers, politicans, shopkeepers, athletes, nuns, people from every walk of life in every nation on every continent, all journeyed to the bank of the Tiber to see, hear and be inspired by the Pope of Peace. One day the Harlem Globetrotters paid a call at Castel Gandolfo. When Pius expressed a desire to see a sample of their basketball wizardry they complied. Lacking a phonograph they began to sing their theme song, *Sweet Georgia Brown,* while bouncing and passing the ball with their inimitable dazzle and dexterity. This thoroughly human and gentle pope was spotted laughing uproariously at the Trotters' antics and tapping his foot to their rhythmic tune.

Romans out late on any given evening who happened to be passing by St. Peter's square would take note of the patch of yellow against the ink black sky, emanating from the second window from the right on the top floor of the Apostolic Palace. A few were even lucky enough to have been passing by on the occasions when Pius XII would come to his window sometime between one and two a.m. to take one more momentary look down over Bernini's colonnade into the deserted and darkened square, and then vanish. A few moments later the light would go out signaling that the pope had finished another workday and had gone to bed.

In the mid-1950's Pius' health, never robust, began to wane. In fact, at the time of his vision of Jesus in December 1954 he was seriously ill and his physicians feared for his life. His recovery was considered miraculous. But in the autumn of 1958 there was to be no miracle. This year the Holy Father had stayed on a little longer at Castel Gandolfo in the vain hope that the clear air would restore his vitality. On Monday morning, October 6, after celebrating Mass, Pius returned to his study. Members of the household were heartened to hear the clicking of his typewriter and then, minutes later, disheartened by a sudden prolonged silence.

When there was no customary, *"Avanti!"* in response to their knock on the door, aides rushed in to discover the pope slumped over his desk. He had suffered a stroke. The light that had given so much hope to a darkened Europe was dimming. At 3:52 a.m. on Tuesday, October 9, it went out forever as the holy soul of Pius XII, Eugenio Pacelli, went to meet the Lord. He had lived for eighty two years, seven months, and seven days and had reigned as Supreme Pontiff nineteen years, seven months, and seven days.

On Friday afternoon Pius XII began his final return to his beloved Rome. Reminiscent of his departure as nuncio from Berlin many years before, crowds of tearful people of all ages lined the route as the cortege slowly wended its silent way down from the Alban hills through the Roman countryside, past the sun-baked brick arches of the Claudian aqueduct, onto the Via Appia Nuova which enters the city through the St. John Gate, to the basilica of St. John Lateran. Father Hugh Eller provides us with a vivid eyewitness account of that solemn event:

"As soon as we saw the body go into the Church, we . . . hurried to join the procession which had been forming in the Piazza San Giovanni behind the basilica. It was so difficult to get through the crowd we had to go around two blocks and come back to join the Friars at their place in the procession. We arrived moments before they started to march for St. Peter's in the Vatican. Because we were so late in joining our group (i.e. all the Friars from the Antonium) we were the very first, right at the head of the whole crowd. . . . Our place in the line of march was about four contingents back of the group of laymen carrying the standards who immediately followed the Italian soldiers. The procession to St. Peter's took two hours or longer and was a glorious spectacle. All the priests and clergy of Rome were in it! Someone told me that today was the first time in several hundred years that a pope was publicly honored by the Italian government in Rome. Today made up for it.

"The crowds were enormous! People in windows; on church balconies; in the Colosseum, and thronging every inch of free space in the streets. The closer we came to St. Peter's, the more dense became the crowd. An area was fenced off in the square to make room for the procession. None of the general clergy were allowed inside the basilica. Only the bishops, etc. who formed the escort immediately accompanying the pope. So as soon as we reached the obelisk in the square, we broke ranks and took up positions in the square."

The whole world grieved. Tributes and expressions of love and gratitude poured into Rome from all corners of the world. But this one from the late Richard Cardinal Cushing of Boston seems to say it best:

Only one whose priesthood had penetrated into his every human power could approach the problems of his daily life with the statesmanship of St. Robert Bellarmine, the theological depth of St. Alphonsus, the simple detachment of St. Francis of Assisi, the monastic devotion of St. Bernard, the self-immolating dedication of the Cure of Ars, the missionary zeal of St. Francis Xavier, and the simple directness and fervor of St. Pius X. These are the qualities which I discovered in Eugenio Pacelli as I learned of his early career as a diplomat in the service of the Church and as I came into official and personal contact with him during his years as a member of the sacred college and as the supreme pastor of souls.

"Theologian, canonist, scholar, linguist, statesman, diplomat— all of these Pius XII was. For all of them he has been hailed and praised. But more than anything else he was a pastor, a good shepherd of souls, selflessly dedicated to the honest interests of the Church and to the greater glory of God."

CHAPTER XI

POPE JOHN XXIII

On October 28, 1958, the conclave unwittingly extended a century-old trend by electing the rotund cardinal, Angelo Roncalli, patriarch of Venice. The trend called for a stout pontiff, with an "r" in his last name, then a thin one, *without* an "r" in his last name, followed by another heavy-set pope, etc. Pius IX was chunky, Leo XIII a rail, Pius X another fullback, Benedict XV wiry, Pius XI a bit stout, Pius XII reed thin, Pope John XXIII tipped the scales impressively indeed. In another contrast to his predecessor, a city boy, Roncalli was a product of the northern farmland.

Early in the morning of November 25, 1881, Signora Maria Anna Roncalli, nee Mazzola, presented her husband Giovanni Battista Roncalli with their fourth child and first son, Angelo Giuseppe. Though the tiny Lombard village of Sotto Il Monte was being drenched by a *tramontana*, Maria Anna left her bed late in the evening of that same day to take little Angelino, as he was already being called, to the old and deteriorating local church of San Giovanni. After a cold and soggy walk through the village of two thousand inhabitants, the Roncallis arrived at the church only to find that the priest, Father Francesco Rebuzzini, was out on a sick call. Undaunted, they waited on a bench in the sacristy, the lonely silence interrupted every few seconds by the clattering of the shutters which had shaken loose on the adjacent building. Because of the high infant mortality rate in those days, it was common practice to have the baby baptized at the earliest possible moment. Around midnight, Father Rebuzzini returned and wearily, but happily, administered the first sacrament to Angelino.

Quite poor but contented, the family lived in a little

apartment in the heart of the town. Like most of the peasant populace of tenant farmers, the Roncallis rented their farmland from a certain Count Morlani. Determined to raise the station of his bride and his brood, Giovanni Battista Roncalli became a fanatical saver. Before the rest of his ten children started to arrive, the farmer had accumulated enough *lire* to buy his own farm and dwelling on the periphery of the town. Though the natural beauty of the area was matchless—the medieval stone houses hugging each other, their orange tile rooftops and an occasional *campanile* creating a picturesque skyline, all basking in the golden Mediterranean sunshine—it was of little compensation at the table. The Roncalli diet was indeed meager with lunch consisting of some bread and a chunk of cheese, and dinner offering the wholesome but unexciting *polenta,* cheap wine, and very occasionally, a little meat. Fruit supplemented the skimpy menu of this close-knit, pious family whose custom it was to pray the rosary aloud and together each evening. Not only did they pray together, they worked together as well, all day long with even the pre-school age children expected to pitch in. Holidays were passed in family pilgrimages to the many shrines in the area.

Illiteracy was the rule in the area since little schooling was available. Wanting something better for their first son, the parents enrolled Angelo in classes conducted by a priest in the hamlet of Carvico, two miles away. Each day the mischievous and humorous Roncalli lad would walk barefoot to the one-room schoolhouse with his loyal chum Battista Ogazzi, who was destined to become the village blacksmith. Late in the afternoon the chunky, spunky Angelo would return to do his stint in the fields. Then it was home to dinner, the rosary, a couple hours of study and on to dreamland.

At age seven, Angelo undertook the study of Latin. When his early efforts proved to be less than *summa cum laude* he was encouraged to concentrate harder by some raps on the head with the priest's copy of Caesar's *Gallic*

Wars. In time young Ronealli came to master Latin, and to love it. (Contrary to popular belief, Pope John XXIII never intended Latin's complete elimination from the Mass, merely a reduction of it in favor of some vernacular usage.) He often, for fun and challenge, quoted in it, wrote poems in it and corresponded in it.

Early on in his life, Roncalli loved to spend a great deal of time in church. Though he loved games and pranks he also had a serious side and it was this side of his character that led him to become the priest's shadow. Angelo just could not wait to be an altar boy. The unusually devout child prayed often, especially on his long walks to school according to his pal, Ogazzi. And the simple prayers he was taught by his beloved Uncle Zaverio he recited each night the rest of his life. At the age of eight Angelo received First Holy Communion and simultaneously this call to the priesthood: *"Egredere de doma tua!"* ("Leave your home!"). He could not get the words out of his thoughts. As pope he once remarked that he could not remember a time when he did not want to be a priest. Once when he returned to the village as a priest, he was heartbroken to find that his boyhood church of San Giovanni had been razed.

While like Eugenio Pacelli in boyish piety, Angelo Roncalli was quite unlike him academically. He was not an especially industrious student. Still, he loved history and especially Church history. And Latin continued to busy him even after he transferred to the *scuola media* (middle school) at age nine in Celano, three miles away over the hill called San Giovanni. This new trek he made daily with his colleague, Pietrino Donizetti, the future mayor of Sotto Il Monte.

Despite his mediocre grades, Angelo was admitted at age fourteen to the diocesan seminary in Bergamo, eight miles distant. Here the black cassock seemed to change the spirited Roncalli into a dedicated scholar. Though the brownhaired, stocky, rugged-faced youth had an irrepressible wit and propensity for uproarious laughter, the quiet monastic daily regimen of seminary life seemed to agree with him. (His classmates used to say that when something struck Angelo funny "he would laugh with his eyes.") At Bergamo the candidates for the priesthood would rise at 5:30 each morn for prayer, meditation and Mass. From 7:30 to 8:30 was set aside for study. This hour was followed by a light breakfast and then by classes the rest of the morning. Toward noon there would be special chores for everyone and a half hour later a big but unfancy meal. In the best seminary tradition the boys would then walk off their meal and have an hour or so for recreation and relaxation. Four hours of classes filled the afternoon. Following this the seminarians would file into the chapel for meditation and communal prayers. Supper wasn't much: bread, some cheese, olives, fresh fruit, coffee. Another visit to the chapel was next and then back to the cell-like bedrooms for some more cramming before lights out at ten.

On holidays Angelo would walk all the way home to Sotto Il Monte where mamma's *polenta* would be a welcome, almost gourmet, treat. All the rest of his priestly life, except for his pontificate, Roncalli would, whenever possible, take his vacations at his ancestral home.

It was at Bergamo that he came to be interested in matters cultural. There he began to appreciate good music. The operas of Gaetano Donizetti, a native of the area, especially delighted him and decades later the lilting arias of *Lucia di Lamermoor* and *L'Elisir d'Amore* could be heard late each night emanating from the stereo set in the pope's apartment.

Soon after he turned nineteen, having established an impressive record of scholarship at Bergamo, Roncalli was chosen for the signal honor of finishing his priestly studies at the pontifical seminary, the Apollinare, in Rome. The excited young man decided to mark the occasion by commencing a life-long spiritual diary. This work was published posthumously under the title *Journal of a Soul*.

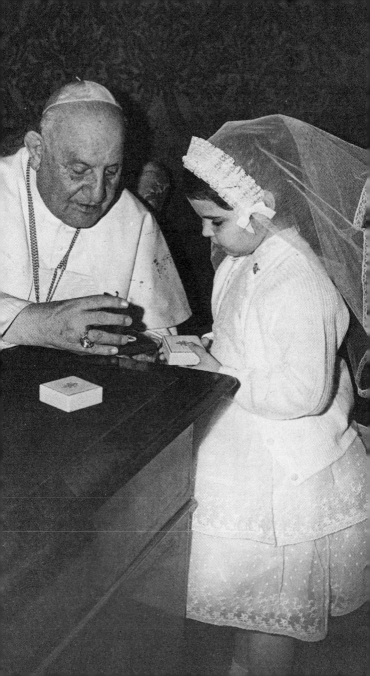

Escorted to the railroad station in Bergamo by his parents and nine brothers and sisters and an assortment of aunts, uncles, and cousins, young Roncalli—kisses, hugs, tears, and a ton of advice behind him—boarded the train for Rome. Later that day, January 3, 1901, the seminarian arrived in the Eternal City. (He could not have dreamed that nearly sixty years later he would also train down from the north to Rome—not to study for the Church, but rather to run it.)

But what a privilege! To study at such a prestigious institution, under the best minds of the Church. One day the northern farmboy and his fellow seminarians were abuzz about a great lecturer who would be talking to them in the afternoon session on some aspect of canon law. An alumnus of the Apollinare, the thin, bony-faced, mysterious, cerebral young priest was said to be the talk of the Vatican and to have attracted the attention of the Holy Father himself. It was the young Father Pacelli who held the class fascinated with his vast knowledge of the topic, his singsong voice, his penetrating eyes.

Roncalli loved Rome. He never quite got over the thrill of living and studying there. Roaming the streets, walking in the pages of the world's biggest history textbook, exploring ruins, visiting catacombs and churches held an endless fascination for him.

Sundays found him taking part in Pope Leo XIII's audiences in the Vatican's St. Damasus Courtyard. Throughout his seminary years, he had many unforgettable spiritual experiences. For the funeral of Leo XIII in the summer of 1903 he managed to get inside the great basilica. Several weeks later he stood with the throng in the sundrenched piazza to see the wisp of white smoke over the Sistine chapel proclaiming the election of Giuseppe Sarto as Pope Pius X. The following week he was back in St. Peter's to watch the medieval panoply of Sarto's coronation. (Half a century later, May 29, 1954 Cardinal Roncalli, patriarch of Venice, was one of the most important invited guests at the canonization of Pius X by Pius XII in the basilica.)

In 1889 the seminarian had met the distinguished Monsignor Count Giacomo Radini-Tedeschi from the secretariat of state who was to profoundly influence his mind and career. Radini was moving up in the Church and had some plans for "the youth from Sotto Il Monte."

Having passed the theology exams in June of 1904, Roncalli was cleared for ordination. The date was set for August 10. While he awaited the great moment, Angelo went on a spiritual tour of the city's holy shrines: the four patriarchal basilicas, the Scala Santa (Holy Stairs), the catacombs, and a couple of hundred of Rome's great churches, among them twin baroque churches which guard one entrance to the immense Piazza del Popolo in the center of old Rome. In the one on the right as you look at them from the obelisk in the center of the piazza (the church of Santa Maria in Monte Santo), the pride of Sotto Il Monte became Father Roncalli. As in the case of Pope Pius XII, the first and last milestones of Roncalli's priesthood would be geographically but a few minutes walk from each other.

More unforgettable experiences awaited the new priest the next day on the occasion of his first Mass which was celebrated over the tomb of the first pope. When Father Roncalli was returning, chalice in hand to the sacristy after his first Mass, he quite unexpectedly encountered the Holy Father, Pope Pius X. A monsignor accompanying Roncalli introduced him to His Holiness as "a brand new priest from Bergamo," Pius's native diocese. Papa Sarto was delighted and reacted with his radiant smile and after congratulating the young cleric began to reminisce about his own Alpine boyhood, the lovely campagna, the gentle people, the churches and their melodious bells, the dialect of the Bergamo region. Then Pius inquired as to when Roncalli would be celebrating Mass for the first time back home. When the pope was informed that it would be August 15, the feast of the

Assumption, he exclaimed: "Oh, how those bells of Bergamo will ring for you! Oh, those bells of Bergamo! Those bells of Bergamo!"

The summer of 1904 was spent in the idyllic surroundings of the Lombard countryside and, as the days grew short, Roncalli's thoughts turned to graduate studies at the Apollinare. By October 1, Father Angelo was back in Rome for some more serious scholarship.

At this time the Bergamo diocese was beset with a variety of problems and Pius X handpicked the man that he thought could best solve them, Monsignor Radini-Tedeschi. Radini's thoughts turned immediately to "that seminarian Roncalli" who had made such an impression on him back in 1899. In a colorful ceremony on January 29, 1905 in the Sistine chapel, Pope Pius X personally consecrated Radini a bishop. Among those invited to participate in the ritual was Father Roncalli who held the Bible upon the shoulders of the bishop-designate during the consecration.

Shortly afterwards the young priest received his first assignment, not the normal post of curate in some country parish but rather as secretary to the new bishop. They would make an odd but effective team: the tall, slim, urbane, articulate patrician Radini-Tedeschi and the short, stocky, rustic, dialectic peasant Roncalli. Bound by a mutual love for the Church and a flaming desire to serve the Lord, the bishop and his aide toiled vigorously in Christ's vineyards.

At the side of the dynamic and indefatigable Radini, Roncalli learned much about such matters as the building and restoration of churches, the establishment of seminaries, the training of priests, fund raising, conducting pilgrimages, and many other facets of the episcopal realms. Roncalli helped his bishop escort groups of *Bergamesi* on pilgrimages to such places as Lourdes and the Holy Land.

Without question he loved his work as the bishop's right hand and a strong father-son bond of love and trust and admiration developed between the two. Accompanying the bishop on his diocesan rounds. Roncalli was able to put together a collection of Radini's sayings, witticisms, and observations which he would someday publish as part of his biography of his superior. Don Roncalli tried to pattern his spiritual life on that of the bishop, for this prelate was considered saintly, brilliant, gentle and extraordinary by all who knew him. Radini was beloved by both his clergy and his flock.

All this serenity was forever shattered however when in 1910 the young bishop, only fifty three, began to decline in health. What was thought at first to be merely a minor intestinal disorder was eventually diagnosed as cancer. Though he would rally for short periods, Radini was to deteriorate steadily. On a sultry morning of August 22, in the year 1914, the prelate passed away in the strong arms of his faithful assistant.

During his decade of service in the Bergamo chancery Roncalli had managed to find time to teach Church history at the diocesan seminary a few blocks away. Now the saddened Roncalli turned to teaching full time there to distract himself from his grief. He enjoyed working with the young priestly aspirants and they, from all accounts, enjoyed him and looked forward to his classes. Also at this time he pursued a personal scholarly interest, i.e., researching the life and writings of St. Charles Borromeo, archbishop of Milan and papal secretary of state in the late 1500's. As part of that scholarship he made frequent trips to Milan's famed *Biblioteca Ambrosiana*. Here he came into close contact with the library's prefect, Monsignor Achille Ratti, the future Pope Pius XI. Roncalli went on to publish several scholarly volumes on the life, times and words of Borromeo. Astonishingly, despite his teaching load and the time and energy required for the work on St. Charles, he also managed to write a five hundred page panegyric on the life of his late bishop which was published in 1916.

Though gaining steadily in prestige and recognition,

never at this time, nor at any future time, did Roncalli forget his humble roots. He truly loved Bergamo and hoped never to have to leave the beautiful northern region. Even as pontiff he would speak often and nostalgically of his ancestral home in conversation and in formal addresses. On the occasion of his election he had in a short talk to the cardinals spoken lovingly of his saintly mamma and hardworking papa and of his virtuous brothers and sisters. And even as pope he would joke that, "of the three ways for a man to ruin himself—wine, women and farming—my father chose the most boring."

But while he had hoped never to leave Bergamo, divine providence held otherwise for him. Indeed he would travel to far off places, and often, in his priesthood and ultimately end his priesthood where it began—in Rome. He began it dressed in black. He would conclude it garbed in white.

When Italy entered the World War later in 1916, Father Roncalli became an army chaplain. Quickly he won the hearts, esteem and trust of the men. Throughout the conflict he witnessed terrible suffering and came to abhor war with every fiber of his being. His encyclical *Pacem in Terris* would, years later, give voice to his sentiments. While in service, he took personal solace in comforting the wounded and the dying around him.

After the guns finally fell silent in 1918, Father Roncalli returned to diocesan work, founding a number of church-affiliated organizations for students, women and returning servicemen in order to keep them close to the Church and away from the atheistic influence of Marx and Lenin. He also lectured frequently during this period and soon after was appointed spiritual director of the seminary at Bergamo. This flurry of sacerdotal activity did not go unnoticed by his superiors and he even drew the admiring attention of Pope Benedict XV.

It was a day in mid-November of 1929 that a telegram arrived summoning Roncalli to the Eternal City to use his exceptional organizational skills for the Church as director of the Society for the Propagation of the Faith in Italy. Although he had long hoped for a pastorate somewhere in the Bergamo diocese, Roncalli accepted this vital post and in it began to travel rather extensively throughout Italy and in Belgium, Austria, Germany, Switzerland and France. Added to this awesome task was a teaching assignment at the Lateran pontifical seminary in Rome.

May 7 of the following year marked Roncalli's elevation to the hierarchy as a papal prelate with the title of monsignor. Pope Pius XI, Achille Ratti, who fondly remembered Roncalli from their Milan days, gave him many important tasks in 1923 for the preparation of the approaching Holy Year of 1925. On every assignment Roncalli demonstrated an exceptional ability and commitment and began to impress more and more the Vatican secretary of state, Gasparri, and the Holy Father himself.

As a consequence, Pius XI sought to use him in higher and more critical diplomatic roles. In 1925, Monsignor (later cardinal) Eugene Tisserant who had been on a recent tour of Bulgaria urged the pope to send a papal representative for the good of the small Catholic community there. Pius chose Roncalli, and to lend more prestige and importance to the post, made him titular archbishop of Areopolis, an ancient, defunct diocese in Palestine and gave him also the diplomatic rank of apostolic visitor.

With his proud parents in attendance, Angelo Roncalli was elevated to the episcopate on May 19, 1925 in a solemn ceremony at the church of St. Charles Borromeo on the Via del Corso in Rome. Later that day the humble Bergamesi were further thrilled when the new archbishop took his parents to the Apostolic Palace for a very private audience with the Supreme Pontiff. Before assuming his post in Bulgaria, the new apostolic visitor escorted his folks back home to Sotto Il Monte where for a few days he could once again enjoy some of mamma's cooking, walk with papa in the golden fields, and each evening talk and sip the *vino locale* into the wee hours, with his brothers and sisters and old friends and neighbors who dropped by to wish him well.

Bulgaria was to be the beginning of a long and fruitful diplomatic career. For his episcopal motto Roncalli took *Obedientia et Pax.* His official rank, as has been mentioned, was that of apostolic visitor since only countries with official diplomatic relations with the Holy See were granted papal nuncios.

Immediately upon his arrival in the Bulgarian capital of Sofia, he began his official task: to assess the state of the tiny Church in that country and to report on it, with recommendations directly to the pope himself and his secretary of state.

He quickly impressed the Bulgarians in many ways. They were particularly awed by the size and quality of the personal library he had imported with him. Since he was great copy with his unusual combination of rustic simplicity and urbane suavity and with his endless supply of witticisms he shortly became the darling of the press corps. The press also often commented admiringly on his library which included the works of the Church Fathers as well as of Dante, Petrarch, the Greek philosophers and tragedians and Italian authors such as Manzoni.

In his guest lectures and sermons he urged the Catholics of the Byzantine rite to improve their relations with the Orthodox majority which came to commend him for his ecumenical ways. So that he might himself relate better, he learned to speak Bulgarian.

He took his message throughout the country, traveling by various means, horseback, rowboat, horse and wagon, through the muddy backroads down rivers and streams, over rugged mountain passes, through rocky defiles. Everywhere he would listen to the problems of the clergy and the people. In every little village he would assure the flock that they had not been forgotten by Rome. Often he met with Orthodox leaders for an exchange of views and ideas, steadily gaining their friendship, trust and respect. These meetings began to fire his life's greatest ambition, i.e. to help bring the separated Christian Church together.

Here in Bulgaria the tireless diplomat established a Catholic Action organization, founded a seminary, helped to build Catholic schools, churches and hospitals.

Late in the year 1934, at the age of 53, Roncalli was reassigned as apostolic delegate to both Turkey and Greece. All Bulgaria and most especially the Orthodox leadership, was upset over the news. Praised effusively in the Bulgarian press for his work, his wisdom and his warm wit, Roncalli took his sad leave on January 4 of the new year. There was a great measure of comfort, however, in knowing that his two beloved housekeepers (his sisters, Ancilla and Maria) would be transferring with him. Thus he would continue to have with him a little bit of that world he so loved, the world of Sotto Il Monte.

On his new job Angelo Roncalli became a great practitioner of "shuttle diplomacy" long before Henry Kissinger coined the phrase. Though there were very few Catholics in Turkey, a country whose government was at the time quite hostile to the Catholic Church, Roncalli nevertheless felt they merited his attention and guidance and made many trips to the capital of Ankara in their behalf. From here he frequently journeyed to his other diplomatic post, Athens, to try to help the fifty thousand Catholics in Greece. These faithful sons and daughters of the Church often suffered for their religious affiliation, and were, as a rule, impoverished and generally ostracized. Roncalli was always happiest when he was busiest and he was exceptionally busy in his latest job trying to unite Catholics of the various rites and fostering a greater rapport with the Orthodox community. For enjoyment and edification the rotund diplomat haunted the great archeological sites, boyishly excited over the opportunity to study *in situ* a civilization he studied so assiduously in the college classroom.

When World War II broke out, Roncalli's residence

served as a sort of clearing house for inquiries from families with loved ones missing in the war. Franz von Papen, the German ambassador to Turkey (and a practicing Catholic) and the apostolic delegate developed a warm friendship. And through this Roncalli was able to help Jews who had fled to Turkey from lands taken by the Nazis. Von Papen, who abhorred Hitler's murderous policies, took serious personal risks in helping Roncalli ship the refugees on to safety in Palestine.

On another occasion the archbishop was appalled to learn that hundreds of Jewish children who had arrived from Germany at the port of Constantinople were being denied asylum by the Turkish government worried about angering the Nazis and forfeiting its cherished neutrality. Through some feverish eleventh hour activity and relentless pressure on the authorities he managed to avert the return of the innocents and have them shipped on to another neutral nation. Nor did he neglect his obligations in Greece during these dark times. After the Nazi-Italian seizure of the ancient land a terrible famine struck the populace. With the oldest and most revered Orthodox prelate, Metropolitan Damaskinos, as his partner, the pope's delegate persuaded the occupation forces to permit Allied food supplies to get through.

It seemed that every decade or so a telegram from Rome would drastically alter the life and elevate the career of Angelo Roncalli and in December of 1944 one arrived declaring his appointment as papal nuncio to Paris, a vital, sensitive position calling for extraordinary diplomatic skills. Before the month was out he was in Paris presenting his diplomatic credentials to President Charles De Gaulle in the Elysee Palace.

By friendly persuasion he soon cooled the antipathy of the new De Gaulle regime toward the French hierarchy which had supported the fallen Vichy government. With his abundant good will and keen sense of diplomacy, Roncalli rapidly emerged as the star of the foreign service corps in the French capital. His excellent command of the language enabled him to feel quite at home on the Seine. His official luncheons and dinner parties were the talk of Paris, not so much for their menus as for their scintillating conversation, their spirit of good fellowship, their laughter (most of which was precipitated by Roncalli's spontaneous one-liners). The nuncio was the first to joke about his own plumpness. Once at a formal affair at the French Academy he observed, "This is a most impressive place indeed. Unfortunately the seats can accomodate only a demi-nuncio."

His popularity with the common folk was even greater. Without a trace of condescension he loved to converse with people from every class and every walk of life. No carpenter, electrician, plumber, gardener, worker of any kind could leave the nunciature in Paris without a glass of wine or some *caffe au lait* with the head of the household himself.

Archbishop Roncalli developed a real fondness for and deep friendship with one worker and on the first Saturday of each month the popular prelate had dinner with him and his wife and their seven children. Robert Schuman, at the time French Minister of Foreign Affairs, described the archbishop as "the only man in Paris in whose company one feels completely at peace and at ease."

During his years in Paris, Roncalli was also a familiar figure in the streets of the capital. Whenever possible and practical, he would walk to his destinations in order to meet the people. Before he left the country for his next assignment, he had visited almost all of France's eighty dioceses, with a pilgrimage every year to his special love, Lourdes. From his youth a dedicated bibliophile, Angelo could often be spotted browsing in the second hand book stalls along the banks of the Seine looking for bargains for his cherished library.

Toward the end of November in 1952 a cable arrived at the nunciature from Monsignor Montini, Pius XII's acting secretary of state for Ordinary Affairs. Roncalli blushed as he read the news that he would be raised to the cardinalate at a consistory in the coming January. This would surely be the culmination, the final honor, the crowning glory to his priesthood. So he thought. Soon after the new year began he also learned that with his new colors went a new assignment, the patriarchate of the diocese of Venice. Another decade, another telegram, another mission. The patriarchate was truly one of the key posts in the entire Church. Earlier in the century Giuseppe Sarto had gone on from this position to the papacy.

To welcome their new spiritual leader the Venetians, long accustomed to such pagentry, truly outdid themselves. Roncalli's arrival in March, 1953, was hailed by a regatta of practically every gondola, launch, barge and *vaporetta* in the fairy-tale city. Balconies and loggias were festooned with municipal, national and papal colors. Everywhere there were flowers. Bands played. School children serenaded the new patriarch with hymns and folksongs.

Contrasting with this lavish display was the cardinal's simple first address to his new flock from the pulpit of St. Mark's cathedral. The people loved him already for his unassuming manner. Even with the local communist government leaders, Roncalli enjoyed from the start a remarkable rapport. He was considered by everyone the "first citizen of Venice."

Despite his rather advanced age, he put in staggeringly long work days, beginning customarily at five a.m. and extending often beyond midnight. As had one of his predecessors, Cardinal Sarto, Roncalli deeply loved the unique beauty of the insular city. Weather permitting, he liked to go up to the roof-top terrace of his residence at dawn to read his breviary, listen to the church bells, and especially to watch the rising sun do its magic to the domes and bell towers, tile rooftops and pastel facades of Venice.

Showing visitors around the city was a special delight

for him. Once, Stefan Cardinal Wyszynski of Poland—recently released after three years of incarceration by the communist regime—was on his way to Rome and decided to stop off at Venice. The Polish primate was met at the station by his colleague Roncalli who took him to see the sights along the Grand Canal. After about an hour of this, Wyszynski suddenly snapped out of his rapture and cried, "I'm going to miss my train!" Cardinal Roncalli reassured him. "Do you see that man in the back of the launch?" he asked. "Well, he's the station master and I've kidnapped him. No train can leave without his approval."

Mornings would often be given over to visiting different parishes in the diocese, while afternoons were frequently reserved for audiences in the patriarchal residence. Under Roncalli's reign thirty new parishes were founded with the cardinal taking an active and keen interest in their progress.

This was the happiest period of his career and in his mind this was surely the last stop on the long and fruitful road of his priesthood. Perhaps after this he could "enjoy a few years of retirement at some quiet monastery engaged in a little personal scholarship or at some seminary in Italy counseling the young priestly aspirants."

Suddenly it was October of 1958 and Pope Pius XII was dying. This fact deeply saddened Roncalli who stayed up even later than usual in order to pray for his pontiff. Over the radio in the early hours of October 9, he heard the sad news: "The pope is dead." After celebrating a Requiem Mass for Papa Pacelli in the basilica of *San Marco* early on October 11, Cardinal Roncalli packed his bags and departed for the funeral and subsequent conclave in Rome. Many among the thousands of his flock who saw him off thought about the possibility of his election, recalling Sarto's election as Pope Pius X fifty five years before.

After participating in Pius XII's funeral and escorting his remains to the crypt beneath St. Peter's, Roncalli whiled away the wait for the start of the conclave with daily nostalgic tours of Rome. The Eternal City was abuzz with speculation over Pius's successor. Among the leading *papabili* were Cardinals Lercaro, Ottaviani, Masella, Ruffini, Siri and one non-cardinal, Archbishop Giovanni Battista Montini of Milan. In the lively betting action in the bars, cafes and men's clubs of the city, Roncalli's name was largely forgotten.

Clad in scarlet (for mourning) instead of their traditional red, fifty two princes of the Church assembled on Saturday, October 25, in the Sistine chapel for the start of the conclave. Each cardinal had a throne with a canopy. The empty one next to the Armenian, Cardinal Agagianian, was a sad reminder of the American, Cardinal Mooney, who had passed away just hours before at the North American College seminary on the Janiculum hill overlooking the Vatican.

Following two days of voting—two ballotings each morning and two more each afternoon—no one had yet received the two-thirds plus one required for election. In Rome and around the world the tension mounted, and so did the speculation. During the morning of the third day, Tuesday, October 28, there was an unexpected but significant trend toward Roncalli. That afternoon's first ballot was decisive. The Church had a new shepherd. The keys of the husky, humble, humorous fisherman of Galilee had been entrusted to the husky, humble, humorous farmer of Sotto Il Monte.

The cardinals had given the world a beautiful surprise. And surprise would be almost the very byword of the new pontiff's entire reign. Even Roncalli's choice of a papal name was startling since for more than five and a half centuries no other pope had chosen it. "I will be called John," he softly proclaimed. Pope John XXIII quickly explained his choice to his astonished electors. It was, he said, a good name, a common name, the name of the Church where he was baptized, the name of the Baptist and of the Evangelist of the Scriptures.

Those who thought that the aged John XXIII was

going to be merely a caretaker pope filling in briefly between Pius XII and the next dynamic pontiff were shortly persuaded to the contrary. Things began breaking fast. For instance, in his first day on the job, Papa Roncalli announced through the Vatican newspaper, *L'Osservatore Romano,* that Monsignor Domenico Tardini would be his secretary of state. Many other higher ranking prelates had been considered more likely choices. Before that first day was up, Pope John had made a great number of other important appointments. Archbishop Giovanni Urbani was given the patriarchate of Venice with the pope's personal exhortation, "Take good care of our beautiful and beloved Venice and her wonderful people!" John set the coronation ceremonies for Sunday, November 9, which was a happy coincidence, for it was the feast day of the saint of Roncalli's personal scholarship, Charles Borromeo.

The white cassock did not alter in the least Roncalli's simple ways nor his penchant for gentle humor. Even as pope he would joke about his size. "But whenever I feel fat," he said one day, "I go and stand next to Cicognani and then I suddenly feel slender again." (Laughing the hardest was the victim of the pope's needle, Cardinal Cicognani, one of the more rotund members of the sacred college.) John once lamented to Archbishop Fulton J. Sheen, "Almighty God knew from the beginning of time that I would someday be pope. You'd think He would have made me a little better to look at!"

Soon after the election, Vatican workers were pleasantly stunned to see the great figure in white walking the grounds, dropping in on the various shops. "This must be thirsty work," he said to one group of laborers and insisted that they take a break and enjoy a glass of chilled white wine with him. Before long he was being affectionately refered to by the Vatican's little people as "Good Pope John."

On one of his tours of his miniature sovereign state the pope was introduced to some more workers. Cardinal

Gustavo Testa was escorting him. When they came to one man, Cardinal Testa announced: "*Santo Padre* (Holy Father), may I present to you Papa, Giovanni." "Who?" the pope asked in amazement. (In Italy it is customary to give the last name first and first name last in an introduction. Giovanni Papa was the man's name.) "Ah," said the amused pope after he caught on. "So there are two Papa Giovannis. Great! I was beginning to wonder how I was going to manage this job all by myself."

At his audience he always had a humorous anecdote or pun for his visitors. Two close aides from the start of his papacy were Monsignor Dell' Acqua and Cardinal Canali and to a group of Venetians one day he joked, "I am daily reminded of my happy days in Venice because I am still surrounded by *Acqua* and *Canali* (water and canals)." He often joked with his cardinals. When he learned that his secretary of state, Cardinal Tardini, frequently referred to him as "the one above" (because the pope's office was upstairs from the secretary's), Pope John kidded: "*Caro Tardini*, let's get straight on one matter. 'The one above' is the Eternal Lord of us all. I am merely the one on the top floor. I must ask you to please stop throwing confusion in the ranks."

All of the humor, however, must not be misinterpreted as a frivolous approach on the part of the pontiff to his solemn task. About his pontifical role he was very serious and to it lovingly dedicated. In fact he was a model for all priests and laymen especially in the corporal works of mercy. Throughout his reign, John XXIII continued to visit the sick, the poor, the imprisoned and the forgotten. His first Christmas in office surprised many, for he chose that occasion to visit the inmates of Rome's *Regina Coeli* prison and later toured the children's hospital *Bambino Gesu* on the Janiculum.

Shortly after his election he demonstrated his outstanding administrative skills by reorganizing the financial administration of the Holy See. Fiscal responsibility was entrusted to Cardinals Tardini, Cicognani and Di Jorio.

It also occurred to John early in his pontificate that the growth of the Church in recent decades called for the creation of a greater number of cardinals to carry on its work. Accordingly, he announced a consistory for December 15, 1958, at which he would create twenty three new cardinals, exceeding by five the limit of seventy set by Pope Sixtus V in 1586. Significantly, and somewhat prophetically, first on the list of new cardinals was Archbishop Montini who would succeed John as Pope Paul VI. (While the pope cannot name his successor, many believed that Montini was John's personal choice to carry on the great work he would begin.) Two American prelates, Archbishop Richard J. Cushing of Boston and John O'Hara of Philadelphia were given the red hat at the same consistory. One year later another consistory added eight new members to the sacred college and fifteen months after that, in March of 1960, Pope John brought the number of papal princes to eighty five. Among those honored in the last group was the first black cardinal, Bishop Laurean Rugambwa of Tanganyika.

Change and reform were to be the hallmarks of John's brief reign. Hurt feelings were sometimes an unfortunate by-product of some of the changes. Determined to infuse more vitality and a fresh point of view into the Church's government, the pope was not unwilling to remove an older cardinal to a less vital post and replace him with a younger member of the sacred college.

Often another by-product of Pope John's measures was shock such as that registered by most of the eighteen cardinals present at St. Paul's Outside-the-Walls on Sunday morning, January 25, 1959. After celebrating Mass in the ancient and venerable basilica, Pope John held a conference of the cardinals in attendance in the dining hall of the monastery attached to the historic church. He chose this occasion to announce his intention to call an ecumenical council (a gathering of cardinals, archbishops, bishops and heads of religious orders from all corners of the globe). John's council, to be known as Vatican Council II, would be the first such gathering in nearly a century, the first since Vatican Council I convoked by Pius IX in 1870. Throughout the long history of the Church there had been but twenty councils, each called to resolve a crisis or enact long overdue reforms within the Church. Some had been convoked to combat heresy, for example, the very first council at Nicea in 325 where the Church fathers were concerned with the suppression of Arianism. Others were summoned in order to formulate new responses to long-standing problems within the Church or to clarify doctrines long held by the Church, e.g. Vatican I in 1869 defined the doctrine of papal primacy and infallibility.

But Pope John had no particular heresies to fight or doctrines to define. His hope was simply to bring the Church into step with the modern world and to promote the unification of the divided Christian world. He wanted merely to "open a window and let some fresh air" into a Church grown musty with, in his view, outdated medieval trappings and disciplines.

All eighteen cardinals present that day were startled at the announcement, some pleasantly so, others, particularly the more conservative among them, not so happily so. The latter instantly perceived this move as not so much a case of opening a window but rather a Pandora's box. Even Cardinal Tardini, the secretary of state, had profound reservations about the idea.

These conservative prelates feared it would give a dangerous forum to the liberal bishops, especially those from the countries that border the Rhine—Germany, Austria, Switzerland, France, the Netherlands and nearby Belgium—through which they might spread their ideas regarding the modern Church, ideas the conservatives found abhorrent and dangerous. Their fears were, it turned out, well-founded for the predominating influence in the measures adopted by the council came from precisely those quarters. (Ralph M. Wiltgen's fine book

on the council implies this influence in its clever title,
The Rhine Flows into the Tiber.)

While this division into two hierarchical ideologies was
to be expected, it nonetheless saddened the pope. Still
his more global aim of Christian unity transcended this
and he exhorted his fellow bishops during the great
period of preparation for the council to "emphasize those
things which unite rather than those which divide."

Hoping to lead the way toward reunion by his own
example, he received in audience the Anglican Archbishop of Canterbury, Geoffrey Fisher, on December 2,
1960. He likewise received visits from clergy leaders of
other Christian denominations. In fact, among the many
commissions Pope John established for the task of preparation for the council, one was the secretariat for pro-
moting Christian Unity. The commission's mandate was
to establish dialogue with other branches of the Christian
community and to invite them all to send observer delegations to the council. Observer delegates at Vatican II
were to number sixty six, with twenty two Churches
represented, giving this council perhaps the most truly
ecumenical air of all the councils over the twenty Christian centuries.

Nearly four years were required to tend to the staggering logistics. There would be nearly three thousand participants, each with a staff of three or four meaning there
would be accomodations needed in or near Rome for
more than ten thousand persons.

Committes were set up for defining the various problems the council should tackle. Some of these groups and
their cardinal chairmen were: the Committee on Theology presided over by Cardinal Ottaviani; the Bishopric
under Cardinal Mimmi; the Sacraments, Masella; the
Liturgy, Gaetano Cicognani; the Eastern Church, Ame-
leto Cicognani; the Missions, Agagianian. Cardinal Cento
directed the committee on the Lay Apostolate while Cardinal Tisserant chaired the group in charge of ceremonies.
In addition, an elaborate no-nonsense timetable had to be

drawn up for the four sessions of the council.

In the weeks and months leading up to the opening of the great assembly, the Catholic Church would be engaged in self examination and evaluation. In the midst of this elaborate and feverish groundwork the octogenarian pontiff found the time and energy to issue his widely acclaimed encyclical, *Mater et Magistra*. The title derives from the opening line of the document: "Mother and Teacher of all nations—that is the Church in the mind of her founder, Jesus Christ." The encyclical was a treatise on the Church's compassion and concern for the working classes.

Halfway through the preparation of the council the Holy Father's joyful anticipation was dimmed by a great personal loss, the death of his 'right arm,' the cardinal secretary of state, Domenico Tardini on June 30, 1961. "Think of how our heart is afflicted by the loss of this beloved cardinal, this closest and strongest helper of the pope in the government of the Holy Church," he brooded in his announcement of Tardini's death from his window over St. Peter's square.

With a good deal of the foundation already laid, Pope John in his Christmas address in 1961 formally convoked the Second Ecumenical Council of the Vatican for the autumn of the following year.

A couple of hours before dawn on October 11, 1962, the pontiff awoke in nervous but joyful anticipation of the council's opening ceremonies. Pushing open one shutter of his bedroom window he was chagrined at the weather, for it was raining and thundering in the inimitable Roman fashion, the precipitation coming down in sheets from the Alban hills. John XXIII stood there for a few minutes with a look on his face akin to that of the Little Leaguer whose game has been rained out. He had waited four years and was disappointed that the planned procession of the bishops through St. Peter's square would have to be moved indoors to the central aisle of the basilica. While there is a misty majesty to St. Peter's cobblestoned piazza in the rain, John had been hoping for it to be sunsplashed for this occasion. With a smile toward the heavens and a shrug of his broad shoulders, the pope knelt at the prie-dieu in his room and prayed till daylight.

Then, after a light breakfast, he had some last minute meetings with his secretary, Monsignor Loris Capovilla, and those in charge of the ceremonies for the day. About 8:20, while walking through the halls of the Apostolic Palace on their way to the back of the cathedral for the start of the procession, the pope and those accompanying him were delighted to see the sun burst through the windows and streak across the marble corridors. The outdoor festivities were put back on.

Now in mid-morning, under a deep blue sky, the endless line of colorfully clad bishops of every nation, in their pointed mitres, slowly made its way over the rain-washed stones, between the barricades holding back the multitudes of faithful, toward the basilica. Behind the more than two thousand bishops and archbishops walked the eighty two princes of the Church, followed in turn by the nine patriarchs of the Eastern rite. Then with the crowd's roar a deafening pitch and hundreds of church bells chiming ecstatically, a huge figure in white was born aloft on the *sedia gestatoria* at the very end of the procession. Solemn music accompaniment was provided by bands in gallant uniforms while press fotogs and tourists alike snapped their lenses incessantly in an effort to record the spectacle for generations yet unborn. Priests and nuns and laymen too, fortunate enough to have secured passes for the top of Bernini's colonnade, leaned precariously over the balustrade for a closer look. Angelo Roncalli had come to the climax of his priesthood, his life. As Rome was growing even older and her pagan ruins across town continued to crumble, the Church, thanks to good Pope John, was being rejuvenated.

Inside the basilica, with the invited observers of the separated Churches already in their places, the long river of purple and red split into two streams with each flowing up into the seats on either side of the six hundred foot long nave.

When John entered, the Sistine choir thrilled everyone with the hymn, *Veni, Creator Spiritus* (Come, Holy Spirit). As soon as the pope had been enthroned, the dean of the sacred college, Cardinal Tisserant began his celebration of the opening Mass in Latin. Certainly the many architects of the centuries-old basilica could never have dreamed that the twentieth century medium of TV would beam a ceremony from here, live, to the farthest reaches of the globe.

Pope John addressed the opening convocation, also in Latin, the official language of the sessions, explaining his hopes for the council, viz. the renewal and updating (*aggiornamento*) of the *Magisterium* or teaching authority of the Church. Speaking against "the prophets of doom," the pope struck an optimistic chord, telling the council fathers how the council was the "hope of mankind," how those separated from the Apostolic See and non-Christians as well were counting on that august body to engender unity and peace among all men and all nations as well as all faiths.

Night eventually fell again on old Rome and on its aging bishop. A full moon smiled down on St. Peter's square. Though it had been a long and strenuous day for John, he was exuberant—and hopeful. Bone-weary he nonetheless obliged the throng which had gathered beneath his window in the vast square chanting for his appearance. When he stepped to the window an indescribably beautiful and inspirational sight greeted him. Down in the floodlit piazza thousands of men in a single line stretching from the steps of St. Peter's far down into the Via della Conciliazione, the broad boulevard which runs from the Tiber to Bernini's colonnade, carried torches. Intersecting this was another line from the center of one colonnade to the other, resulting in a colossal golden cross. It was a most emotional and never-to-be-forgotten experience for all and for the pope himself who in a brief, impromptu address from his window recounted the great events of the day, closing with the gentle exhortation, "get home safely" and the humble request to "give your children a hug and a kiss from the pope."

Two days later the council fathers got down to business. It was fascinating to hear the ancient Latin tongue of the Caesars become a living language once again in twentieth century Rome. But since not all spoke it fluently or understood it well, printed transcripts translated into each one's native tongue were provided so that the bishops could participate more fully. This first session, as would be all future ones, was attended by bishops not only of the Latin rite but also by those from the Uniate and Eastern rite Churches with their own unique traditions and rituals but who still acknowledge the supreme authority of the pope. Also in attendance by papal invitation were delegates from the Coptic Church of Egypt, the Syrian and Russian Orthodox Churches, the Anglican, Lutheran, Calvinist, Pentecostal, Congregationalist, Methodist and Quaker Churches, and the secretariat of the World Council of Churches. An Ecumenical Council indeed!

The first session ended on December 8, 1962 after having sanctioned change in public worship to render it "more vital and informative." In the days following, the bishops flew back home to their dioceses.

In the meantime, good Pope John had been stricken with a dreadful illness and knew in his heart that he would not survive to inaugurate the second session. Though the pontiff was left in constant agonizing stomach pain, he fought back with all the might of his sturdy peasant frame for the next six months. But his affliction was soon to triumph.

Around noon on June 3, he slipped into a coma. That warm evening Cardinal Traglia celebrated a Mass in the square, attended by a hundred thousand of the pope's flock. Throughout the Holy Father's sickness, messages of tribute flowed into the Vatican from heads of state of every ideology, of every creed, from the old and young, the rich and poor, the mighty and the lowly. A Jewish friend of mine consoled me in those sad days with, "You know he's our pope, too." Just as the Mass was ending and the multitude was praying for a miracle, Pope John XXIII broke the heart of the world with his last breath *Ite, missa est.*

On June 21, the cardinal again advised the world from the balcony of St. Peter's: *"Habemus Papam!"* "We have a pope!" Giovanni Battista Montini, who was John's first cardinal, was the man to whom the sacred college looked to complete the stupendous task undertaken by Angelo Roncalli. Montini was to reign as the gentle and saintly Pope Paul VI. (The tradition of stout-slim had been perpetuated.) We shall consider the life and pontificate of Paul VI shortly. At this point, however, perhaps we could examine the work and decisions of Vatican Council II.

Paul called the council to a second session on September 29, 1963. It was to run almost ten weeks, to December 4, and be remembered largely for its reconfirmation of the principle of collegiality, i.e., the governance of the Church by the bishops together with the pope, the bishop of Rome, and under his primacy. From September 14 of 1964 to November 21 of the same year ran the third session and from September 14 of 1965 to December of that year the fourth and final session.

All together, the council ratified sixteen documents. One called for a greater sharing by the bishops in the exercise of ecclesiastical authority. Another revised the sacred liturgy to allow broader congregational participation. This document also replaced Latin with the vernacular in certain parts of the Mass. A third emphasized the importance of the Sacred Scriptures in the life and liturgy of the Church, helping to narrow the gap between Catholics and Protestants regarding divine revelation.

Other decrees involved such things as a continued condemnation of atheism, but a simultaneous call for compassion and understanding toward atheists because "they are also God's creatures"; a greater respect for religious freedom; a pledge to work toward Christian unity; the modernization of the religious life of monks, priests, brothers and sisters; reforms in the intellectual and spiritual training of seminarians; the reaffirmation of the laws of priestly celibacy; the exhortation to the world of communications to use the various media for moral purpose; and a call for greater participation of the laity in the apostolate and ministry of the Church.

All over Rome there are the great architectural and artistic works commissioned by countless popes. As mentioned earlier, these are easily recognized as papal works by the initials *P.M. (Pontifex Maximus)* after the patron's name. John was the personal architect of Vatican II and the farreaching effects of the council are his chief monument.

CHAPTER XII

POPE PAUL VI

Uncharacteristic of everything else in Rome except for automobile drivers, the conclave moved fast. Shortly past noon on Friday, June 21, 1963 the waiting throng in St. Peter's square raised a mighty roar as suddenly the tall glass doors leading to the central balcony of the basilica swung open. Moments later the multitude erupted again in joy, for standing directly under the name of the Borghese Paul V, engraved across the entablature of the facade of St. Peter's was the new Supreme Pontiff. *"Habemus Papam!"*

The slim figure in white, almost lost in the colossal baroque backdrop, stood motionless, savoring the delightfully deafening welcome to his new diocese from his Roman flock and from his sons and daughters from around the world. His slight frame, his graceful, stately manner, his gaunt, bespectacled face, his enigmatic air, his paternal gestures evoked memories of Pacelli. One Roman signora was heard to gasp incredulously, *"E' tornato Papa Pio Dodicesimo!"* ("Pope Pius XII has come back to us!"). The providential preparation of Giovanni Battista Montini for the Supreme Pontificate had been completed. The reign of Pope Paul VI had begun.

Pretty Giuditta Alghisi Montini presented her soft-spoken husband, Giorgio, with their second son on September 26, 1897 in the sleepy village of Concesio in the Italian Alps. The eighteenth century house at Via Vantini 14, where Signora Montini brought a future pope into the world, still stands. Four days later the happy parents took the *bambino* to the little church of Sant' Antonio where the pastor, Father Giovanni Fiorini baptized

Giovanni Battista Montini.

The Montinis also had a townhouse on Via Trieste in the city of Brescia, seven miles away. Giorgio was well known in the area, and throughout Italy in fact, as a talented lawyer, a courageous journalist and a distinguished member of Parliament where he represented the Popular Party from 1919–1926. During this same period the energetic Montini was in the forefront of the movement to heal the wounds between Church and State. (It was this same Popular Party that was suppressed by Mussolini and then emerged, after the war, under the leadership of Alcide De Gasperi, to lead Italy's new republic under the name of the Christian Democratic Party.)

In the years from 1881 to 1912 Giorgio worked as the publisher and editor of the Brescian daily, *Il Cittadino*. By politics a liberal progressive, Montini remained in the face of scorn, derision, threat, vilification, a staunch defender of the Catholic Church. Signor Montini was to have a profound influence on his new son. For it was from his father that Giovanni Battista got his organizational talents, his interest in the great social questions, and in philosophy and in writing. From his delicate, shy and pious mother, much involved in Catholic women societies of Brescia, the boy got his love of the poor, for two or three days of Giuditta's week were given over to ministering to Brescia's impoverished.

Within a few weeks after the new baby's arrival, however, the parents' joy turned to sadness and worry when the doctor advised that the extremely frail infant be given a "change of air" (the time-honored Italian panacea). Dejectedly the Montinis handed over their little son to wet-nurse Clorinda Perretti in nearby Bovezzo until he was thirteen months old. Even then it was against the doctor's wishes that Giuditta brought him back to Brescia. Giovanni was later to spend another stretch at Bovezzo and was never to forget his "other" mother. Once as cardinal he paid a nostalgic and emotional visit to Clorinda who still referred to him lovingly as *"il piccolino"* (little one).

As a result of his fragile health, due largely to a pulmonary weakness, Giovanni Battista's childhood was to be somewhat sheltered. Still he managed to attend the demanding Cesare Arici school, run by the Jesuits, throughout his elementary and high school years. Fortunately the school was close to home. From the outset, little Montini was an extraordinary student. In most of his courses he finished at the head of his class.

The pale, thin lad with the big eyes, high forehead and pointy features was by nature serious and, due to his health problems and a natural shyness, something of a loner. Yet his classmates recall how he nevertheless loved exercise, especially running and bicycle riding, though he did neither very well. He was then, and remained throughout his life, a light eater. Doctors' restrictions forced him to take it easy to avoid getting run down for he was especially vulnerable, they thought, to pneumonia—or worse. Thus sidelined much of the time, Montini consequently read a lot to distract himself. Soon he became compulsively bookish.

One resident of Concesio, Luigi Bolognini, points out that deep inside this angelic tyke, however, raged a volcanic spirit. To illustrate Giovanni Battista's spunky side, the old timer relates how one day a tough farm boy of Concesio tied a frying pan to a cat's tail. Everyone howled at the creature's frantic efforts to free itself. Everyone, that is, but little Montini. *Giambattista,* as everyone called him, ordered the boy to stop torturing the cat. The farmboy brushed him back brusquely. Whereupon Montini leaped upon the much bigger lad and the two began to go at it, fists flying wildly.

Giambattista was unabashedly prayerful, stopping even in the middle of a game to recite the Angelus prayers when he heard the bells of the village church. And he was quick to invite his comrades to join in.

In the classroom young Montini impressed peers and

professors alike with his logical and analytical mind, with his extensive and precise vocabulary, and his prodigious, photographic memory. Articles he wrote for the school paper had an unusual maturity and polish.

At seventeen, Giambattista began the next phase of his studies at the *Liceo Arnaldo da Brescia*. The *liceo* is practically the academic equivalent of our junior colleges. At the Arnaldo, Montini attended few classes, his still fragile condition compelling him to study for his exams at home. This separation from his classmates, however ungregarious he was, distressed him deeply.

Vacation periods were passed with the family in their mountain retreat where Giovanni hiked and ran, in an effort to build up his weak frame, with his older brother, Ludovico, who like his father went on eventually to Parliament, and his younger brother, Francesco, a future doctor. (You may recall our discussion some pages back of how young, frail Eugenio Pacelli's vacations were similarly spent.)

Whether in Brescia, or in the summer country villas in Concesio or Verolovecchia, life in the Montini home was a quiet one but one abundant in good, intelligent, sophisticated conversation about social issues, cultural matters, political and world affairs. There was plenty of warmth and love and piety. The family prayed the rosary together daily.

In his eighteenth year, his family and friends were concerned when it became obvious that Giambattista was wrestling with some inner problem. By now he had already confided to his old friend, Father Persico back at the Arici school, his plans to enter the priesthood. The following year he graduated the liceo with highest honors and, with Italy at war, was soon after drafted for military service. Montini's record of poor health resulted in an exemption freeing him to enter the seminary. Here the parallel with Pacelli's life continues, for Giacinto Gaggia, bishop of Brescia and a family friend, granted the priestly aspirant permission to live at home and attend the seminary as a day student. At the seminary Montini quickly excelled in his studies of philosophy and theology. At home, through exposure to the conversation of his father's friends and a steady exchange of ideas and diverse viewpoints, he progressed rapidly in his understanding of the political and social forces of the world.

Montini dearly loved children and throughout his seminary years he spent as much time as he could working with them, teaching catechism to the candidates for First Holy Communion and likewise to the older children preparing for the sacrament of Confirmation. Since these classes were held after school hours the young seminarian began with the proverbial two strikes against him. Yet Giambattista quickly won their respect, trust and affection. His heart went out particularly to the poor and the sickly among them.

Ordination day came on May 29, 1920. Bishop Gaggia took a special delight in bringing into the priesthood the gifted son of his dear friends, the Montinis. On the followng morning, family, friends and neighbors gathered in the beautiful *Santuario della Grazie* in Brescia to attend Father Montini's first Mass. There was hardly a dry eye to be seen when the village bookworm gave Communion to his beloved mamma and papa.

After a few weeks vacation Father Montini drew the assignment of curate in the village church of Verdanuova down the road from Brescia. Though his days as a curate were to be few, there were enough of them to get the picture of a new priest immensely popular with his parishioners. One day the thin cleric was out walking in his long black cassock and broad brimmed black hat. A local farmer spotted him and was alarmed at his emaciated appearance whereupon he gave him a chicken and a couple of dozen eggs. The chicken Montini toted in one hand while in the other he carried his hat upside down, now filled to the brim with fresh eggs.

In late autumn of that year Bishop Gaggia informed the new priest that he was being sent to Rome for a "good rest and perhaps some light study." But once ensconced at Rome the boundlessly energetic Montini entered the Lombard pontifical seminary for advanced theological studies and also took courses in philosophy at the renowned Gregorian University. Not content with having a few idle minutes on his hands each day, the frail priest enrolled in literature courses at the University of Rome. Notice the difference in Montini's understanding of and Gaggia's concept of "rest." But the truth was that the bright, scholarly priest thrived spiritually, intellectually and physically on this incredible regime.

His tremendous capacity for scholarship was brought to the attention of Monsignor Giuseppe Pizzardo from the Vatican secretariat of state. Seeing a future diplomat in the trim Lombard, Pizzardo got him accepted to the prestigious Academy of Ecclesiastical Nobles, training ground for prelates and papal nuncios. From here they went off to their diplomatic posts in the great European capitals. Among the illustrious alumni were such names as Gioachino Pecci, Giacomo della Chiesa and Eugenio Pacelli. Here at the Academy, Montini concentrated on studies in diplomacy and in English, German and French.

Continuing to show exceptional promise, Montini attracted the attention of the higher ups in the secretariat and at the age of 25 in May of 1923 his studies were interrupted again by an assignment as attache to the nunciature in Warsaw. He was at the time the youngest Vatican diplomat. As should have been foreseen, however, the brutal climate of the Polish capital proved perilous to him and after five months he was sent back to the Eternal City.

In October he was appointed *minutante* in the Vatican secretariat. Rising all the time in esteem among his peers and superiors, Montini resumed his studies at the Academy. Some of the other young priests and monsignori that Father Montini worked side by side with at that time were Francis Spellman, Alfredo Ottaviani and Domenico Tardini. Pope Pius XI was pope and his secre-

tary of state was the dynamic Cardinal Pietro Gasparri.

A tireless worker himself, Montini was most compatible with the many other workaholics of the Vatican state department. Gasparri, for example, was known to wrap himself, fully dressed, in a few afghans, fall on his bed for a few hours and begin another twenty hour day in the vineyards of the Lord. Work was life for this unusual breed. And it was exciting, too, for the decade of the twenties was a sort of Golden Age in Vatican diplomacy with the signing of countless concordats and the negotiating of rapprochements with many nations. Everyone in the secretariat, even the minutantes, were thrilled to be making history for Christ and his Church.

Though he carried out his work with his customary elan, Father Montini could not set aside his fervent desire to work with or even just be with the poor, the sick, the suffering. The parish priest inside this papal diplomat preferred saving souls to poring over dossiers, and he one day confided this to his patron, Pizzardo. A light bulb went on at once in the monsignor's mind for he knew of just the post as an ideal outlet for Montini's desires. The slender cleric from Brescia was soon after appointed spiritual advisor to the Roman branch of FUCI (the Italian Federation of Catholic University Students).

This latest assignment would prove to be truly a labor of love for Montini and would bring out a gregarious side of him not seen before. Montini worked with FUCI for the period from 1924 to 1934. His charges took to him at once. They affectionately called him *Don G.B.M.* (after his initials). They loved to walk with him, talk about life, pick his brain about religion, philosophy, politics. They enjoyed impromptu soccer matches and foot races with the ascetic figure in the black soutane. Don G.B.M. organized trips to foreign countries for both university men and women and used these sojourns to introduce the students to the wondrous religious shrines of Europe.

As did Roncalli, Father Montini organized a social action group of university students to go out to minister to Rome's depressed areas especially in the quarter of Porta Metronia not too far from the Lateran basilica. One day each week the group would bring food parcels along with clothes, shoes, blankets and medical supplies. On some occasions the young missionaries and their chaplain would be jeered by anti-clerics but they remained undaunted because an old man's grasp of hand, a child's grin, a mother's "God love you" more than offset the taunting. At this juncture in his priestly career, Father Montini lived a short distance from the Vatican out on the ancient Aurelian Highway.

The fascist authorities hated FUCI which, with its message of love, peace and brotherhood, stood in the way of their converting all youth to the cause of totalitarianism. FUCI's efforts on the campuses were challenged by the rival organization GUF (Fascist University Groups) whose style was militaristic, bellicose and nationalistic with a penchant for uniforms, parades and drills. Frequently and violently they broke up FUCI gatherings and in some of these clashes the slim chaplain himself was roughed up. A particularly violent attack on a FUCI rally took place in 1931 in the town of Macerata in central Italy. Montini received some minor injuries in that one. As a result of these thugs' activities, the police began to shut down FUCI clubs all over Italy. Pius XI responded to this suppression of Church-affiliated youth groups with his eloquent encyclical, *Non Abbiamo Bisogno*. The Fucini, though suppressed, remained an honest voice, a sort of national conscience, an intellectual elite under their articulate chaplain who now stood even higher in their esteem for having been at their side in the trenches against the GUF. Montini continued to write articles for their weekly newspaper, *La Sapienza*.

In the late twenties and early thirties Father Montini shared a residence with another priest, Father Bevilacque, on the Via Terme della Deciane just up from the Circus Maximus on the Aventine hill, where Peter and Paul often walked.

The Ides of March 1933 brought with them a new assignment for Montini. He was being moved up in the state department. But he was never to lose his concern for and interest in the Catholic student organization. As cardinal many years later he was to recall fondly his FUCI days: "All I know I owe to those dear young, courageous friends of my early priesthood. They were for me a stimulus, a living lesson in fortitude and idealism which I could never have learned from books." And his young flock was never to forget him. Some, in later years, even named sons after their spunky former spiritual director.

In the late thirties, with Europe inching ever closer to the holocaust, the priest from Brescia continued his work in the secretariat, arriving each morning at the Vatican's Porta Sant' Anna, passing through the stately courtyard of San Damaso, climbing to his office on the third floor of the Apostolic Palace to tackle the problems assigned to him. In these peaceful surroundings, in this eye of the hurricane, the future pontiff toiled.

With the passage of time he received increasingly more important assignments, getting his diplomatic training at the hands of the outstanding secretary of state, Cardinal Gasparri, who had served three great pontificates. Montini also worked under two other brilliant secretaries of state, Cardinal Eugenio Pacelli and then under Pius XII's foreign policy chief, Cardinal Luigi Maglione who died in 1944 and was never replaced. (When Maglione died, Pius XII became his own secretary of state, not through any lack of confidence in others but because of his unlimited capacity and desire for work, and because he was a well-trained diplomat himself. A good share of the duties of the office, however, went to the two under-secretaries, Montini and Tardini.)

Throughout the war, especially toward its end, and on into the post war era, Montini's office served as a crossroads and a sanctuary for people with problems. Montini worked hard to help refugee Jews who had shown up at the Vatican gates seeking asylum. One day in 1942 an Italian Jewish family, Aldo Mopurgo, his wife, mother and four year old son arrived in Rome having fled from northern Italy. They were advised to seek a meeting with "the little mountain" ("Montini" in English), in the Vatican. There the frightened Mopurgos were cordially received and reassured by Montini, who helped them secure a visa for Ecuador. The family remained in South America until 1946 and then migrated to the United States, settling in Long Island, later becoming naturalized citizens. "The little mountain" worked closely with Papa Pacelli in aiding innocent victims of the war, especially those of the Jewish race. Montini organized, administered and developed the largest Church-related assistance program for refugees (the wounded, the displaced, the missing) in history.

In the post war years, with Pius more tied up with audiences for all kinds of groups (Pius placed a high priority on making himself accessible to his flock), Montini became more and more the one sought out by diplomats, cardinals and even heads of state. In this capacity, Montini with his quiet but winning ways proved to be a special asset as a sort of public relations man for the Holy Father. As a result, he was particularly dear to Pacelli's heart. Gratefully, the pontiff in 1952 offered the red hat to both of his top aides, but astonishingly the two declined lest with the cardinalate go new assignments in some distant diocese or curial department. They loved their roles, they loved the pope they served, believed in his goals and wanted to stay on to the end of their lives or his reign whichever would come first.

Toward the end of 1954, Pope Pius XII named Monsignor Montini as archbishop of Milan. It was clearly the Holy Father's wish to move his aide's career along, to broaden his hierarchial experience, some people said to enhance his future papal candidacy. Though deeply saddened to leave the pope ("Today I am an orphan," is the way he expressed it), Montini nevertheless took the positive view that at long last he had the opportunity for a pastoral priesthood, the chance "to cast his net for the souls of men."

Milan was a key post in the Church and Montini would spend eight years there. In preparation for his new task he was consecrated archbishop and given the symbolic pectoral cross by the bearded Gaul, Cardinal Tisserant. Pius XII would have done the honors himself but was ailing and confined to bed at the time. Nonetheless he participated in the splendid service by delivering live over a specially rigged public address system a ringing panegyric of Montini along with the pontiff's warmest best wishes for health, happiness and success in the north.

Archbishop Montini's departure from Rome was a rather heartrending one. Having come here initially on the advice of his bishop in Brescia "for a little rest," he had made his life and career here for more than three decades. He loved Rome, her aged stones, her friendly people. He had become quite thoroughly Romanized. Before departing, he gifted his longtime housekeeper, Maria, with a sewing machine and a bicycle and sent her back with his gratitude and his blessing to her beloved Abruzzi. Then early on a rainy day in January of 1955 Montini bid Rome *Arrivederci* and left by rail from the city's Stazione Termini.

"And so I came to Milan," wrote St. Augustine who was converted there in the city of Constantine's edict. The see of Milan was already famous for three great bishops: St. Ambrose (390), St. Charles Borromeo (1564) and Achille Ratti (Pope Pius XI) just a few decades earlier. It was indeed a mighty challenge for Montini. Pius XI once reflected, "It is easier to be pope than to be bishop of Milan." His implication was clear. This sprawling diocese in the province of Lombardy was a political hotbed, an industrial, communistic, hedonistic, modernistic, cynical, anti-clerical stronghold.

Later that same dismal January 5, Montini arrived in Lodi in the neighboring province of Emilia. At the station there he blessed a crowd of workers behind the barricades and responded to their hearty welcome with his twinkling eyes and saintly smile. From Lodi he crossed over the Lambro River into Lombardy and then ordered his driver to park the vehicle. He disembarked for a few minutes to get down on his knees in prayer and then to kiss the wet soil of his new diocese. Word quickly spread about this holy and symbolic act and the Milanese, even some of the most cynical, were impressed by it.

Though making his entrance on a rainy, sleety day, the 140th bishop of Milan still rode in an open car "so the flock can see its shepherd." Thus he arrived at the piazza in front of the *Duomo* (Milan's ancient gothic cathedral), with the city's two other landmarks, *La Scala* and *La Galleria*, looking on. Despite the weather, the square was filled to overflowing and Montini received a rousing welcome. Then inside, thirty thousand more heard his first address from the high pulpit. From the cathedral he rode to the archepiscopal palace where that night he hosted at dinner, by personal invitation, more than a thousand of the city's poor.

While eager to tackle Milan's massive problems, Montini was not to get the chance right away. Because of the drenching he received in his arrival he became ill soon after. Fearing pneumonia, the doctors recommended a Swiss "change of air." With no intention of wasting the opportunity, Montini spent his convalescence with his nose buried in a wide variety of books and journals on Milan. For someone who had never administered a little country parish, the task must have seemed formidable if not mind-boggling. Archbishop Montini was now in charge of almost a thousand parishes spread out across a vast territory, a territory of urban and suburban areas, of Alpine villages and small farms, of a million and a half population.

Back on his feet, Montini crossed the Alps to plunge into the sea of work that awaited him. Sundays were given over to the goal of a personal visit to each of the nine hundred and seventy parishes. And were it not for other more pressing matters that pulled him away frequently, and for occasional illness, he would have made good on his commitment. Archbishop Montini wanted the people to know him and he wanted very deeply to know them, but the attitudes of Milan worked against this hope. No one could blame him if he were a bit frightened after his long, rather sheltered life in the Vatican enclave. But "fear" was not in his personal lexicon. He was resolved to win back to the Church from communism and materialism, the factory workers, housewives, executives and children that had been lost. He visited the industrial districts and promised the workers that he would try to be a good archbishop for them, that he would stand with them against exploitation by the big industrialists. In his first address in the Duomo he had promised to "defend the workers with zeal and solidarity, as a shepherd and father, whenever and wherever there is suffering and injustice or a legitimate aspiration to social betterment."

Sometimes when he received weak or even hostile reactions in the factories, instead of retreating, he would stride right into the midst of the rank and file with that characteristic, arms open, paternal gesture of his. His popularity with the working class grew steadily with the result that it greatly annoyed the right wingers. One night in January, 1956, the episcopal residence was struck by neo-fascist fire bombs.

Montini spent a good part of his first-two years watching the Milanesi drift further and further from the arms of the Church and he resolved to reawaken their faith, their sense of their Christian roots. Preparations were under way for a city-wide spiritual retreat and included committees on press and publicity, financing, preaching, overall organization. There was to be a three week mission with each parish actively involved. By late October of 1957 the walls of Milan were covered with posters and the streets festooned with banners all proclaiming: "People of Milan, From the 4th to the 24th of November a thousand voices will speak to you of God!" Actually Montini had enlisted the preaching services of 1,290 clerics including three cardinals (Lercaro, Siri and Urbani), twenty five archbishops (himself included), six hundred priests, five hundred ninety seven religious and sixty five seminarians. Cardinal Giacomo Lercaro came from Bologna followed by his twenty "flying friars" employing trucks equipped with altars, confessionals and loudspeakers.

There was, to be sure, vehement opposition from the capitalists who denied the missionaries permission to preach in the factories because they thought the essential message would be inflammatory against them, a sort of "Workers, throw off your chains" theme. Then, too, there was opposition from the communists who thought the contrary, viz. that it would be a message of submissic to authority, to employers, in the name of peace. Th communist daily of Milan repeatedly attacked it as a act of exploitation of the poor and the ignorant.

Nevertheless the ambitious crusade went full stea ahead. Special programs were arranged for the variou occupations: one for dancers, another for bartender others for bellhops, police, professors, students, ca drivers, athletes, and so on. All of Italy watched closel listening each evening to the Vatican radio's coverage o the event, reading the progress reports daily in the country's leading newspapers. Montini's daily sermor was broadcast each night.

All preachers were instructed to stress the positive formidable truths of Christianity, to avoid negativism, controversy, politics. Tact was stressed. Called by the media, "the Great Mission," the colossal project aimed to strengthen the faith of those still loyal to the Church and to win back those who had fallen into agnosticism or atheism. In his own addresses, the architect of the mission, Archbishop Montini, asked the fallen away to forgive the Church for failing them, for being in a way responsible for their disenchantment. This unusual and startling conciliatory approach was most effective. "Whatever and however many may have been our faults in the past, forgive us, but then *please* listen to our message from Christ."

For three solid weeks the preachers took their gospel to the people not only in the churches but also out in the squares and parks, streets and theater lobbies, slums, airports, railroad stations, shopping districts, hospitals and prisons. Some still recall Montini in those days as having "fire in his eyes" and liken him to Paul the Apostle, and his mission to the early days of the Church.

Initially there was a great and excited response to the crusade. But even the archbishop was compelled to admit that the effects were largely ephemeral when the Milanesi soon after slipped back into their hedonistic ways and renewed the hectic chase for material goods. Still, he concluded, it had been all worth the effort for surely some of the flock had been reclaimed and was it not Christ himself who said that there would be more rejoicing in heaven over the recovery of one lost sheep than over a hundred in no need of saving.

By the time he left Milan, Montini had also earned the label of "Builder of Churches" having completed the construction of seventy seven churches, and initiated work on twenty more in and around the city. All of this he had done the better to bring the Church to the people and to break down their spiritual isolation. There were under Montini's direction many chapels erected in high rise housing projects and he was able to persuade many architects to include chapels in their building plans.

He also strengthened the Catholic publications of the diocese and inaugurated a new magazine, *Diocesi di Milano*, and even frequently wrote for it, at the same time inviting writers of all ranks and various ecclesiastical ideologies to contribute. Deeply interested in the arts, Montini would often celebrate special Masses for painters, sculptors, writers and entertainers. Because of this interest he was thought, rather mistakenly, to have a great deal of influence in these areas. As a result, people seeking help in furthering their careers in these areas were often urged to get help from Montini. Added to his crowded schedule was his personal involvement in the corporal works of mercy, visiting the sick, the poor, the imprisoned.

Montini had become widely recognized and admired as a man of outstanding intellectual stature, piety and ability. He was thoroughly familiar, through more than thirty years work there, with the machinery of the Vatican. Consequently, upon the death of Pius XII in October of 1958, when the cardinals were deadlocked for a time over a successor, they very nearly went outside their own ranks for a pontiff as Montini's candidature was seriously put forth for consideration. (The last time the electors had gone outside the sacred college for a new pope was in the case of Urban VI of Naples in 1378.) But the conclave ultimately elected Roncalli, patriarch of Venice, as Pope John XXIII. Just two months later, John, in his first of three consistories, elevated Archbishop Montini to the sacred college.

When soon afterwards John decided to call a general council, he turned to Cardinal Montini to play an important role in the preparations. At the council itself, Montini's role was one of peacemaker between the progressives and the conservatives among the Church fathers. And as Pope Paul VI, Montini was largely responsible for the council ending, as French writer Jean Guitton so eloquently put it, "in a magnificent gothic arch the apex of which requires bending and giving on both sides for the mutual goal of unity."

As a cardinal, Montini began to travel rather extensively, a duty he loved, on behalf of the Church. First there was the goodwill tour of the United States in early June of 1960 which took him to New York and his old colleague, Francis Cardinal Spellman, and then on to

Chicago, Boston, Philadelphia, Washington and lastly to South Bend, Indiana for an honorary doctorate from Notre Dame. That same odyssey took him to Latin America before his return to Italy. In the summer of 1962 he toured Africa where he was edified by the simple but deep religious fervor of the natives. Ignoring the barriers of South Africa's apartheid policy, Montini participated in ground-breaking ceremonies for the *Maria Regina Mundi* church in the black district of Johannesburg. Many of the blacks were moved to tears at the unprecedented sight of a white prelate in their midst and felt loved and remembered by Rome.

The Cardinal loved and worried about his priests and sought to share his experiences, knowledge and wise counsel with all two thousand of them. Often he would write encouraging pastoral letters to them and every Thursday morning was set aside as open house for them at his residence. Each priest felt, and rightly so, singularly important to his superior and would leave the office with Montini's *"grazie della visita"* ("thanks for coming") pleasantly ringing in his ears.

And his lifelong devotion to and fondness for children did not diminish in the face of his awesome responsibilities. Montini took an active interest in the schools and colleges of his diocese.

At Milan he set a furious daily pace which would serve as the model for his day-to-day timetable in the chair of Peter. Up at six thirty, he would open his day with his private Mass served by his devoted aide, Monsignor Macchi, following which he would take the role of altar boy for the monsignor's Mass. Next he would say part of his priestly office, and follow this with a skimpy breakfast at which he would speed read all the local and national newspapers. From this point until one in the afternoon, Montini would meet with his aides, grant audiences, be on the phone with pastors all over the diocese. Never did he show the least sign of wear. Visitors never failed to be struck by his appearance, his slim build, his marble complexion, his stately posture, brisk walk, long, thin hands, gentle gestures, sing-song voice, warm but penetrating eyes and wan smile. Prayer and meditation took him up to two p.m. and the main meal of the day. Then in the best Roman tradition there was a short nap.

Upon awakening he would retire to his private chapel to finish his breviary. By four thirty he was back at his desk writing pastoral letters, or articles for *Diocesi di Milano*, or next Sunday's sermon. At eight or half past there was a very light supper and then some television watching of the nightly newscast. Some time after nine he could be found reciting the rosary aloud with the priests of his residence. And after that back in his study for a lot more work. Unwinding took the form of reading (he had an insatiable appetite) and later in listening to classical music on his stereo set. Two a.m. was generally bed time and then four and a half hours of fitful sleep.

Giovanni Battista Montini was happy and fulfilled in his work but he was distressed in the first few months of 1963 over the illness of beloved Pope John and deeply saddened in May when the gravity of the Holy Father's illness was revealed.

On Friday, May 31, Cardinal Montini was informed that there was no hope and that the pope had asked for him. That night he emplaned for Rome in the company of the brothers and sisters of the dying pontiff. They landed in Fiumicino airport west of Rome where a Vatican car was waiting to whisk them to the Apostolic Palace. Arriving at the sad threshold they all knelt at the bedside to pray. Pope John was unconscious but then, regaining lucidity, he recognized his old friend and they spoke affectionately and nostalgically for a few moments. This was to be their last terrestrial meeting. Then to his grieving siblings John said: "Remember mamma? Remember papa? I am going to be with them soon."

On Saturday night, June 1, the cardinal returned to his

diocese and at midnight, in rainswept Vigorelli stadium, before a crowd of twenty thousand, he celebrated a Mass for the moribund Papa Roncalli. Hours later, on Pentecost Sunday, Cardinal Montini delivered in the cathedral a moving panegyric on the stricken pope. The following night, June 3, Pope John XXIII entered the ages and unknowingly (or was it knowingly?) sharply altered the life of Giovanni Battista Montini.

Montini did not return to Rome for the pope's funeral. He had stayed on instead in Milan to tend to the myriad of problems there. This was not a breach of propriety. Montini had gone to Rome when it really counted, to bring his friend one last measure of joy in his life. With the conclave to elect a successor to John fast approaching, Cardinal Montini flew to Fiumicino once again, this time with his right hand, Monsignor Macchi. Some of his aides had urged him to make decisions on some important impending diocesan matters "in case you don't return from the conclave." "No, No, I'll be back, and then we'll. . . ."

It was early morning, June 16, when they landed and they drove immediately the half hour ride to Castel Gandolfo where Montini was to be the overnight guest of Dr. Emilio Bonomelli, director of the papal villa on Lake Albano.

Dawn broke and the cardinal from Milan, having spent a restless night despite the Edenic environment of the Alban hills, moved on to Rome. By now the Eternal City was electrified with rumors, most of them about the most *papabile* of all the princes of the Church, Giovanni Battista Montini. Indeed his credentials would be difficult to match: a vigorous progressive but at the same time a proud traditionalist, a man of lofty intellect, of piety unsurpassed, possessed of great organizational talents, a young sixty six, a linguist, trained in Rome, knowledgeable about the curia, experienced as a diplomat and, for the last eight years, as an administrator.

Everywhere he went in the ancient streets the people

whispered, many times quite audibly, *"Il Papa!"* Even in his visit to his alma mater, the Lombard pontifical seminary, on Wednesday, June 19, in the hours between the morning Mass of the Holy Spirit attended by all the cardinals and the five p.m. opening of the conclave, Montini could not escape the prophecy. One excited seminarian, Luigi Serentha, called out as the cardinal was leaving, *"Arrivederci Milano, Eminenza!"* ("Goodbye to Milan, Your Eminence!").

Many believed that John's dying hope had been that the sacred college would see fit to replace him with the thin, erect solemn Lombard. That sultry June morning, eighty of the eighty-two members of the college had made their solemn entrance into St. Peter's still clothed in purple mourning vestments for the Mass of the Holy Spirit at which they invoked Divine guidance upon their decision in the conclave. Then in late afternoon, when Rome is at her honey-colored best, the cardinals entered into conclave to select the next bearer of the keys.

While Montini entered as the distinct favorite he also went in under the burden of the rather accurate proverb: "He who enters a pope, exits a cardinal." The two rounds of balloting that took place in the Sistine the following morning, proved inconclusive. Likewise the two late Thursday afternoon. But the first vote on Friday, the fifth of the conclave, transferred to Cardinal Montini the keys of Peter.

After the brief but highly emotional acceptance ritual, and after having announced his choice of a name, the new pope, Paul VI, proceeded to the central balcony of St. Peter's to impart his first blessing *Urbi et Orbi,* to the City and to the World.

On the day after his election, Pope Paul addressed the Catholic world by radio, promising to carry out all the programs initiated by his predecessor, committing himself to the *aggiornamento,* i.e., renewal, which John XXIII had called for.

From the beloved and admired Papa Roncalli, Paul

had inherited Vatican Council II which would be re-convening in but a few months. Of all the matters that awaited the Holy Father's attention, the council had to get top priority.

The council was guided to its conclusion on December 8, 1965 and from that point on Paul saw as his major task the carrying out of all its mandates and recommendations. John had aimed some of his reform program at the Roman curia, that complex of congregations, offices and tribunals that constitute, in effect, the pope's cabinet. Pope Paul got started by restructuring the Sacred Congregation of the Holy Office, giving it the new name of the Sacred Congregation for the Doctrine of the Faith. He also made clearer its duties and dominion. In those first hectic days, the Supreme Pontiff also abolished the Index (the Church's list of forbidden books), and announced that the beatification courses of his predecessors John XXIII and Pius XII were being inaugurated.

With some reform ideas of his own Pope Paul created, in February 1965, twenty seven cardinals, increasing the membership of the sacred college to the all-time high total of one hundred and three, making it more representative of the universal Church, with forty three nations now represented. Then in June of 1967 he raised the number to one hundred and eighteen.

Early in his reign too, Pope Paul VI adopted a policy of detente with the communist world, hoping to foster a meaningful dialogue with "our atheistic sons and daughters." Of course the possibility that such a policy could ease the pressure on the Church in those countries was not wasted on Paul. All of this was part of the theme of his first papal encyclical, *Ecclesiam Suam*, in 1964.

Paul's reign was marked from the very beginning by a spirit of ecumenism and by a continuing effort to foster understanding and warm relations with the clergy and laity of all faiths. This spirit was especially exemplified by his travels. Of all the popes of the Church, Paul VI quickly became, and by far, the most traveled.

In January of 1964, in the footsteps of the apostles, Paul journeyed to the Holy Land where he had a number of cordial conferences with the Orthodox patriarch, Athenagoras I of Constantinople. Paul VI was the first pope since *the very first pope* to visit the war torn land of Jesus, the first in five centuries to meet with an Orthodox patriarch. The two religious leaders met again in July of '67 in Istanbul and once again in October of the same year at the Vatican. This marked the first visit to Rome by a patriarch of Constantinople since the year 1451. Along these same lines, i.e. the cultivation of better relations among all religions, the pope established in May 1964 a new curial department, the secretariat for non-Christians.

Taking to the airways once again in December of 1964, Pope Paul left Da Vinci airport outside of Rome for the Orient. In Bombay he was received warmly by multitudes of the Christian faithful and by tens of thousands more of various creeds. His speeches to the people of India stressed that "we must begin to work together to build our common future."

Amidst the most extensive security measures in the history of the New York Police Department, His Holiness on October 5, 1965 landed at John F. Kennedy airport outside the city and motorcaded into midtown Manhattan. At noon the Pontiff made a call on President Lyndon B. Johnson in the Presidential suite at the Waldorf Astoria. Cheering thousands hailed the frail pontiff all along the route to the United Nations headquarters where he met with other world leaders before stepping to the podium of the great assembly hall to deliver his moving exhortation for peace. There he urged all nations to disarm, warned them of the awful threat of nuclear war, and spoke against the "balance of terror." Again and again throughout his speech he exclaimed and implored, "No more war!"

Later Paul stopped at St. Patrick's cathedral for a sentimental meeting with longtime pal, Francis Cardinal

Spellman. After dinner at the cardinal's residence, Paul celebrated Mass before an overflow crowd of eighty thousand in cavernous Yankee stadium. Many millions more watched the historic event via television and stayed glued to their sets as the papal cortege made its way out to the fair grounds in Flushing Meadows where the pope stopped to visit the Vatican pavilion at the World's Fair, the highlight of which was Michelangelo's *Pieta'*.

On December 4 of that year, with improved interfaith relations now even higher on his list of goals, Pope Paul met with the non-Catholic observers at the council for an unprecedented ecumenical bible service for Christian unity on the eve of the council's closing.

Within weeks of this significant event, in February of 1966, Michael Ramsey, the archbishop of Canterbury and head of the Anglican Church, journeyed to Rome for an ecumenical dialogue with the pope. Two years later the pope sent his warmest best wishes to the Tenth Lambeth Conference of Anglican bishops and also to the Fourth General Assembly of the World Council of Churches. To both convocations the Holy Father sent a delegation of Catholic observers.

December, 1966, found the pope in the Tuscan city of Florence to comfort the flood victims of the Arno.

May 1967 marked the fiftieth anniversary of the Blessed Virgin's appearances to three peasant children in the picturesque village of Fatima, Portugal. On the thirteenth of that month, Pope Paul made a one day pilgrimage to the village to pray at the Marian shrine there and to converse briefly with the sole survivor of those celebrated events, Sister Lucy.

Two months later, on July 25, Paul flew to Turkey to visit once again with Athenagoras I and to tour the ancient city of Ephesus and the site of a house where the Blessed Virgin Mary is said to have spent the final years of her terrestrial life. Thirteen months later, August of 1968, there was a three day papal visit to Bogota, Columbia for the International Eucharistic Congress.

And almost a year after that he made a transalpine trip to Geneva to address the leadership of the World Council of Churches. At every turn he seemed to be making history, this man who had had to struggle so to survive his first year on earth.

Over the course of his long reign Pope Paul continued to implement the enactments of the council in various documents. His *motu proprio,* "*Ecclesiae Sanctae,*" on August 6, 1966 set revised norms for the four council decrees on the pastoral office of bishops, the ministry and life of priests, the adaptation and renewal of religious life, and the missionary activity of the Church.

Another *motu proprio,* "*Catholicam Christi Ecclesiam*" issued in January of '67 established both the council of the laity and the commission for justice and peace. On June 23 that year the pontiff released his encyclical, "*Sacerdotalis Caelibatus,*" reaffirming the Church's discipline of priestly celibacy.

Pope Paul authorized the activities and publications of the secretariat for interfaith affairs. His reign vigorously embodied the thinking and spirit of the council. Yet with all this fervor for and devotion to the unfulfilled dreams of his predecessor, Paul frequently had an inexplicably "bad press." While John was simply adored by the media, Paul was often attacked, even vilified, by the same element. Once, about ten years into his reign, Paul wearily confided to Archbishop Fulton J. Sheen that ". . . each night I lay my head down upon a pillow of thorns." Some publications used to headline thinly veiled suggestions that the pope should resign. Even the normally friendly New York Daily News ran an article in September 1976 with the heading, *Pope Paul at 80: Time to Go?*

But Paul was not without his defenders. Father James V. Schall, S.J., who teaches part of the year at the University of San Francisco and the rest of the time at the Pontifical Gregorian Institute in Rome had this to say while Pope Paul still reigned:

"My own feelings about Paul VI is rather that he is the most intelligent pope in modern times in terms of analytic penetration and awareness of precisely the intelligence aspect of the faith. Coming as he did immediately after John XXIII and more especially after the myth of John, Paul has tried to exercise papal authority in primarily an intellectual way. No one who reads carefully the vast and remarkable work he has produced—and all say he does most of his own writing—can doubt that Paul is one of the most underestimated men of our time. We really do not expect to have such an 'intellectual' as pope. On almost any theological or cultural issue on which he is criticized, Paul reveals much more insight than his critics. Many will doubt if we should have such an intelligent pope precisely because the intellectual tends to rely too much on persuasion and the appeal of truth by its own force. The number of times Paul returns to this notion that truth should be believed for its own sake is remarkable. This is the key, I think, to why he does not 'exercise' authority. In this he is more Thomist and rational than Augustinian. He is reluctant to believe that men, especially Christians, more especially academics, clerics, and religious, will not be convinced by clear argument. I cannot help but admiring such a quality. I suspect, as the years pass, we will come to wonder how we had such a perceptive pope and why it was that a good part of the Catholic world wasted its energies disagreeing with him, when history is proving him basically right.

"Among his critics there is the anti-*Humanae Vitae* school, which judges the validity of his papacy on this one issue. And in this case, with much superficial analysis, he is seen to have been wrong. Yet, what is frightening about *Humanae Vitae* is not how wrong it was but how right. We have seen in these past twelve years, laws and mores come about pretty much as Paul predicted. When the period began, the doctor who induced abortion was illegal. When the period ends, the one who does not is more and more held to violating a woman's 'rights'."

Even had Paul been inclined to resign, which I am confident he never was, he would not have wanted to run the risk of letting the world think that the chair of Peter can be manipulated by the Gallup Poll. For the papacy, while of this world is at the same time *not* of this world. Were one to listen to the extreme right one would conclude that Paul was a maniacal liberal, while the extreme left would have us think that the same man was a fire-breathing reactionary. This contradiction in itself ought to tell us of the responsible moderation of Pope Paul VI. "Too weak," some charged, and pointed to the celebrated Lefebvre case. But this simplistic diagnosis fails to take into account that Paul sharply, though as diplomatically as possible, rebuked the activities of the French arch-bishop.

The truth is that he was brilliant, farseeing, courageous and the ideal man for the role of stabilizing the convul-sive Church which he inherited. As did his ancient name-sake, Paul frustrated and confounded his critics by his rejection of expediency and his embrace of the truth however painful that may have been to him personally. Like a true intellectual, he tended to believe that it is better in the long run to be on the side of truth even when the truth is manifestly unpopular.

Constantly and tirelessly engaged in the pursuit of world peace, Pope Paul offered his services as a mediator and the Vatican as a site for peace talks to resolve the Vietnam war in May of 1968. It was two months later that he issued the encyclical, *Humanae Vitae,* banning artificial birth control methods for Catholics and confirm-ing traditional Church teaching, which precipitated the emotional storm to which Father Schall alluded.

The following year, 1969, Paul took to the airways again with a trip to Geneva, Switzerland in June for an appearance at the Protestant World Council of Churches, and two months later with a two day visit to Kampala, Uganda, which marked the first time a pontiff ever visited Africa.

The eighth year of his reign, 1970, was marked by his continued efforts toward Christian unity, his appeals for world aid for Pakistan following cyclone and tidal wave catastrophes there, and by another odyssey to the world's Catholics, this time to the Philippines, Australia, Iran, Indonesia, Hong Kong, Ceylon and East Pakistan.

In 1971 he received Hungary's Cardinal Mindzenty following the prelate's exile for treason charges dating from 1949, for which he had been under house arrest for nearly two decades. On September 30, he opened the World Synod of Bishops.

1973 saw stepped up papal ecumenical efforts with Pope Paul co-signing with Coptic patriarch, Shenouda II, a plan to set up a commission to expedite the move for Christian unity and the Dalai Lama of Tibet being received at the Vatican in the first audience ever scheduled between a pope and the head of the Buddhist community.

The Holy Year of 1975 was particularly demanding on the ailing and aging pontiff when the influx of two million pilgrims called for more frequent audiences and other public activity on the part of the Holy Father in addition to the ordinary, merciless burdens of his office. For Americans at least, the high point of the Jubilee Year was the canonization ceremony in St. Peter's square on Sunday, September 14, making Mother Elizabeth Seton the first American-born saint.

During Italy's national elections in early 1976 the pope spoke out vigorously against the communist threat urging Italian Catholics not to vote for that party's candidates.

"Troubled and tormented" was how he referred to the Church in one of the audiences he held in July of 1977. He could have used these words to describe himself as he grew increasingly anguished, now in the twilight of his reign, over such matters as Archbishop Marcel Lefebvre's contempt of papal authority and the reforms mandated by Vatican II, liberalization of abortion laws in Italy and abroad, world wide terrorism. It was in October of that year that he offered himself as a willing hostage in exchange for eighty six hostages held by terrorists aboard a German airliner. But '77 held some joyous moments too: his meeting with the archbishop of Canterbury, Donald Coggan, in April; the consistory naming four new cardinals; the canonization of Bishop John

Nepomucene Neumann in June; and the formal observance of his 80th birthday in September.

With his strength slipping away, Pope Paul in 1978 missed his public Holy Week services for the first time but did manage to summon the energy to celebrate the Easter Mass in St. Peter's square. His arthritic condition had worsened to the point by this time that he was all but paralyzed and each step had to be taken with assistance and excruciating pain. This was clearly evident in the public ceremonies on June 21, marking the 15th anniversary of his election. On July 14, in a very weakened condition, the Holy Father left the Vatican for his traditional two-month summer stay in the hill town of Castel Gandolfo. When on Saturday, August 5th, the weakened pontiff suffered another severe flare up of arthritis, his doctors insisted that he cancel the next day's appearances and confine himself to complete bed rest. Sunday dawned to find matters worse. Toward the end of a pain-wracked day, the pope was stricken by a heart attack while listening to Mass offered in his private chamber by his personal secretary, Pasquale Macchi. Four hours later, in the seventeenth-century papal palace perched high over tranquil Lake Albano, Pope Paul VI, while reciting the Lord's Prayer, died, his right hand, with what little strength remained, clasping that of Father Macchi.

Back in the briefing hall of the Vatican press center, Father Pierfranco Pastore, acting head of the Vatican press service, sobbing, made the official announcement: "With profound anguish and emotion I must inform you that Pope Paul VI passed away at 9:40 tonight, Sunday, August 6 (3:40 p.m. New York time) at the papal summer residence in Castel Gandolfo."

As the announcement was made all the lights in the medieval town went out and a crowd of hundreds gathered in the main square directly in front of the palace. Heavy black chains were dragged across the main portals of the building signifying that the world-wide affairs of the Church were suspended until a new pope was chosen.

Paul's reign was a long, historic and productive one. Despite his advanced years and physical afflictions, his mind was to the end as keen as it ever had been and his zeal for his task as fiery, resulting in continued productivity from the chair of Peter. His remarkable ability to maintain Church unity in the face of numerous ecclesiastical ideologies and to avert heresy and schism antagonized to no end those who would love to witness the demise of the Church.

To those who spread rumors of the pope's intention to resign or step down "for the good of the Church," Paul calmly responded, "I am *Il Papa*, the father, and a true father never retires." He intended to and did serve until his last breath, acting as the guardian of dogma and morals, the repository of the principles which ensure the integrity of his "family" and the sanctity of souls. He went on representing Christ in this world and serving as the earthly father of all. He touched the hearts of many with his fatherly compassion, gentleness and encouragement. Yousuf Karsh, the renowned photographer of the prominent people of our era saw some of Paul's immediate predecessors in him: the gestures, build and austerity of Pius XII; the warmth, vision and openness of John XXIII. And like his predecessors, even when they were well along in years, Paul was possessed of incredible vitality.

As the Pilgrim Pope, Paul VI toiled relentlessly and untiringly for peace around the globe. He expanded the Vatican's diplomatic relations to more than one hundred nations, including some communist lands. He continued to encourage dialogue between Rome and the other Churches of Christianity, between Rome and all the other faiths, between Rome and the atheistic world. In the late twilight of his reign his one overriding hope was to bequeath to the one who followed him to the chair of Peter a vibrant, prospering Church, as free from error and division as he could make it through his stewardship.

I was in Rome on assignment for some papers and magazines in the States to cover the events that would take place in the days and weeks after Paul VI's death. The following chapter consists of excerpts from my journalist's diary in which I recorded my impressions of the interregnum.

CHAPTER XIII

EXCERPTS FROM A ROMAN DIARY

Rome

7 August, A.D. 1978

Sede Vacante. With these words on its masthead and its pages bordered in black, *L'Osservatore Romano,* announces the sad news that the see of Peter is vacant. Across the Tiber and around the world people mourn and pray for the repose of the pontiff's soul and for God's guidance and blessing upon the Church.

Since yesterday afternoon when the bulletin was issued a multitude of journalists, commentators, photographers and technicians have been converging on Rome to cover the three momentous events which will soon transpire: the funeral of the late pope, the election and the coronation of his successor. Every hour brings more members of the sacred college of cardinals, other prelates, the ordinary clergy, thousands of religious and multitudes of the faithful to the city of Peter, all with their own roles to play in this imposing drama.

Around the clock the Vatican radio plays solemn and mournful music, interrupted only by special bulletins. Papal power has been suspended. The sacred congregations of the Church government limit their activity to the most routine matters. No bulls, briefs, concordats, nothing of consequence may be signed, for while the cardinals are at this time the trustees of papal power, they cannot exercise it.

Here in Rome the mood is a somber one as the *cives Romani* await the return of their bishop's mortal remains. The usual gaiety of the city is not in evidence. Instead the residents of the Eternal City and their guests walk with a heavier step and move about with a subdued spirit today—especially all around me here in St. Peter's vast square. This is the second time in months that the normal, incomparable vitality of the city has been sapped by a death. Last spring the tragedy of Aldo Moro, Paul VI's good friend, cast a pall of gloom over this normally happy city.

What changes the calender can bring! What prophecies it can fulfill!

We were present in Castel Gandolfo a year ago, August 15, the joyful feast of the Assumption, when the Holy Father, bolstered in spirit by the outpouring of affection for him from the villagers and their visitors, said that he would like to make an appointment to meet with all of us same time, same place next year. Then suddenly his mood became quite melancholy as he added: "But who knows if I, old as I am, can hope to mark this feast day with you again. If God wishes it, I will. But I see the threshold of the beyond approaching."

9 August, A.D. 1978
A.M.

It is late morning of a summer Wednesday in the Eternal City. In this morning's paper Bishop Giuseppe Caprio, the Vatican's assistant secretary of state, revealed that before departing the Vatican for Castel Gandolfo on July 14, the pope had said to him, "We are leaving, but we don't know if we will be coming back." Paul seems to have been convinced indeed that he would not be celebrating another feast of the Assumption, at least not on earth.

My tour group (I work as a guide here in July and August) had come from great distances to see and hear the *living* Pope Paul VI but God had willed otherwise. Now they stand in the sweltering heat of the square— some seeking relief in the cool, marble forest of Bernini's columns—along with tens of thousands of their fellow Christians, waiting for the chance to pay tribute to the Pilgrim of Peace. They stand in sad resignation to the fact that in a few days, when their time in Rome is up, they and the religious articles they have purchased will be going back home *sine benedictione apostolica*.

P.M.

Even though the siesta period has ended, the shops of Rome remain closed, their metal corrugated shutters still lowered. The pulse of this normally pulsating city is stilled. As the shadow of the greatest shrine in Christendom lengthens across the enormous square and threatens to reach out into Via della Conciliazione, the evening sun casts an apricot glow over Rome Eternal. A policeman I've known for years has just informed me (it's 7:05 now) that the funeral cortege is at the moment stopped in Piazza San Giovanni in Laterano before the basilica of the same name. This is altogether fitting, for it is the cathedral of the Roman diocese and consequently the pope's episcopal seat. I have learned from the same source some of the details of the solemn motorcade from Castel Gandolfo.

The papal cortege left the summer villa at three minutes to six, proceeded down the Via del Papa, the nickname given by the residents of the hill town to the road which connects with the new Appian Way. The latter runs parallel to the venerable and picturesque (and ruin-rich) *Via Appia Antica*. Because of the recent political turmoil in Italy, security was at a maximum all along the route with four police helicopters constantly watching over things from above. Crowds many persons deep lined the curbs all along the way as the motorized procession rolled slowly across the lovely Roman countryside. With all the roads intersecting with Appia Nuova blocked off, traffic was backed up throughout the area.

Before thousands of the faithful overflowing Piazza

San Giovanni (according to accounts coming over the transistor radios around me), the diocesan vicar general, Cardinal Ugo Poletti, is at the moment delivering a eulogy to "our bishop and father."

Ten more minutes have passed and the body of the terrestrial leader of Christianity is now being conducted down the Via Merulana toward the greatest symbol of ancient paganism, the Colosseum.

Here in St. Peter's the throng thickens with each second as the cortege wends its way through the streets of Renaissance Rome and at 7:30 passes the church of Santa Maria in Vallicella where little Eugenio Pacelli, later Pope Pius XII, served as altar boy.

Now at 7:34, the first vehicle of the procession enters into the colonnade's embrace. We all watch transfixed as the cypress coffin of the pope is removed from the hearse and is borne into the hall by the same throne-bearers who on hundreds of more joyous and triumphant occasions had carried the pope on the *sedia gestatoria* through the crowds to the accompaniment of *"Viva il Papa!"* While the enormous bell in the left tower of the facade tolls for the deceased pope, cardinals, other prelates and clergymen accompany the remains to the foot of the main altar where they are taken from the wooden coffin and placed —dressed in full pontifical robes and mitre—upon a low catafalque. Word has been passed that the doors of the basilica will re-open tomorrow morning at seven and that the public will have two full days in which to pay its last respects to a pontiff known for his simple manner and brilliant mind and whom history will surely judge as one of the giants of the papacy.

Most of us will be back early tomorrow morn.

11 August, A.D. 1978

A.M.

This morning's papers carry the news that the sacred college of cardinals will meet August 25 for the start of its secret conclave in the Sistine chapel from which will emerge the 263rd pope.

We have been here in St. Peter's square since dawn. As I write on my clipboard in the shade and cooling mist of one of the twin baroque fountains (the one to the left as you face St. Peter's) the crowd of mourners waiting to pass the bier has reached many tens of thousands and spills back out through the huge iron gates of the main entrance and cascades down the cordonata into the piazza. A short time ago I myself stood at the bier and in that fleeting moment savored many vivid memories of the Holy Father. I saw him borne into the hall for another audience. I saw him lift an infant into his arms and take it for a brief airborne ride while a million flashbulbs illuminated his handsome Lombard features. I saw him make the sign of the cross with his slender hand. I saw him at the podium of the United Nations pleading: "War never again!" I saw him on the steps of an Al Italia jet embarking on another of his pilgrimages. I saw him—a slim figure in white—at his window on the top floor of the Apostolic Palace returning the waves and love of the Sunday noontime crowd down in the square. I saw him at Castel Gandolfo smiling at my three little boys lining the rail as he passed through the gardens of his summer villa. I saw him on Easter Sunday of 1977 at the altar set up for outdoor Mass and heard him expressing again and again to the quarter of a million of his flock gathered before him, *"Buona Pasqua! Buona Pasqua! Buona Pasqua!"* I saw him with that gentle gesture of his as if to say, "Come to me, *figli carissimi."* I saw him and heard him at Castel Gandolfo on August 15 wishing us a blessed feast day yet expressing his fears that this would be his last Assumption observance. I saw him last spring agonizing through the long, heartbreaking Aldo Moro tragedy. I saw him practically carried up the steps to the altar by two young monsignori in the waning weeks of his life suffering from a painful and crippling arthritic condition. I saw him now in eternal repose.

12 August, A.D. 1978

P.M.

It is symbolic, it would seem, that the shadows are already lengthening across the square as a hundred thousand of us await the start of the first open-air funeral for a pope in the Church's long history. The final curtain of the final act of the long and glorious reign of Paul VI will within a few hours fall, and the mortal remains of the gentle pontiff will be returned in accord with his wishes, to the "true earth."

Great numbers of priests, monks, nuns, seminarians in a wide variety of colored cassocks and habits seem impervious to the withering heat of a Roman summer afternoon. Some are leading clusters of the faithful in a recitation of the rosary, a prayer form to which Pope Paul had been deeply devoted.

Bishops and other Church dignitaries are starting to fill in the section of seats to the left of the altar which has been set up on the first landing of the staircase leading up to the basilica. In keeping with the ecumenical spirit which characterized Paul's pontificate, there will be many leaders from the various Christian denominations in attendance. Former Archbishop of Canterbury, Dr. Michael Ramsey, is expected along with patriarchs from the Orthodox sees of Constantinople, Cyprus, Alexandria and even Moscow. In the section to the right will sit Rosalynn Carter and Senator Edward Kennedy from the United States and delegations from more than a hundred other countries. Other than these two groups it would appear that those with the best vantage point from which to watch the cardinals concelebrate the funeral Mass would be the stony saints high upon the twin colonnades of Bernini.

A decade and a half ago, on another sunny summer day, in this same piazza, midst even more ritual and panoply, the coronation of Giovanni Battista Montini as Pope Paul VI took place. Today some of the same cardinals who shared in the joyful task of escorting Paul to the throne of Peter have the sad role of conducting him to a humble grave near Peter's tomb.

The procession is beginning to exit from the basilica. The simple wooden casket is being borne upon the shoulders of the *sediarii* while the singing of the Sistine choir fills the air and is wafted softly upward to the rain-washed azure skies. Now the coffin has been set down on a tapestry, which appears to be a Persian rug, in front of the altar. A white candle has been lit alongside the casket and an open copy of the New Testament has been placed upon it, both serving to symbolize eternal life in the Lord.

Carlo Cardinal Confalonieri, the 85-year-old dean of the sacred college, has begun to chant the opening prayers of the Mass, assisted by more than a hundred other princes of the Church equally divided on either side of him and around the altar. Psalm 64 is the first solemn hymn of the Mass.

Young seminarians from different lands, studying at the various pontifical seminaries in Rome, have been assigned readings from the lectern. What an unforgettable and inspirational moment for them, for their priestly futures, for their loved ones watching via live satellite television coverage!

Cardinal Confalonieri has stepped to the microphone now to deliver, in an aged but clear voice, a eulogy to his Holy Father and old friend. Many of us are choked with emotion as the cardinal commends Papa Montini for his "great spirit, keen intelligence and heart filled with goodness," for his role as a "true prince of peace."

The Mass continues, with some prayers recited even in Aramaic, the ancient native tongue of our Lord and his apostles. Dusk is fast asserting itself as the two hour service draws to a close. As the *sediarii* lift Papa Montini upon their shoulders for the last time and a small group of relatives and cardinals prepare to escort the body of the pontiff to its place of final repose, the crowd erupts into wonderfully incongruous applause and waving of handkerchiefs, the same two ways they had used to express their love to His Holiness in life. I shall never forget these joyful shudders now racing through me.

"*Addio, Papa Paolo. Grazie di tutto.*"

13 August, A.D. 1978
Noon in St. Peter's Square

Today's issue of *L'Osservatore Romano* carries the headline: THE WORLD WEEPS FOR ITS FATHER, and the subheadline: A Great Heart is Stilled.

"It's hard to believe he's not there anymore," I overheard one Roman matron whisper in Italian to her husband as they stood in the long line before me. The line was edging its way into the basilica, up the main aisle, and down the spiral marble staircase which leads to the *Tombe dei Papi*, the extensive grottoes where most of the 262 pontiffs of the Church are buried.

We make our way slowly along the curving narrow corridor now. There is a bit of stir just ahead at the crypt containing the sarcophagus of Pius XII. Directly across the little hallway is the iron gate leading to the tomb of St. Peter, the humble fisherman-pope from the shores of Galilee. A few yards past Pius we come upon another illuminated crypt with a sarcophagus engraved simply: *Joannes XXIII.*

I am swept along by the endless line now and within a moment find myself standing before two modest sarcophagi with the bodies of two popes from the 1500's, Marcellus II and Julius III. Within a moment I find myself at the grave of Papa Montini. It is situated, like Pius' and John's, in a brightly lit alcove. But unlike Pius and John, Paul lies in the ground itself with a simple yet impressive marble slab covering the grave. It is not completely flat but rather pitches forward and is engraved only with the words: *Paulus VI PP* (Paul the Sixth, Pope and Pontiff), the way he signed all documents during his pontificate. My wife squeezes my hand. We nod our heads in prayer. We ponder the joy Paul has brought into our lives and the lives of our children. We thank God for him. We pray for him. We pray for the Church.

I make a mental note that within a few feet of one another lie the three popes of my lifetime: Pius XII, John XXIII and Paul VI.

17 August, A.D. 1978

A.M.

I drove down to the Vatican earlier this morning to pick up today's copy of *L'Osservatore Romano*. It is still bordered in black on every page. The major story today is the full text of the late pope's will:

September 16, 1972; 7:30 a.m.

"Into your hands, O Lord, I commend my spirit. My soul doth magnify the Lord." Mary!
I believe. I hope. I love.

The last three phrases could be considered the hallmarks, the guidelines of Giovanni Battista Montini's life. The passage continues, bearing another date:

June 30, 1965

I ask pardon for all that I have not done well. To everyone, I give peace in the Lord.

I greet my dearest brother, Ludovico, and all my close ones and all my relatives and friends and those who helped my ministry. To all my co-workers, thanks. To my secretary of state particularly.

I bless with special charity Brescia, Milan, Rome, the entire Church. "How pleasing are your tabernacles, Lord."

My every possession belongs to the Holy See.

May my personal secretary, dear Father Pasquale Macchi, dispose for some benefit and give as mementoes some from among my books and little objects to deserving persons.

I do not desire any special tomb.

Just some prayers that God may be merciful towards me. "In you, Lord, I have hoped. Amen, Alleluia!" To all, my blessing, in the name of the Lord.

PAUL, POPE PONTIFF VI

21 August, A.D. 1978

A.M.

An article on the front page of today's *Daily American* satirizes the Roman's propensity for friendly wagers on various contests, even on papal elections. According to the writer, Ladbroke's (the British bookmaker) has installed Cardinal Sergio Pignedoli, head of the secretariat for non-Christians, as the 5–2 favorite, with Cardinals Baggio and Poletti going off at 7–2. My hunch is Paolo Bertoli, another curia cardinal.

P.M.

At lunch today I overheard two Romans discussing the election. One said that some of the papers claimed inside information that the cardinals were set to stun the world with the election of Cardinal Bernardin Gantin, the 58-year-old black African prelate. The other fellow scoffed that this was the paper's ploy to sell more papers.

Many Vatican watchers are, however, conceding a possible change to another Third World prelate, Argentina's Cardinal Eduardo Pironio. Most observers seem to think, though, that the Italian string of pontiffs—the last non-Italian elected to the pontificate was Adrian VI, a Dutchman, in 1552—will be continued.

25 August, A.D. 1978

P.M.

Though it is really too beautiful to be indoors we have remained so this afternoon, as have so many others throughout Italy and thirty other countries including the U. S., so that we might watch, via the miracle of television, the cardinals dressed in their mourning purple vestments entering the conclave.

At 4:30 in the afternoon, Monsignor Virgilio Noe, master of ceremonies of the conclave, utters the Latin words, *"Extra omnes,"* ("Everyone out"), and the conclave officially begins.

This afternoon there will be no balloting, only prayers to the Holy Spirit for divine guidance. In the morning the first vote will be conducted and perhaps by this time tomorrow the *Sede Vacante* will have ended and the Church will have a new Supreme Pastor.

26 August, A.D. 1978

A.M.

This morning's *Il Messagero* entices its readers with the headline: *Oggi prima fumata* (Today the first smoke), then goes on to frustrate them with the subheadline: *Sara' nera* (It will be black).

P.M.

We joined the multitude in the square in late morning and it's already past noon with no signal from the conclavists.

Now there's a stir in the throng. The pipe is emitting smoke. The stir crescendoes to a tumult. But 'tis in vain. *Il Messagero* was right. *E' nera.*

We are back, after a light Roman repast of bread, cheese and a little *vino bianco,* in St. Peter's square waiting for history.

Late afternoon, and the sun is playing its special magic on the travertine of the colonnade and the honey-colored brick of the Apostolic Palace. There must be a quarter of a million people here now.

Again, smoke coming from the Sistine chimney! But what color? Some are shouting, *"Bianco!"* Others are muttering, *"Nera!"* Confusion reigns. I hear cries of, *"Viva il Papa!"* They send chills through me. The last time I heard them, Paul VI had appeared.

The smoke continues to pour out of the skinny pipe. More and more are convinced that it's white. There's a crackle over the public address system. In several languages the crowd is being exhorted to "keep your eyes on the window." There can be no doubt now!

Almost an hour has passed since first we saw the smoke and the wait is torturous. Now the huge glass doors of the central balcony have swung open and at the microphones is the senior cardinal deacon, Pericle Felici, a *papabile* himself. The crowd hushes itself to a resounding silence. Here it comes!

"Nuntio vobis magnum gaudium," ("I announce to you a great joy,"), *"Habemus Papam!"* ("We have a pope!").

Suddenly I am mindful of Luigi Barzini's observation that the Italian people love a good show and I think to myself, "What greater and more moving and more inspiring spectacle could one ask for than this?"

Felici continues: *"Reverendissimum Dominum, Dominum Cardinalem Albino Luciani!"* ("The most reverend Lord, Lord, Cardinal Albino Luciani!"). We are informed that the new pontiff has chosen the double name of *Giovanni Paolo.* Pope John Paul is dramatically honoring, by his choice of name, his two predecessors on the chair of Peter.

The roar is deafening! They must hear it cross town at the Colosseum, up and down the Tiber, on all the seven hills. *"Viva il Papa! Viva il Papa!"* Then there he is! A frail figure, arms upraised, palms heavenward much like Paul before him. He's wearing glasses, like Pius XII. He's not stout, I'm thinking, and there's no *"r"* in his name. Another tradition is broken. Men and women and children alike are waving their handkerchiefs at their new Holy Father and he is waving back, smiling.

Waiting patiently, lovingly even, for the tumult to subside, the new pope is about to impart his first apostolic blessing *Urbi et Orbi,* to the city and to the world. Silence is restored now and we await Papa Luciani's blessing: "May the Holy Apostles, Peter and Paul, in whose power and authority we trust, intercede for you with the Lord. May the Lord God Almighty grant you indulgence, absolution and pardon for all your sins. And may the blessing of Almighty God, Father, Son and Holy Spirit, descend upon you and remain with you forever." "Amen! Amen!"

So then. We have a pope. Long live the pope!

CHAPTER XIV

POPE JOHN PAUL I

Albino Luciani, the eldest of the three children of Bertola and Giovanni Luciani, was born in 1912 in the northern diocese of Belluno at Forno di Canale, now called Canale d'Agordo, a hamlet in a scenic but impoverished valley in the Dolomites, just thirty three miles south of the world-renowned luxury skiing resort of Cortina d'Ampezzo. The brick mountain farmhouse where Albino entered the world and was to spend his boyhood is today just about the same as it was two-thirds of a century ago. Of two stories, it has a charming outside stone staircase that leads to the second floor, an orange-tiled rooftop and weather-bleached wooden shutters. Inside, the dwelling is rather peasant-like, unadorned, its worn wooden staircase leading to the upper rooms. It has been occupied for many years now by Albino's married brother Edoardo (something of a local celebrity himself, having served three terms as *sindaco* or mayor of the community back in the mid-sixties) along with his wife, Antonietta, and their daughter, Saveria. The couple's five sons and their other four daughters have all married and left the homestead. Albino's sister, Antonia, is married to a bricklayer. They have two children and live near Trento.

A few days after his birth the future pope was taken by his devoutly Catholic mother to be baptized in the quaint village church of St. John the Baptist built in the year 1300. Ironically, the father of the 262nd successor of St. Peter was an itinerant laborer who spouted an old-fashioned anti-clerical socialism. (One old timer of Canale d'Agordo who remembered Luciani's father grumbled at the news of the election of his townsman that "this election is a scandal. He's a very good and holy man, but his father burned crucifixes in his stove!") Nonetheless, Bertola insisted on bringing up the children in the Catholic Church.

The elder Luciani like the other men of the village had difficulty in finding steady work. A bricklayer by trade, he worked part of the year in Switzerland and tried to save enough to see the family through the other long months of unemployment. Eventually he found fairly steady work as a glass-blower on the island of Murano in Venice. While an activist in the local chapter of Italy's Socialist party, Signor Luciani, to his everlasting credit, did not oppose Albino's later decision to enter the seminary. The boy's mother was a scullery maid who had a fervent devotion to the Blessed Virgin and imparted her love for prayer and the Church to little Albino.

Frail throughout his boyhood, Albino was nonetheless a playful, energetic youth who was popular with his peers. At school he quickly showed himself to be highly intelligent and exceptionally gifted in verbal skills. Without prodding from his instructors he read intensely, a habit he was to continue all his life. Writing also delighted him and from some of his compositions in the fourth grade of elementary school we get a glimpse of life in the Luciani household.

In one theme he described the family diet of *polenta* (corn bread grits), barley, macaroni, vegetables and "only rarely a little meat." The youngster said that he especially liked *carfoni,* a local dessert. On some evaluations from his teachers to his parents he was described as diligent, studious and bright but also at times a "bit too vivacious." "Oh, he was a mischief-maker all right, and a great fellow to pal around with," recalls Santo Del Bon, a boyhood chum of Albino. "We were always getting into scraps." Disarmingly lovable and innocent, the slender Luciani once made the following entry in his diary, confessing to his mother that he had once lied to her.

"Dear Mamma," he wrote, "You sent me to Cencenighe to buy medicine and gave me twelve lire. On the way home I lost two lire and told you that it cost seven lire instead of five. I could never find the courage to confess that I lost two."

Often he would stroll across the gorgeous landscape of the rolling northern countryside, book in hand, and purposely lose himself off some beaten trail where he could better indulge his favorite pursuits of literature, composition and contemplation. In his writing he exhibited the innate gift of clarity and purity of expression which was to lead to something of a writing career in his priesthood. "Had I not become a priest," he used to tell friends, "I would have loved to have been a journalist."

Like his predecessors in their boyhoods, young Luciani could be found in the early morning hours serving Mass as an altar boy in the parish church. Though he could clearly see a vocation to the priesthood evolving here, the boy's father, his contrary ideology notwithstanding, did nothing to obstruct it. During his twelfth year, Albino began formal studies for the priesthood at the minor seminary in nearby Feltre. From there he moved on to the major seminary of Belluno to study philosophy and theology. Upon completion of these rigorous studies he was ordained a priest on July 7, 1935. Before he even drew a parish assignment Albino was designated by his bishop for advanced studies at the Gregorian University in Rome. Here he worked for the next two years toward a doctorate in theology and was lauded by his professors and advisers for his brilliant dissertation on the origin of the soul in the thought of the Italian philosopher, Antonio Rosmini. Degree in hand, Father Luciani returned to Canale d'Agordo in the summer of 1937 to serve as curate in his boyhood church.

An eloquently simple style of expression was a vital asset to the new parish priest in his popular homilies to the simple folk of the community. Father Luciani became accustomed to making a point from the pulpit via interesting stories and fascinating anecdotes which his flock loved. Added to his parish duties was his teaching assignment at the local technical school where he instructed the youth in religion. And not long after, since he had developed such a scholarly reputation, he was given the post, despite his tender age, of vice-rector and professor of dogmatic and moral theology, canon law and sacred art in the diocesan seminary of Belluno. For the next ten years he filled the roles of parish priest, high school teacher, seminary professor, and administrator, revealing an extraordinary capacity for hard work and long hours which would result in his steady progress up the ecclesiastical ladder.

Continuing his arduous duties at the seminary, Luciani, in early 1947, took a position with the chancery office serving first as pro-chancellor, then pro-vicar general, and in a short time vicar general of the diocese. Later that year in recognition of his organizational skills and methodical approach to his every assignment, his superiors put him in charge of arrangements for the synod of the diocese of Feltre and Belluno. And in the following year he was made director of the diocesan catechetical office as well as arrangements chairman for the 1949 Eucharistic Congress of Belluno. Once again the writer in him surfaced when he recorded his views and experiences in catechtical work and set them forth in a small book which has had seven editions since, *Catechesi in Briciole* (Catechism in Crumbs). The book won acclaim for its concise, appealing, lucid style and its profound Christian message.

Luciani was a boyish forty-six years of age when on December 15, 1958 word arrived from Rome that he had been elevated to the episcopate and named bishop of Veneto. Twelve days later, Father Luciani was back in the familiar surroundings of the Eternal City to be consecrated in St. Peter's by His Holiness, Pope John XXIII, himself.

His episcopal career was soon to be noted for its feverish pastoral activity. He wasted no time in organizing

the clergy and the various Catholic societies into a federation that would collaborate closely with the bishop for the welfare of the diocese. When time permitted during this period he turned again to his old passion for writing. For the monthly magazine, *Messaggero di S. Antonio*, Luciani wrote a series of open letters addressed to celebrated figures in history and literature through which he would indirectly preach to his flock. These were later gathered into a 350-page book under the title *Illustrissimi* (To the Illustrious).

To Charles Dickens he wrote: "I am a bishop who has taken up the strange job of writing every month to some illustrious person. Your books have pleased me immensely because they are pervaded with a sense of love for the poor. Against them stand the oppressors, whom you disgrace with your pen dipped, as it is, in the genius of righteous anger and irony."

To Sir Walter Scott: "Honor to this Scotsman! I say this sincerely despite your little arrows shot now and then at the Catholic Church that I so love. This, however, is most understandable in you as a Presbyterian of indubitable good faith. Nonetheless the good that you have done remains as does your exemplary life. Sir Scott, I wish that Christians, especially young Christians, will understand you and follow you in those peaceful regions of spirit and fantasy where you love to live and make your reader live."

To Pinocchio: "When I was seven I read of your adventures for the first time and I delighted in them so that I reread them many times. It was that in you, as a child, I recognized myself. In your environment, I recognized my own. In the journey toward independence, as with all adolescents, dear Pinocchio, perhaps even you will knock against a hard rock, i.e. the problem of faith. In fact you will breathe anti-religious arguments as you breathe the air whether at school or in the factory. . . . If your faith is a heap of good grain, there will be a whole army of mice ready to assault it. If it is a house, a pick ax will try to tear it down piece by piece. You must defend it. These days one only keeps the faith one defends."

Letters also went out to the archduchess, Maria Theresa of Austria, G. K. Chesterton, Mark Twain and a host of other *'illustrissimi.'* This is what the good and humble bishop wrote to his divine Lord: "Dear Jesus, I have been criticized. Some have said, 'He is a bishop. He has been writing letters left and right, and yet not a single line has he for Christ.' You know that with you I try always to maintain a continuous dialogue. To translate it into a letter, however, is difficult. These are personal things. And also these are often such small things. It seems I've left out most of what one could say about You, that I've said badly what one should have said better. But there is this comfort: the important thing is not that one should write about Christ, but that many people should love and imitate Christ. And luckily, despite everything, this still happens." The volume was popularly received and acclaimed for its spiritual content and appealing format.

When Pope John convoked the Second Vatican Council in the autumn of 1962, Luciani returned once more to the city that already held so many memories for him. At the council he supported its reforms and, when he went back to his diocese, he worked vigorously for their acceptance and implementation.

Obedience had characterized his whole priesthood and when the controversial encyclical, *Humanae Vitae,* was published he at once exhorted his flock and his priests and even fellow bishops to accept, without hesitancy or reservation, its message, saying in effect that Rome had spoken and there should no longer be any doubt.

December 15 seems to have been a rather special date in the personal calendar of Albino Luciani, for on that day in 1969 he was named by Pope Paul VI to succeed Cardinal Urbani as patriarch of Venice. When on February 3 of the following year he went to take possession of his new see the whole city, in festive array, warmly welcomed him though he had cancelled the triumphal procession of gondolas on the Grand Canal that tradition-ally escorted the new patriarch to his cathedral, St. Mark's basilica. Luciani insisted on walking the streets and bridges to St. Mark's. Here was a pastor truly in his element, strolling with and among his people.

With his gentle ways and low-key style the new patri-arch impressed and won the affection and trust of his people at a time when Venice was beset with many serious problems. The industrialization of inland Venice had created a pressing need for priests and churches, a need which Luciani filled within a few years with his dynamic and inspiring leadership. On the insular part of the city, which was thought to be slowly drowning in the Adriatic and consequently slowly being evacuated, the beaming and optimistic prelate brought a new spirit of hope and resurgence to the islanders' morale. Luciani was enthralled by the unique, fairy-tale beauty of the lagoon city, and worked closely with the civil authorities in their efforts to get engineering advice and economic aid for the city.

Pope Paul VI himself showed that he shared the Venetians' concerns for their city's troubles when he visited their bishop in September of 1972. Midst much fanfare and colorful pageantry and before a huge crowd in St. Mark's square, the pontiff surprised everyone when he placed his ermine stole on the shoulders of Luciani. Taking this as a broad hint on the part of the pope that he would soon be elevating their patriarch to the cardi-nalate, the people went wild with joy (and the shy Luci-ani's face flushed with embarrassment). Their interpreta-tion of things proved accurate when, on March 5, 1973, in a consistory at the Vatican, Paul VI included the name of Bishop Luciani of Venice among the thirty nine new cardinals he was appointing. Later that month the popu-lar Luciani received the red hat, symbol of membership in the sacred college.

As a prince of the Church, he intensified his already

herculean daily work schedule. For the next three years he served as vice-president of the Italian Episcopal Conference. Cardinal Luciani startled his countrymen who had come to know him as an efficient but mild-mannered prelate when during the fiery divorce issue in Italy in the mid-seventies he quickly and forcefully suppressed two Catholic organizations of the diocese for their support of divorce. There should have been no surprise, however, for his whole career had thus far clearly shown that on matters of faith and Catholic doctrine Cardinal Luciani was intransigent. For the regional magazine, *Il Gazzettino,* he wrote a strongly worded article denouncing divorce entitled: "Divorce, a Sacrament in Reverse." In it he warned that the option of divorce would hang like a sword of Damocles over conjugal love "generating uncertainty, fear, suspicion," and that it would eat at the very fabric of society.

The cardinal used his patriarchal chair to speak out and write on many theological issues. Writing in *L'Osservatore Romano* January 23, 1974, he elaborated at length on the responsibility of theologians and urged them not to abuse their liberties in seeking truth by treating theology as "a mere human science instead of the sacred science that it is." He cautioned them against the temptation of self-aggrandizement at the expense of the welfare of the Church by coming up with new "discoveries." (The quotation marks are his.) In another article he urged priests to live their priesthood by word and deed following the example of Christ who had prayed intensely and continually and showed Himself always to be "gentle, humble, chaste and poor."

As the true pastor he had always wanted to be, he loved his flock, enjoyed visiting with the children in their schools, the workers in their plants, the farmers in their fields, often greeting them with the idiomatic, *"Come va?"* ("How's it going?"). They felt a certain closeness of identity with him when they would see him peddling his bicycle through the streets or down some country road or walking through snowdrifts to pay a call on some families.

As patriarch of Venice he attended special meetings in the Canal City of Vatican delegations and emissaries from the Anglican, Lutheran and Pentecostal Churches and the World Council of Churches. Once he walked for twenty five minutes from his residence to the meeting site of an ecumenical commission carrying a cake for the participants.

Throughout his hierarchial career, Luciani allowed himself just seven days vacation a year, time which he almost invariably spent at Pietralba where there was a Marian shrine which he used to visit as a boy with his mother. At Pietralba he would happily do as the Pietralbans did. Lunch would be a brown bag affair, dinner he would take at the tiny local trattoria. Mornings he would walk the outdoor markets gabbing with the ladies, joking with the vendors. Afternoons might be spent reading and snoozing under the shade of an ancient tree. Evenings were almost always sure to find him playing *bocce* (a lawn bowling game) with the men. For the remainder of the year his chief source of relaxation was stealing a half hour late in the evening to listen to recordings of Vivaldi and other Baroque masters.

This was the man, the plain, simple, practical man, whose fellow princes of the Church selected to inherit the mantle of St. Peter. And when the results of the election were announced that sultry day in the Sistine he accepted with characteristic obedience, humility and wit. To the smiling Jean Cardinal Villot who approached the pontiff-designate with the ritual question, "Do you accept?" Albino Luciani at first replied with a wry grin. "May God forgive all of you for what you have done in my regard," he said, then gave his assent.

Evidently the cardinals had sought a pastoral pope this time, in the style of John XXIII, one of affability and doctrinal conservatism. With respect to his viewpoints, Luciani had long and clearly been on record as vigorously opposed to marriage for priests, ordination of women, abortion, divorce, liturgical excesses. He was an implacable foe of communism. He could see no reconciliation possible between Marxism and Catholicism and in national elections had openly used his pulpit to urge his flock to vote against the communist party's candidates. At the same time he had developed an image as a fervent champion of the poor.

Like Paul VI and Pius XII before him he was ascetic in his personal habits. Like John XXIII, he was gregarious by nature. When he was presented to the world for the first time as pope from the central balcony of St. Peter's, John Paul I waved happily with both hands and flashed his matchless boyish smile, the smile that was to become the trademark of his month-long reign, the *September Pontificate* as some have called it.

On the following morn the Holy Father, who had spent the first night of his reign in the monastic cell reserved for him during the conclave, had breakfast with the one hundred and ten cardinals who elected him. Later in the morning John Paul, who had never worked in the Vatican's corridors of ecclesiastical power, celebrated Mass with his electors in the Sistine chapel, after which he spoke to them, in Latin, from a small throne in front of Michelangelo's *Last Judgment*, spelling out what course he would take as pope. He said that he intended "to devote all our ministry as priest, teacher and pastor to the teachings of the Second Vatican Council." He gave indication that he would be principally a pastoral pope, more concerned with spreading the gospel, while running the Vatican largely on the advice of those more familiar with the Church bureaucracy. "I don't know anything about this job," he kept candidly confessing.

At noon that same day, Sunday the 27th of August, the slightly built, handsome, bespectacled pontiff, a lock of his gray hair falling on his forehead, went to the central balcony again to address the throng which had late the day before given him such a roaring welcome to his new diocese. Again he charmed them with his simple conversational style of speaking. First he praised Pope Paul as "a great and humble man" and promised to continue his predecessor's program. Then the Holy Father explained his choice of a papal name and startled knowledgable onlookers by dispensing with the regal "we," traditionally employed by Supreme Pontiffs, in favor of the more colloquial pronoun, "I." He explained that his two immediate predecessors had both had a profound influence on his priesthood and his life, citing Pope John's elevation of him to the episcopate and Pope Paul's nomination of him to the college of cardinals. "I do not have the wisdom or the heart of Pope John nor the preparation or culture of Pope Paul," he modestly insisted. "But I am here in their place and I must try to serve the Church. I hope you will help me with your prayers."

Then he told of his surprise and his emotions at his election the day before: "Yesterday morning when I came to the Sistine to vote tranquilly, I never dreamed of what was about to happen. As soon as the danger began for me two colleagues nearby reassured me with words of encouragement. One said to me, 'Courage. If God gives you a burden, He also gives you the help to carry it.' And another colleague said, 'Don't worry. In all the world there are so many people who pray for the new pope.'"

After his talk, he imparted his apostolic blessing to the enthusiastic faithful, many of whom chanted the Latin responses back to him. As indicated by his choice of an unprecedented double name (which by the way the Romans found too much of a mouthful and quickly came up with their own abbreviated version, *Gianpaolo*) Papa Luciani would give the chair of Peter his own special, original touch. For example, he decided against the centuries-old coronation rite and even a simpler enthronement ceremony in favor of a Mass, on Sunday,

September 3, at which he would be invested with the *pallium,* a strip of white wool with black crosses on it signifying authority, to mark the beginning of his life as Supreme Pastor which is how he referred to himself and how he viewed his new role. Throughout his life he had an aversion to pomp and circumstance, but on one matter he quickly relented when he realized he was disappointing the people. He had tried to do away with the ceremonial portable throne, the *sedia gestatoria,* at public functions but this meant that many in the great crowds that came to the general audiences would not be able to get a good look at him.

These audiences, though so few in number, are among the most memorable in recent papal history for the special touch which John Paul gave to them. Sometimes he would summon school children up to the podium to help him make a particular point in his weekly talks. Papa Gianpaolo's constant, radiant, infectious smile whipped up excitement in the crowds. His fatherly ways did likewise. Even his departures were special. He would take his leave from all public functions chuckling, waving, giving his blessing and calling out to the crowd, "Be good now. Calm down."

Even in formal meetings, John Paul put everyone at ease with his warm and simple manner. On September 21 the Holy Father received in private audience fifty American bishops and astounded them when he threw the meeting open to questions. (Such sessions in previous pontificates were marked by formality and protocol.) The stunned bishops sat there in silence momentarily until Auxiliary Bishop Anthony Mestice of New York agreed to serve as translator. "Come on, you guys," Mestice implored, "ask something!"

Pope John Paul's simple yet profoundly spiritual talks at his general audiences provided some clues as to where his pontificate would have been directed. Twice in his short reign he stressed the importance of the virtue of obedience in the Church. On September 23, when he took formal possession of his own diocesan cathedral of St. John Lateran, he remarked, "One of the most important moments of my life was when I put my hands in those of my bishop and said, 'I promise.' From that point on I felt committed for all my life (to obedience)." This was taken by many as a message from the Supreme Pontiff that he expected no less a commitment from every priest, monk, brother and nun.

He also indicated that he would put an end to liturgical abuses that had developed in the post conciliar period and that programs aimed at helping the poor would get a genuine priority. On the matter of world peace, he hinted at a more active Vatican role in international efforts toward that goal and also informed his close advisers that he was thinking about visiting the Middle East to get personally involved in reestablishing harmony there.

John Paul ran the Vatican as a country pastor would his parish. He would rise at five a.m., read his Office and meditate for a half hour, celebrate Mass in his little private chapel off his bedroom, breakfast very lightly and then plunge vigorously into the eighteen hour workday that awaited him.

On Thursday morning, September 28, he received the African cardinal, Bernardin Gantin, president of the pontifical justice and peace commission, met with several department heads of the Roman curia, and later a group of bishops from the Philippines. Around one in the afternoon he broke for a brief lunch (eating, as usual, "like a canary," as one aide described the pope's frugal diet) and then tended to some paper work and correspondence. In a letter, his last one, to Bishop Hugo Aufderbeck of East Germany, he wrote, curiously, of longing "for the blessed existence of eternity after the sometimes arduous pilgrimage of life."

Cardinal Jean Villot, whom Pope John Paul had kept on as secretary of state, went over some diplomatic business with His Holiness until some time around eight in the evening. At nine, the pope put in a long distance friendly phone call to an old chum, Cardinal Giovanni Columbo of Milan, who said later that he had detected no sign of fatigue or illness in the pontiff's voice.

Around ten that night, he spoke his last terrestrial words to an aide, Father Diego Lorrenzi, who had just informed him that a young Roman communist had been shot at a political gathering earlier in the evening. This news deeply upset the pope who lamented, "Even the young are killing one another now." Moments later he walked toward his austerely furnished bedroom on the fourth floor of the Apostolic Palace. He settled into his simple fourposter bed with a copy of *The Imitation of Christ,* a fifteenth-century devotional book by Thomas à Kempis and some papers with notes on them for future homilies and speeches.

When at five thirty the following morning the Holy Father failed to appear in his private chapel for his prayers, Father John Magee, his secretary, went to see what the problem was. With mounting anxiety, Magee knocked on the bedroom door for a couple of minutes and finally opened it to look in. He saw the pope, slumped forward, the reading light still on. The priest tried to awaken him, but quickly realized that Pope John Paul I was dead. The brief, sunny, promising reign of Papa Luciani was ended. John Paul I, who would have observed his sixty-sixth birthday on October 17, had died in his sleep from a heart attack.

For the second time in as many months Rome became center stage of the world as the shocked and grief-stricken cardinals arrived in the Eternal City to choose another from among their ranks to fill the shoes of the fisherman while a mourning and incredulous world watched and waited.

First, though, they had to tend to the sad task of conducting their beloved John Paul, whose reign was the shortest since 1605 when Leo XI served just twenty seven days, to the tomb. At an outdoor Mass on October 4, that was almost a carbon copy of the papal funeral rites back in August except for the lack of sunny skies, Pope John Paul I was eulogized by the eighty-five-year-old dean of the sacred college, Cardinal Carlo Confalionieri. "Providence took him away from us so suddenly," Confalionieri lamented. "Now we are all left with our eyes turned upward, wondering about the inscrutable designs of God." The cardinal called the pontificate of John Paul "a dialogue of love between father and children," praising the pontiff as "the perfect teacher, catechist and pastor," citing his concern for peace, for the oppressed, for the poor, for the suffering. He compared John Paul to "a meteor that unexpectedly lights up the heavens and then disappears, leaving us amazed and astonished."

At the close of the simple rite, as the coffin of John Paul, who had always insisted, "I am just a poor man accustomed to little things and to silence," was being borne past the diplomatic corps and heads of state from around the world into the basilica, the crowd burst into applause, tears streaming down their faces.

The private burial rite in the basilica's crypt began with the chanting of Psalm 117 ("Rejoice in the Lord, for He is good") and soon Albino Luciani came to the last stop on that "arduous pilgrimage of life," in a small tomb just across the corridor from the two predecessors he had loved and honored with his choice of a pontifical name. He had been but a month in the chair of Peter, but that brief span had been long enough to win the hearts of the Romans and the world. His death had been enough to break them.

CHAPTER XV

POPE JOHN PAUL II

In Rome and around the world all eyes were once again focused on the slender smokestack of the Sistine chapel. With Mass, solemn prayer and meditation, and other prescribed ritual the second conclave of the tumultuous summer of '78 began at 4:30 p.m., Saturday, October 14. One hundred and eleven princes of the Church once again closed themselves off from the world to fulfill the most important duty of their high office by choosing the next vicar of Christ on earth.

As voting began the next morning, crowds were already gathering in the square in hope of seeing, sometime around noon, a puff of white smoke. But the emissions from the Sistine roof after both balloting sessions that day were black. Sunday had, disappointingly, come and gone and the *Sede Vacante* continued.

On Monday it appeared to be more of the same as, shortly past midday, more unwelcome black smoke announced the inconclusive action of the morning. That evening, however, at 6:19, unmistakably white smoke poured from the celebrated chimneypipe to a roaring response from the throngs assembled in the cobblestoned piazza. By radio and by word of mouth news of the white smoke raced through all the quarters of Rome, bringing countless thousands more out of the city's pastel-colored *palazzi* and into the square to join the excited early birds.

Twenty four minutes after the smoke had risen into the evening sky, Cardinal Pericle Felici stood on the ornate central balcony and waited for a semblance of silence. His sly grin indicated a certain boyish delight in stretching out the tension as he delayed some moments more at the microphones. Then he began what would prove to be a particularly historic and world-shaking announcement. *"Habemus Papam!"* he exclaimed in deliberate and exquisite Latin. At this point he was interrupted by another happy uproar which soon subsided in anticipation of the name of the elected. And then Felici, who had twice this summer been considered a prime *papabile* himself by Vatican watchers in the media, delivered the news heard round the world: *"Cardinalem Carolum Wojtyla!"*

The crowd, the vast television audience, the press, the clergy, the political world were all caught completely off guard. "Who was Wojtyla?" "A non-Italian pope?" "Incredible!" "Impossible!" Some in the crowd quickly consulted their roster of cardinals published in all the newspapers that day and learned that the new pope was the young (58) cardinal from Poland, Karol Wojtyla, the archbishop of Cracow. "A pope from behind the Iron Curtain?" "Pure fiction, right out of Morris West's novel, *Shoes of the Fisherman!"*

But, even to the shock of Wojtyla himself, it was pure fact rather. When he had arrived at Da Vinci airport a week earlier he laughingly counseled the press photographers, who were taking no chances and were snapping every cardinal who came through the terminal, "Stop wasting your film, boys. My chances of election are nil."

Now Cardinal Felici concluded his happy task by announcing the name that the new Supreme Pontiff had chosen: *"Qui sibi nomen imposuit, Ioannem Paulum Secundum!"* ("Who has taken for himself the name of John Paul the Second!"). Another stunner! At this tribute by the new pontiff to his beloved predecessor the multitude went simply wild with joy. This was indeed a summer to end all summers. A series of events to test the credulity of even the most gullible. The summer of the three popes. The summer of Paul, John Paul and John Paul II.

When word reached Poland, which was instantly

thanks to the miracle of Marconi, there was exultation throughout the long-suffering land. In the pope's home see of Cracow there was dancing and singing in the streets well into the night. At Wawel Castle, where Polish kings once lived, the great Sygmunt bell, rung only on historic occasions, pealed joyously as did church bells all across the eastern European, communist-governed country. The small town where Wojtyla was born and raised erupted in celebration. People were throwing open their shutters and hanging precariously from their windows to proclaim the news out of Rome to neighbors across the alley and to passersby in the streets and squares, "They've made our Lolek pope!" Thousands rushed into the streets snakedancing, hugging one another, toasting their pope, laughing and crying all at the same time. Some men fetched their accordions and started a Polka festival. Others mounted soapboxes and delivered impromptu, yet stirringly eloquent panegyrics about their countryman, who at the moment was being vested, in a little room just off the far away Sistine, in white cassock and skullcap and red cape for his introduction to the world. Others chose to gather at the ancient church of Karol Wojtyla's boyhood.

Poland's top communist officials, who had for years jousted in ideological battles with the courageous prelate, wired their felicitations to the new pope and announced that they were lifting travel restrictions, clearing the way for thousands of Poles to go to Rome for the installation of John Paul II.

Around the globe millions of people sat transfixed before their television sets waiting for an electronic look at the man who had, by his election minutes earlier, ended the long Italian tenure on the papal throne.

Meanwhile, back in Rome, some *Sanpietrini*, the maintenance workers of St. Peter's, at 6:48 were extending from the balustrade of the central loggia a red and white drape. Another long thirty two minutes passed while the piazza filled to overflowing. Groups of enthusiastic and agile youths had scampered up onto the four large lampposts that surround the obelisk in the center of the piazza. A few fortunate faithful had squeezed together on the vantage point afforded by the pedestal of that needlelike Imperial trophy from Egypt which had witnessed the martyrdom of the first Holy Father twenty centuries earlier and a couple of hundred yards away.

The sweet climate of a typical Roman October evening had surely swelled the turnout. Nearly an hour had passed since the white smoke and still no pope appeared. Some then began to whistle so as to beckon "those inside the Vatican to come on out." Others started to clap rhythmically for the same purpose. Soon the whistling and applauding crescendoed to a thunderous pitch.

Finally, at quarter past seven, with the harvest moon full and red and romantic against a dark blue velvet sky, the high glass doors of the balcony to the right of the central loggia opened and suddenly there were purple-robed cardinals swarming all over it, smiling and waving to the cheering people below. A second or two later and the same thing was happening on all the other side balconies both left and right of the center signaling the imminent appearance of the pope.

Powerful floodlights set up by the television crews bathed the facade in a whitish glare and the clock over the left bell tower showed precisely seven twenty. Just then, Pope John Paul II, having already concluded the first hour of his pontificate, strode into view to a deafening ovation.

Visibly moved, tears glistening in his large blue eyes, the silver haired, robust, muscular, handsome new bishop of Rome gestured paternally and lovingly to his deliriously happy and curious flock. It seemed that the resounding welcome would never let up but after several minutes the pope succeeded in delivering the first words of a brief talk: "Jesus Christ be praised!"

Renewed booming applause constrained the pope to remain smilingly silent again for a few moments and then he began anew, telling the crowd that their eminences, the cardinals, had called a new bishop of Rome, that they had summoned him from "a country far away." Continuing to speak in elegant Italian, he won the hearts and respect of the Romans at once when he paused and said, *"Se mi sbaglio, mi corregerete"* ("If I make a mistake, please correct me").

"With fear I received this nomination," the pope explained, "but I have accepted it in obedience to our Lord and to the Mother of God." Then with eyes still misty from the never-to-be-forgotten welcome his new diocese had given him, John Paul II raised his hand and imparted the traditional solemn blessing, *Urbi et Orbi,* closing a most memorable day in a year of memorable days in Rome. The 263rd successor of St. Peter had begun his universal ministry.

The day had seen the election of the first non-Italian to the chair of Peter in 455 years; the first pope ever from Poland, a nation whose fervor for Roman Catholicism has been unsurpassed, perhaps unequaled, for a millennium; the first pope from a communist nation; the youngest pope in modern times. But the question remained on the lips of the world long into the night: "Who is Karol Wojtyla?" Let us in the ensuing pages try to piece together the answer.

South of Warsaw, the capital of Poland, about a hundred and seventy miles, lies the industrial village of Wadowice. It was here in this community of fifteen thousand people, on May 18, 1920 that Karol Josef Wojtyla, the future Roman Pontiff, was born to Karol and Emelia Kaczorowska Wojtyla. Today, on the tower of the parish church in the picturesque town marketplace is a huge poster of Wadowice's most famous native son, John Paul II, successor of St. Peter. On one side of the picture is the white and red flag of Poland; on the other, the white and yellow standard of Vatican City. The morning after the election of the Polish cardinal, the pastor of the church went down to the rectory cellar and retrieved the parish baptismal register for the years 1917–1927 and made the following striking notation next to the name of Karol Wojtyla: *Elected to the See of Peter, October 16, A.D. 1978; has taken the name John Paul II.*

Karol, whose boyhood pals knew him by the affectionate nickname of Lolek, was a remarkably versatile lad with a first rate mind in the classroom and exceptional ability on the athletic field. He played goalie for his elementary school soccer squad. Lolek was always tall and sturdy for his age and loved the strenuous activity of running, cycling and hiking.

On many occasions he would follow a workout with a swim in the swift waters of the Swaka River. This rare combination of class scholar, class athlete and class wit distinguished himself in his every youthful endeavor. Academically he excelled in the deep courses like philosophy and religion and in the exacting courses like Latin and Greek.

Young Wojtyla was already in his high school years considered something of an authority by many on the philosophy of Kant. Enamored of Homeric verse, Lolek could quote the blind Aegean poet at length. And he always seemed to be ready with an appropriate Latin proverb for every situation. As class comedian, he could always be found on the school grounds in the middle of a cluster of youths which would every few seconds burst into gales of laughter at another of Lolek's outrageous stories or hilarious jokes. One of his schoolmates, Wiodzimierz Piotowski, today a physician, tells how "everyone was crazy about Lolek, especially the girls. With his sunny disposition and lively conversation you couldn't help but like him."

Yet there was a very serious, deeply contemplative, private side to the popular blond schoolboy. Many had observed a special spiritual quality about him and how much time he liked to spend in church at prayer. Therefore it came as no grand surprise to Lolek's comrades when he decided to study for the priesthood.

A certain extraordinary maturity had come to Lolek early in life perhaps out of the tragedies that marked his first two decades. When he was just nine years old his mother died in childbirth. In his early teens he lost his beloved older brother, Edmund, a doctor who had contracted a fatal case of scarlet fever from one of his patients. Though the Wojtyla family bond had always been strong, the boy and his Dad became particularly close in their bereavement. They subsisted on the elder Karol's meager army sergeant pension.

After finishing at the top of his high school class in the late 1930's, the young scholar enrolled at the famous Jagellonian University in Cracow where he majored in Polish literature and where in his spare time, he began to write poetry. At the university he also joined a little theatre group, the Rhapsodic Theatre, which would put on morality plays for small intellectual audiences.

In 1939 the rumble of tanks and the thump of jackboots echoed across the land and Poland found itself partitioned by Nazi Germany and the Soviet Union. During the Nazi occupation there was a crackdown on the intelligentsia and the academic community and on all cultural activities. With education now irregular, difficult, and sometimes dangerous, Karol suspended his studies and went to work in a quarry in Cracow but continued his work with the "cultural resistance movement." The group went underground, performing for handfuls of people in private apartments.

Already rugged physically, Karol became even more so from the punishing outdoor labor at the quarry, through Poland's sub-zero winters. In the cold months, before setting out for work, he would smear his face with a thick layer of vaseline to guard against frostbite. In 1957 a prominent Polish magazine, *Znak*, published a poem entitled "Quarry" by Andrzej Jawiew (the pen name of Karol Wojtyla). Returning home one evening in 1941, Karol found himself alone in the world at the age of 21. His father had died in bed. After the funeral the kind family of Juliusz Kydrynski, a dear friend of young Karol, insisted that Wojtyla move in with them.

Later that same year Nazi troops began herding hundreds of thousands of Polish Jews from all regions of the country into the Warsaw ghetto to facilitate their dispatch to Auschwitz and the other extermination camps. Wojtyla, deeply distressed over the persecution of the Jews, became active, often at great personal peril, in efforts to hide them from their Nazi tormentors. Karol had had close personal ties to the Jewish community of Wadowice from boyhood. Jerry Zubrzycki, a high school classmate of Wojtyla's, today recalls that Karol lived in danger daily of losing his life. "He would move about the occupied cities taking Jewish families out of the ghettos, finding them new identities and hiding places. He saved many families threatened with execution."

During this same period, young Wojtyla was leaning more and more to giving his life to the Church. Then in 1943, with seminaries being suppressed by the occupational authorities, Karol, along with four other young aspirants, took up residence in the home of the archbishop of Cracow, Cardinal Sapieha, where for the next two years, under the direction of the cardinal himself, they studied for the priesthood. After the war, they completed their studies in philosophy and theology at the Cracow diocesan seminary and were ordained in 1946.

Autumn of that year brought a pleasant and exciting surprise for Father Wojtyla, when he was notified of his selection for doctoral studies at the Angelicum in Rome. Over the next two years he deeply impressed his mentors with his keen intellect and scholarly ways. The talented priest's dissertation, written in Latin, was a brilliant piece of research and analysis on "The Problems of Faith in St. John of the Cross," Spain's sixteenth century Carmelite mystic. Excerpts from the document were published as articles in a number of academic journals.

Father Wojtyla returned to his beloved homeland at the end of the summer of 1948 and promptly drew an assignment as curate in a suburban parish and a simultaneous one as chaplain to university students in Cracow. In both posts he quickly became enormously popular, especially with the youth. Often he would spend his off days and weekends with them hiking in the woods, mountain climbing, bicycle riding, skiing, canoeing, swimming—all the while sneaking in discussions of spiritual themes.

His superiors recognized something special in Karol Wojtyla and in early 1949 nominated him for another doctoral program, this one in theology at the theological faculty of the University of Cracow. With his exceptional ability Wojtyla continued to draw the attention and the accolades of diocesan authorities and in 1954 he was given a professorship at the Catholic University of Lublin, which had published in full his second doctoral dissertation, a complex work, in Polish, entitled: "An Assessment of the Possibility of Erecting a Christian Ethic on the Principles of Max Scheler."

All this time, Karol continued to do parish and chaplain work, giving many spiritual retreats for students. His theatrical experience enhanced his work on the classroom podium and his ministry in the pulpit. A dynamic lecturer and eloquent preacher, he was able to hold his classes and his congregations spellbound. Astonishingly, with all these pressing duties he still found the time and the energy to produce several books on faith and morals. This exceptional burst of scholarly and pastoral activity combined with Wojtyla's outstanding piety and spirituality was not wasted on his superiors in the Polish hierarchy who were for a long time already eyeing him for even more important and more challenging tasks.

While on a canoeing trip in July of 1958 he received an urgent message to report to the residence of Archbishop Baziak of Cracow where he learned to his amazement that he had been named auxiliary bishop of the diocese. The new post did not prevent him from maintaining ties with the university students who practically revered him. Often he would drop in on meetings of their various fraternities and societies. And even as a prelate he still loved to go off with them for hiking or skiing holidays.

Four years later, at the Second Vatican Council, Bishop Wojtyla gained international attention with eight outstanding speeches, the talk on religious liberty and freedom of conscience the most widely acclaimed of them all. Before hundreds of prelates who fancy themselves as fine orators, Wojtyla's rich and resonant voice boomed his ringing Latin phrases to the farthest reaches of the spacious basilica.

While still a young man, 42, as the hierarchy views age, Karol Wojtyla was made archbishop of Cracow and in this role too he maintained his close involvement with all the classes of Polish society. He held frequent conferences with labor groups, student unions, artists, academics and especially with young priests. Each morning there was an open house policy at the episcopal residence. What few leisure hours were left to the consummate scholar were spent in reading and writing. Archbishop Wojtyla avoided any show of luxury but kept a chauffeur only so that in traffic jams his precious time would not be wasted but could rather be spent working on papers. A flip-up desk counter in the back seat provided a sort of episcopal "office on wheels." One other little extravagance was an extensive personal library that contained volumes in an array of languages.

As was his practice throughout his priesthood, he always rose at daybreak. He would shave with a plain safety razor, repair to his small chapel for meditation, celebrate Mass with an aide, take breakfast in the kitchen and at the same time speed read the morning papers, and conclude things with a walk of a few miles through the neighborhood. "Indefatigable," was how his staff described him. They could never quite resist shaking their heads in disbelief as they observed and participated in his eighteen to twenty hour work days.

Often he would be on the road visiting the many parishes of the sprawling archdiocese. Wherever he went, Wojtyla met with an enthusiastic welcome and an outpouring of love from the flock for its shepherd. In him the intellectual community in particular felt they had a true friend and a champion of their welfare against a hostile state. Certainly no one could ever accuse Wojtyla of being a snob but such is the profundity of his thought that he has always delighted in the company of scholars, thinkers and literati.

Wojtyla also kept in close touch with the Jewish community and often hosted their leaders at his home. On occasion he spoke in their synagogues and always sought to help them with their problems. For example, the orthodox rabbis informed Wojtyla that their congregations were experiencing difficulty in obtaining Kosher meat. With a few phone calls placed to the right persons in the government the matter was resolved with dispatch.

This would not have been possible had the Catholic prelate, who was quick to do verbal combat with the communist authorities, not had a diplomatic side. Though known for his bitter opposition to the ideas of communism, he resisted excessive, overkill, counterproductive language in his public statements against the ideology. "He's not an extremist," says John Cardinal Dearden of Detroit, "but a very balanced man on critical issues. He looks at the different angles and does not carry fixed positions." Surely this befits a man who has spent his life developing his mind the better to penetrate the higher distinctions. Without ever compromising his repudiation of the communist system, Wojtyla has always firmly believed in the value of a Christian-Marxist dialogue. "I am always for dialogue," he says. "There is too much monologue in the world." Though the regime long viewed the archbishop as a thorn in their side because of his influence on the people and especially on the young, the fact is that while frequently and openly and loudly denouncing censorship, religious persecution, anti-Semitism and other forms of oppression and all the other harassments suffered under a communist state, Wojtyla, as archbishop, still deftly managed to bring about a measure of detente between the Church and State in Poland.

Pope Paul VI held Wojtyla in high regard for all of this along with his work on Church reforms launched at the Second Vatican Council and in 1967 raised him to the cardinalate.

According to Richard T. Davies, former United States ambassador to Poland, the communist government wasted no time attempting to establish a rivalry between the two Polish cardinals, Wojtyla and the bluntly outspoken critic of the regime, Stefan Cardinal Wyszynski, primate of Poland—a rivalry they could afterwards exploit. But Wojtyla was their equal in wiliness. When prominent European dignitaries visited Poland, officials would try to take them to Wojtyla's residence first. Aware that they were trying to use him in an insult to Primate Wyszynski, for whom Wojtyla had a deep filial love and esteem, the new cardinal would either be conveniently out of town or waiting out front in his car, an old Volga, offering to act as escort to the primate's quarters. Much to the chagrin of regime officials they could do nothing to diminish the strong bond between the cardinals.

As cardinal, too, Wojtyla continued with his scholarship and his writing. Long a serious student of phenomenology, Cardinal Wojtyla wrote a major book on the subject in 1969 entitled, "The Individual and the Deed." Then, in 1972, he published "The Essentials of Aggiornamento," a study of the realization of Vatican II.

At the World Synod of Bishops in Rome in 1974, Cardinal Wojtyla impressed his colleagues further with his profound statements on evangelization. Pope Paul VI, that same year, extended an invitation to the cardinal to conduct the Lenten retreat for the pontiff and his household.

Wojtyla had also developed a reputation as an energetic traveling prince of the Church. He twice visited the United States, the first time in 1969. Wherever he went, he was given wildly enthusiastic receptions by huge crowds, especially in the Polish parishes of the United States and Canada. He had an abundance of charisma and a certain capacity to electrify the air wherever he appeared. Cardinal Wojtyla paid his second visit to the States in July of 1976 when he led a delegation of twelve Polish bishops to the International Eucharistic Congress in Philadelphia. That month he also spoke at Harvard University where he so impressed the summer student body that the following day's issue of the *Harvard Crimson,* the campus newspaper, ran his picture on the front page with the caption: "The Next Pope?"

Early in 1977 Cardinal Wojtyla realized another triumph over the communist government of Poland when he dedicated the first Catholic church in the postwar industrial town of Nowa Huta. This town was supposed to be a propaganda showplace, planned as the first real socialist urban development in Poland, and there was to be no church built to mar the showplace. For two decades the people had petitioned for a church. The communists steadfastly refused. Civil unrest followed, but still no church. Cardinal Wojtyla and his closely knit fellow bishops of the country put relentless pressure on the authorities who at last yielded. One hundred thousand cheering, weeping Poles turned out for the dedication ceremonies on May 15 and heard their dauntless cardinal say that, "Nowa Huta was originally intended to be a city without God, without a church. But the will of God and of the people working here have together achieved a victory, a victory of God's power!"

When the State stepped up its campaign against the Church later that year, the cardinal escalated his anticommunist rhetoric, calling upon the people to defend the faith against all threats and intimidation. "It is our duty to defend our faith, which is threatened in our homeland by a program of atheism which bears various names and uses various methods," he warned.

Thanks to the intrepid and inspiring leadership of its cardinals and bishops and clergy, the Church of Poland, reminiscent of the infant Church in Imperial Rome, flourished all the more, the more the government tried to suppress it. In many parishes, attendance at Sunday Mass is today so heavy that Masses must be scheduled all day and into the evening. Vocations to the priesthood are also flourishing despite the tactics of the regime.

Perhaps having seen what wondrous things Karol Wojtyla had done for the Church in Poland against such formidable obstacles is what persuaded the cardinals in conclave that he could do likewise for the universal Church. Perhaps they saw as equally important as his scholarly, theological, ecclesiastical credentials, his charming, warm and interesting personal manner that would—as John Paul I's had done—capture for the chair of Peter and for the Church the hearts and esteem of the world.

Certainly the media love him for the excellent copy he provides with his many ingratiating personality traits, not the least of which is his wry wit. Once on a visit to Milan he was asked about his passion for and indulgence in the sport of skiing. "Is it becoming to a cardinal to ski?" a reporter inquired. "It is unbecoming to a cardinal to ski badly," Wojtyla shot back with a wink. Then he turned the tables on the journalist and inquired, "How many of the Italian cardinals ski?" When he received no reply, the husky eastern European prelate noted, "In Poland forty percent of the cardinals ski." Reminded that Poland had only two cardinals, Wojtyla laughed and said, "In our country Wyszynski counts for sixty per cent."

He is especially fond of good puns and like the Lolek of old, is still a marvelous story teller. He has astounding recall and is fluent in Polish, Latin, Italian, English, Spanish, French and German. Wojtyla has always been known as a great listener, an endangered species in the modern world. Once at a conference of bishops, Cardinal Wojtyla said nothing. When this was afterwards pointed out to him, he replied, "I'm here to represent the listening Church."

Photographers for the media appreciate the photogenic qualities of the tall, tanned, handsome, ruggedly built pontiff whose craggy face seems to have been hewn out of a block of granite. His generous shock of white hair, his eyes that can laugh at something before a smile can be traced on his lips, and his broad smile that when it does come is radiant, are all positive personal attributes of this popular pope who has a remarkable but disconcerting ability to read or write while conversing and yet later can recall every detail of the conversation.

John Paul loves to sing and has a beautiful baritone voice. Several years ago when he was schussing down the slopes of the Tatras mountains he came upon an injured fellow skier and helped in getting her to a hospital. That evening a group of persons who had been on the slopes earlier in the day visited the woman at her bedside and serenaded her. It wasn't until after they had left that a nurse informed her that the guitarist in the group was the archbishop of Cracow.

His Holiness has confided to old friends that he hopes to continue skiing "if they (the Vatican protocol people) will let me." Rumors abound in Rome that during his first winter in the chair of Peter, he did manage to slip away for a few hours of clandestine skiing on hills a little north of Rome.

As cardinal he customarily walked five miles a day. One Polish member of the curia says he wouldn't be surprised to see John Paul II jogging in the Vatican gardens before long. The Holy Father plays more than a fair game of tennis and according to insiders has had a few workouts already on the Vatican courts. He is also an enthusiastic swimmer and, as is no secret, thoroughly appreciates the new swimming pool recently installed at the papal summer retreat of Castel Gandolfo.

Unlike many of his recent predecessors who "ate like canaries" according to their own admissions, Papa Wojtyla has an appetite to match his frame, which one journalist described as that of a "rugby front-row forward." To the traditional continental fare of a buttered roll and a cup of thick coffee, Pope John Paul II prefers a hearty breakfast of ham or bacon and eggs, some toast, hot cereal and juice. Two Polish nuns from the Sacred Heart Convent in Rome have been brought in to help with the meals.

A few days after his election, the pope, like Morris West's fictitious pontiff in *Shoes of the Fisherman,* put on the simple black cassock of a parish priest so that he might slip undetected out of the Vatican and into the streets of the Eternal City to visit a very close, ailing friend, Polish bishop Andrezej Deskur, in a Roman hospital without causing any fuss.

This is Karol Wojtyla. This is the man the cardinals had turned to in one of the saddest hours in papal history, the one man among them magnificently prepared by Providence, in their judgment, to assume the awesome burdens of the pontificate, the pope who would expedite the rapprochement between the Vatican and communist nations that was begun under Popes John XXIII and Paul VI, the pontiff who would complete the implementation of Vatican II's mandates and prepare the Church to enter her Third Millennium, the Holy Father who would by his gregarious nature inherit the universal popularity of his amiable predecessor and thereby gain for the Church and the papacy the world's esteem.

On Sunday, October 22, 1978, under cloudy skies, Pope John Paul II, in a simple but solemn installation rite on the steps of St. Peter's basilica, attended by more than a quarter of a million persons crammed into the vast piazza, officially assumed the throne of Peter, the Prince of the Apostles. Like his predecessor, the new pope had decided against the traditional crowning with the beehive-shaped papal tiara. Instead, the young pontiff donned a simple white wool stole signifying his role as the bishop of Rome.

Dignitaries from a hundred and two nations, including Henryk Jablonski, President of Poland, and emissaries from Protestant and Orthodox Churches attended the ceremony, which was beamed back to the pope's homeland and to fifty other countries via satellite television.

Waving the red and white flag of their communist land as the former archbishop of Cracow was installed as spiritual shepherd of the world's seven hundred thirty million Catholics, Polish pilgrims chanted their ancient felicitation: "May he live a hundred years!"

After the installation ritual, His Holiness, Pope John Paul II, concelebrated Mass with a hundred and twelve cardinals. Because of the political terrorism that had plagued Italy so, thousands of security men were posted in the square and atop nearby buildings to protect the dignitaries. Throughout the three hour ceremony, helicopters buzzed overhead.

Following the proceedings, the pope, who since his election less than a week before had already broken with a great deal of papal protocol, upset tradition—and the security people—again when he walked to the edge of the broad marble steps to acknowledge the cheers from the overflowing, handkerchief waving multitude. When a small boy stepped from the large group of Polish pilgrims along the rail, two Vatican guards tried to turn him back, but the Holy Father beckoned him forward ("Suffer the little children to come unto Me"), accepted the boy's gift of a bouquet of flowers, and leaned over to tousle the lucky lad's hair and give him a paternal bear hug.

So began the reign of Pope John Paul II. In the short while that he has held the keys of Peter, Papa Wojtyla has lost little time in stamping the papacy with his own exuberant personality. At papal audiences he walks among the crowds giving vigorous handshakes, takes children into his arms and tosses them into the air. He has initiated Polish broadcasts over Vatican radio and become, like Paul VI before him, a pilgrim pope. John Paul II has already made several trips abroad: to Mexico in January of 1979 to attend the Conference of Latin American Bishops, a triumphant return to Poland in June and a history-making six-city tour of the United States in October.

Pope John Paul II takes his title as bishop of Rome as more than a figure of speech and has shown that he intends to be a diocesan bishop as well as the universal pastor. In partial fulfillment of his diocesan role, John Paul has spent Sunday afternoons from the start of his reign in visitations to the parishes of Rome.

As when he was a priest, a bishop, a cardinal, Karol Wojtyla still enjoys going out to the people. One day last February he was strolling in the streets just beyond the Vatican walls and passed a souvenir shop where Miss Vittoria Ianni works as a salesgirl. Spotting the pontiff just outside the shop engaged in a chat with some workmen, Vittoria ran out and, having summoned the courage and the nerve, exclaimed to the Holy Father: "I'm getting married next Sunday. Will you perform the ceremony?" He smiled and said, "Yes," leaving the girl and all the witnesses in happy disbelief. The following week in the Vatican's Pauline chapel, where Michelangelo's frescoes also adorn the walls, John Paul II, Supreme Pontiff of the Church, joined in Holy Matrimony Vittoria and Mario Maltese, 23, a clerk for a burglar alarm company. After the Mass at which the pope delivered a beautiful homily on the sanctity of marriage, he gave the couple his personal wedding gifts: to the bride, a painting of the Madonna; to the groom, a beautiful leather-bound copy of the Bible. Then the radiant and spunky Vittoria blurted one last request of His Holiness, "May I give you a kiss?" The pope smiled broadly and quickly replied, "Why not?"

From the moment of his election, Pope John Paul II

has shown himself to be a strong and decisive shepherd. In the interest of continuity after all the shock waves of the summer of '78, he quickly reappointed all the top officials to their posts in the curia, including Jean Cardinal Villot as secretary of state. (Cardinal Villot, a Frenchman who was originally appointed in 1969 under Paul VI, died in March of 1979 and has been succeeded by Agostino Casaroli.)

While calling fervently for Christian unity the second John Paul has also made it clear that the Church of Rome does not intend to dilute its doctrine and compromise its essential practices in order to achieve that accord. In response to a call from the Anglican Church for intercommunion, he has insisted that Christians should not share the sacrament until fundamental differences in doctrine and practice are resolved.

Another example of the pontiff's decisiveness was his recent secret meeting with dissident Archbishop Marcel Lefebvre, leader of a movement opposed to the changes in the Mass and in other Church matters enacted by the council. Though he listened understandingly and cordially to the Gallic traditionalist, the pope concluded the meeting with an ultimatum to Lefebvre to accept papal authority or leave the Church.

Unworried about his popularity ratings, Pope John Paul II has taken tough stands on such controversial ecclesiastical issues as priestly celibacy, clerical garb for religious and the laicization of priests. As of this writing, he has yet to grant a single request for laicization and has taken pains to remind priests that they are morally bound to honor their original commitment to God and to exercise maturity in moments of weakness. He has been particularly outspoken in favor of a return to orthodoxy and discipline in the Church's seminaries.

His first encyclical, *Redemptor Hominis* (Redeemer of Man), issued in March of '79 was interpreted by many as a sort of forecast of his reign. The document called for an expanded role by the Church in the universal quest for human rights, warned against the apotheosis of technology and the spiritual dangers of materialism, scorned the reckless exploitation of the earth's resources for industrial and military purposes and the resulting destruction of man's natural environment.

John Paul wrote that "rational and honest planning" was needed for the earth, adding that the progress of technology required "a proportional development of morals and ethics." In the letter the pontiff deplored the inequities imposed on persons and nations by certain economic practices. "Some societies are rich and highly developed," he stated, "while others are suffering from hunger, with many dying each day from starvation and malnutrition. Hand in hand go a certain abuse of freedom by one group, an abuse linked precisely with a consumer attitude uncontrolled by ethics." He makes it clear, however, that he is not against progress but merely opposed to paying a disproportionate price for it, that he has nothing against the system of capitalism but denounces greed. These were all themes that he reiterated to the United Nations General Assembly when he addressed them on his visit to the States in October of '79.

With respect to issues of Church doctrine, the encyclical was a reaffirmation by Pope John Paul II of the major principles established by Paul VI. The letter stressed the sanctity of the life of the unborn, the Church's opposition to artificial means of birth control and the sacredness of the marriage bond.

There are signs that Wojtyla would like to make the strong, stable cohesive Polish Church a model for all of Catholicism. And as his predecessor had intended, the pontiff hopes to play an active role in peace negotiations between feuding nations in South America, the Middle East and in the other troubled spots around the world. From boyhood devoted to the intercession of the Blessed Virgin, the Holy Father has begun a papal crusade of sorts to foster increased Marian devotion. In fact, his first encyclical concluded with an eloquent tribute to the Virgin Mary and to her central role as Mother of the Church. This, then is Karol Wojtyla, Pope John Paul II.

Long may he reign!

Postscript

As this book goes to press another papal cyclone season is approaching.

In 1979 Pope John Paul II set a new papal record of four trips abroad in one year, including an unexpected one to Turkey. This year, 1980, it appears that he will at least match that record.

- He has already visited six African countries: Zaire, Congo, Kenya, Ghana, Upper Volta and Ivory Coast in an 11-day tour May 2-12.

- He went to France May 30-June 2.

- He is on his way to Brazil this July.

- And a trip to the Philippines with perhaps several other stops, is anticipated in November.

If he introduces no surprise trips before the end of this year and does go to the Far East as expected, by stopping in only two countries there Pope John Paul II will equal the record of 17 countries visited by Pope Paul VI in his entire 15-year pontificate.

Long live the pope!

THE ROMAN PONTIFFS

Christ chose *St. Peter* to be the leader of the apostles, his vicar on earth, the visible head of the Church, the first pope; he promised and conferred on him the office, powers, duties and prerogatives of the chief shepherd (Matt. 16:16–19; John 21:15–17). These powers, duties and prerogatives were not personal to Peter alone, but belonged to his office as the chief shepherd; hence, they passed on to his successors in that office, viz., the bishops of Rome. St. Peter established his see there about the year 42. He later left Rome for a short period to do missionary work in the Holy Land and to preside over the Council of Jerusalem about 51. He was martyred at Rome about 67. Established by St. Peter as the seat of the papacy, Rome is the principal see of the Roman Catholic Church.

In the listing which follows, information includes the name of the pope, in many cases his name before becoming pope, his birthplace or country of origin, the date of accession to the papacy, and the date of the end of his reign which, in all but a few cases, is the date of death. Double dates are used to indicate time of election and coronation. (Source: *"Annuario Pontificio,"* 1979)

St. Peter (Simon Bar-Jona): Bethsaida in Galilee; d.c. 67.
St. Linus: Tuscia; 67–76.
St. Anacletus (Cletus): Rome; 76–88.
St. Clement: Rome; 88–97.
St. Evaristus: Greece; 97–105.
St. Alexander I: Rome; 105–115.
St. Sixtus I: Rome; 115–125.
St. Telesphorus: Greece; 125–136.
St. Hyginus: Greece; 136–140.

St. Pius I: Aquileia; 140–155.

St. Anicetus: Syria; 155–166.

St. Soter: Campania; 166–175.

St. Eleutherius:[1] Nicopoli in Epirus; 175–189.

St. Victor I: Africa; 189–199.

St. Zephyrinus: Rome; 199–217.

St. Callistus I: Rome; 217–222.

St. Urban I: Rome; 222–230.

St. Pontian: Rome; July 21, 230 to Sept. 28, 235.

St. Anterus: Greece; Nov. 21, 235 to Jan. 3, 236.

St. Fabian: Rome; Jan. 10, 236 to Jan. 20, 250.

St. Cornelius: Rome; Mar. of 251 to June of 253.

St. Lucius I: Rome; June 25, 253 to Mar. 5, 254.

St. Stephen I: Rome; May 12, 254 to Aug. 2, 257.

St. Sixtus II: Greece; Aug. 30, 257 to Aug. 6, 258.

St. Dionysius: (?); July 22, 259 to Dec. 26, 268.

St. Felix I: Rome; Jan. 5, 269 to Dec. 30, 274.

St. Eutychian: Luni; Jan. 4, 275 to Dec. 7, 283.

St. Caius: Dalmatia; Dec. 17, 283 to Apr. 22, 296.

St. Marcellinus: Rome; June 30, 296 to Oct. 25, 304.

St. Marcellus I: Rome; May 27, 308 or June 26, 308 to Jan 16, 309.

St. Eusebius: Greece; Apr. 18, 309 or 310 to Aug. 17, 309 or 310.

St. Melchiades (Miltiades): Africa; July 2, 311 to Jan. 11, 314.

St. Sylvester I:[2] Rome; Jan. 31, 314 to Dec. 31, 335.

St. Marcus: Rome; Jan. 18, 336 to Oct. 7, 336.

St. Julius I: Rome; Feb. 6, 337 to Apr. 12, 352.

Liberius: Rome; May 17, 352 to Sept. 24, 366.

St. Damasus I: Spain; Oct. 1, 366 to Dec. 11, 384.

St. Siricius: Rome; Dec. 15 or 22 or 29, 384 to Nov. 26, 399.

St. Anastasius I: Rome; Nov. 27, 399 to Dec. 19, 401.

St. Innocent I: Albano; Dec. 22, 401 to Mar. 12, 417.

St. Zozimus: Greece; Mar. 18, 417 to Dec. 26, 418.

St. Boniface I: Rome; Dec. 28 or 29, 418 to Sept. 4, 422.

St. Celestine I: Campania; Sept. 10, 422 to July 27, 432.

St. Sixtus III: Rome; July 31, 432 to Aug. 19, 440.

St. Leo I (the Great): Tuscany; Sept. 29, 440 to Nov. 10, 461.

St. Hilary: Sardinia; Nov. 19, 461 to Feb. 29, 468.

St. Simplicius: Tivoli; Mar. 3, 468 to Mar. 10, 483.

St. Felix III (II):[3] Rome; Mar. 13, 483 to Mar. 1, 492.

St. Gelasius I: Africa; Mar. 1, 492 to Nov. 21, 496.

Anastasius II: Rome; Nov. 24, 496 to Nov. 19, 498.

St. Symmachus: Sardinia; Nov. 22, 498 to July 19, 514.

St. Hormisdas: Frosinone; July 20, 514 to Aug. 6, 523.

St. John I, Martyr: Tuscany; Aug. 13, 523 to May 18, 526.

St. Felix IV (III): Samnium; July 12, 526 to Sept. 22, 530.

Boniface II: Rome; Sept. 22, 530 to Oct. 17, 532.

John II:[4] Rome; Jan. 2, 533 to May 8, 535.

St. Agapitus I: Rome; May 13, 535 to Apr. 22, 536.

St. Silverius, Martyr: Campania; June 1 or 8, 536 to Nov. 11, 537[5] (d. Dec. 2, 537).

Virgilius:[6] Rome; Mar. 29, 537 to June 7, 555.

Pelagius I: Rome; Apr. 16, 556 to Mar. 4, 561.

John III: Rome; July 17, 561 to July 13, 574.

Benedict I: Rome; June 2, 575 to July 30, 579.

Pelagius II: Rome; Nov. 26, 579 to Feb. 7, 590.

St. Gregory I (the Great): Rome; Sept. 3, 590 to Mar. 12, 604.

Sabinianus: Blera in Tuscany; Sept. 13, 604 to Feb. 22, 606.

Boniface III: Rome; Feb. 19, 607 to Nov. 12, 607.

St. Boniface IV: Marsi; Aug. 25, 608 to May 8, 615.

St. Deusdedit (Adeodatus I): Rome; Oct. 19, 615 to Nov. 8, 618.

Boniface V: Naples; Dec. 23, 619 to Oct. 25, 625.

Honorius I: Campania; Oct. 27, 625 to Oct. 12, 638.

Severinus: Rome; May 28, 640 to Aug. 2, 640.

John IV: Dalmatia; Dec. 24, 640 to Oct. 12, 642.

Theodore I: Greece; Nov. 24, 642 to May 14, 649.

St. Martin I, Martyr: Todi; July 649 to Sept. 16, 655 (date of his death; he lived in exile from June 17, 653).

St. Eugene I:[6] Rome; Aug. 10, 654 to June 2, 657.

St. Vitalian: Segni; July 30, 657 to Jan. 27, 672.

Adeodatus II: Rome; Apr. 11, 672 to June 17, 676.

Donus: Rome; Nov. 2, 676 to Apr. 11, 678.

St. Agatho: Sicily; June 27, 678 to Jan. 10, 681.

St. Leo II: Sicily; Aug. 17, 682 to July 3, 683.

St. Benedict II: Rome; June 26, 684 to May 8, 685.

John V: Syria; July 23, 685 to Aug. 2, 686.

Conon: (?); Oct. 21, 686 to Sept. 21, 687.

St. Sergius I: Syria; Dec. 15, 687 to Sept. 8, 701.

John VI: Greece; Oct. 30, 701 to Jan. 11, 705.

John VII: Greece; Mar. 1, 705 to Oct. 18, 707.

Sisinnius: Syria; Jan. 15, 708 to Feb. 4, 708.

Constantine: Syria; Mar. 25, 708 to Apr. 9, 715.

St. Gregory II: Rome; May 19, 715 to Feb. 11, 731.

St. Gregory III: Syria; Mar. 18, 731 to Nov. of 741.

St. Zachary: Greece; Dec. 10, 741 to Mar. 22, 752.

Stephen II (III):[7] Rome; Mar. 26, 752 to Apr. 26, 757.
St. Paul I: Rome; Apr. (May 29), 757 to June 28, 767.
Stephen III (IV): Sicily; Aug. 1 (7), 768 to Jan. 24, 772.
Adrian I: Rome; Feb. 1 (9), 772 to Dec. 25, 795.
St. Leo III: Rome; Dec. 26 (27), 795 to June 12, 816.
Stephen IV (V): Rome; June 22, 816 to Jan. 24, 817.
St. Paschal I: Rome; Jan. 25, 817 to Feb. 11, 824.
Eugene II: Rome; Feb. (May), 824 to Aug. of 827.
Valentine: Rome; Aug. of 827 to Sept. of 827.
Gregory IV: Rome; 827 to Jan. of 844.
Sergius II: Rome; Jan. of 844 to Jan. 27, 847.
St. Leo IV: Rome; Jan. (Apr. 10), 847 to July 17, 855.
Benedict III: Rome; July (Sept. 29), 855 to Apr. 17, 858.
St. Nicholas I (the Great): Rome; Apr. 24, 858 to Nov. 13, 867.
Adrian II: Rome; Dec. 14, 867 to Dec. 14, 872.
John VIII: Rome; Dec. 14, 872 to Dec. 16, 882.
Marinus I: Gallese; Dec. 16, 882 to May 15, 884.
St. Adrian III: Rome; May 17, 884 to Sept. of 885. Cult confirmed June 2, 1891.
Stephen V (VI): Rome; Sept. of 885 to Sept. 14, 891.
Formosus: Portus; Oct. 6, 891 to Apr. 4, 896.
Boniface VI: Rome; Apr. of 896 to Apr. of 896.
Stephen VI (VII): Rome; May of 896 to Aug. of 897.
Romanus: Gallese; Aug. of 897 to Nov. of 897.
Theodore II: Rome; Dec. of 897 to Dec. of 897.
John IX: Tivoli; Jan. of 898 to Jan. of 900.
Benedict IV: Rome; Jan. (Feb.) of 900 to July of 903.
Leo V: Ardea; July of 903 to Sept. of 903.
Sergius III: Rome; Jan. 29, 904 to Apr. 14, 911.
Anastasius III: Rome; Apr. of 911 to June of 913.
Landus: Sabina; July of 913 to Feb. of 914.
John X: Tossignano (Imola); Mar. of 914 to May of 928.
Leo VI: Rome; May of 928 to Dec. of 928.
Stephen VII (VIII): Rome; Dec. of 928 to Feb. of 931.
John XI: Rome; Feb. (Mar.) of 931 to Dec. of 935.
Leo VII: Rome; Jan. 3, 936 to July 13, 939.
Stephen VIII (IX): Rome; July 14, 939 to Oct. of 942.
Marinus II: Rome; Oct. 30, 942 to May of 946.
Agapitus II: Rome; May 10, 946 to Dec. of 955.
John XII (Octavius):[8] Tusculum; Dec. 16, 955 to May 14, 964 (date of his death).
Leo VIII:[8] Rome; Dec. 4 (6), 963 to Mar. 1, 964.

Benedict V:[8] Rome; May 22, 964 to July 4, 966.

John XIII: Rome; Oct. 965 to Sept. 6, 972.

Benedict VI: Rome; Jan. 19, 973 to June of 974.

Benedict VII: Rome; Oct. of 974 to July 10, 983.

John XIV (Peter Campenora): Pavia; Dec. of 983 to Aug. 20, 984.

John XV: Rome; Aug. of 985 to Mar. of 996.

Gregory V (Bruno of Carinthia): Saxony; May 3, 996 to Feb. 18, 999.

Sylvester II (Gerbert): Auvergne; Apr. 2, 999 to May 12, 1003.

John XVII (Siccone): Rome; June of 1003 to Dec. of 1003.

John XVIII (Phasianus): Rome; Jan. of 1004 to July of 1009.

Sergius IV (Peter):[9] Rome; July 31, 1009 to May 12, 1012.

Benedict VIII (Theophylactus): Tusculum; May 18, 1012 to Apr 9, 1024.

John XIX (Romanus): Tusculum; Apr. (May) of 1024 to 1032.

Benedict IX (Theophylactus): Tusculum; 1032 to 1044.

Sylvester III (John): Rome; Jan. 20, 1045 to Feb. 10, 1045.

Benedict IX: (second time); Apr. 10, 1045 to May 1, 1045.

Gregory VI (John Gratian): Rome; May 5, 1045 to Dec. 20, 1046.

Clement II (Suitger, Lord of Morsleben and Hornburg): Saxony; Dec. 24 (25), 1046 to Oct. 9, 1047.

Benedict IX:[10] (third time); Nov. 8, 1047 to July 17, 1048.

Damasus II (Poppo): Bavaria; July 17, 1048 to Aug. 9, 1048.

St. Leo IX (Bruno): Alsace; Feb. 12, 1049 to Apr. 19, 1054.

Victor II (Gebhard): Swabia; Apr. 16, 1055 to July 28, 1057.

Stephen IX (X) (Frederick): Lorraine; Aug. 3, 1057 to Mar. 29, 1058.

Nicholas II (Gerard): Burgundy; Jan. 24, 1059 to July 27, 1061.

Alexander II (Anselmo da Baggio): Milan; Oct. 1, 1061 to Apr. 21, 1073.

St. Gregory VII (Hildebrand): Tuscany; Apr. 22 (June 30), 1073 to May 25, 1085.

Bl. Victor III (Dauferius; Desiderius): Benevento; May 24, 1086 to Sept. 16, 1087. Cult confirmed July 23, 1887.

Bl. Urban II (Otto di Lagery): France; Mar. 12, 1088. to July 29, 1099. Cult confirmed July 14, 1881.

Paschal II (Raniero): Ravenna; Aug. 13 (14), 1099 to Jan. 21, 1118.

Gelasius II (Giovanni Caetani): Gaeta; Jan. 24 (Mar. 10), 1118 to Jan. 28, 1119.

Callistus II (Guido of Burgundy): Burgundy; Feb. 2 (9), 1119 to Dec. 13, 1124.

Honorius II (Lamberto): Fiagnano (Imola); Dec. 15 (21), 1124 to Feb. 13, 1130.

Innocent II (Gregorio Papareschi): Rome; Feb. 14 (23), 1130 to Sept. 24, 1143.

Celestine II (Guido): Citta di Castello; Sept. 26, 1143 to Mar. 8, 1144.

Lucius II (Gerardo Caccianemici): Bologna; Mar. 12, 1144 to Feb. 15, 1145.

Bl. Eugene III (Bernardo Paganelli di Montemagno): Pisa; Feb. 15 (18), 1145 to July 8, 1153. Cult confirmed Oct. 3, 1872.

Anastasius IV (Corrado): Rome; July 12, 1153 to Dec. 3, 1154.

Adrian IV (Nicholas Breakspear): England; Dec. 4 (5), 1154 to Sept. 1, 1159.

Alexander III (Roland Bandinelli): Siena; Sept. 7 (20), 1159 to Aug. 30, 1181.

Lucius III (Ubaldo Allucingoli): Lucca; Sept. 1 (6), 1181 to Sept. 25, 1185.

Urban III (Uberto Crivelli): Milan; Nov. 25 (Dec. 1), 1185 to Oct. 20, 1187.

Gregory VIII (Alberto de Morra): Benevento; Oct. 21 (25), 1187 to Dec. 17, 1187.

Clement III (Paolo Scolari): Rome; Dec. 19 (20), 1187 to Mar. of 1191.

Celestine III (Giacinto Bobone): Rome; Mar. 30 (Apr. 14), 1191 to Jan. 8, 1198.

Innocent III (Lotari dei Conti di Segni): Anagni; Jan. 8 (Feb. 22), 1198 to July 16, 1216.

Honorius III (Cencio Savelli): Rome; July 18 (24), 1216 to Mar. 18, 1227.

Gregory IX (Ugolino, Count of Segni): Anagni; Mar. 19 (21), 1227 to Aug. 22, 1241.

Celestine IV (Goffredo Castiglioni): Milan; Oct. 25 (28), 1241 to Nov. 10, 1241.

Innocent IV (Sinibaldo Fleschi): Genoa; June 25 (28), 1243 to Dec. 7, 1254.

Alexander IV (Rinaldo, Count of Segni): Anagni; Dec. 12 (29), 1254 to May 25, 1261.

Urban IV (Jacques Pantaleon): Troyes; Aug. 29 (Sept. 4), 1261 to Oct. 2, 1264.

Clement IV (Guy Foulques or Guido le Gros): France; Feb. 5 (15), 1265 to Nov. 29, 1268.

Bl. Gregory X (Teobaldo Visconti): Piacenza; Sept. 1, 1271 (Mar.

27, 1272) to Jan. 10, 1276. Cult confirmed Sept. 12, 1713.

Bl. Innocent V (Peter of Tarentaise): Savoy; Jan. 21 (Feb. 22), 1276 to June 22, 1276. Cult confirmed Mar. 13, 1898.

Adrian V (Ottobono Fieschi): Genoa; July 11, 1276 to Aug. 18, 1276.

John XXI (Petrus Juliani or Petrus Hispanus):[11] Portugal; Sept. 8 (20), 1276 to May 20, 1277.

Nicholas III (Giovanni Gaetano Orsini): Rome; Nov. 25 (Dec. 26), 1277 to Aug. 22, 1280.

Martin IV (Simon de Brie):[12] France; Feb. 22 (Mar. 23), 1281 to Mar. 28, 1285.

Honorius IV (Giacomo Savelli): Rome; Apr. 2 (May 20), 1285 to Apr. 3, 1287.

Nicholas IV (Girolamo Masci): Ascoli; Feb. 22, 1288 to Apr. 4, 1292.

St. Celestine V (Pietro del Murrone): Isernia; July 5 (Aug. 29), 1294 to Dec. 13, 1294; d. 1296. Canonized May 5, 1313.

Boniface VIII (Benedetto Caetani): Anagni; Dec. 24, 1294 (Jan. 23, 1295) to Oct. 11, 1303.

Bl. Benedict XI (Niccolò Boccasini): Treviso; Oct. 22 (27), 1303 to July 7, 1304. Cult confirmed Apr. 24, 1736.

Clement V (Bertrand de Got): France; June 5 (Nov. 14), 1305 to Apr. 20, 1314. (First of the Avignon popes.)

John XXII (Jacques d'Euse): Cahors; Aug. 7 (Sept. 5), 1316 to Dec. 4, 1334.

Benedict XII (Jacques Fournier): France; Dec. 20, 1334 (Jan. 8, 1335) to Apr. 25, 1342.

Clement VI (Pierre Roger): France; May 7 (19), 1342 to Dec. 6, 1352.

Innocent VI (Etienne Aubert): France; Dec. 18 (30), 1352 to Sept. 12, 1362.

Bl. Urban V (Guillaume de Grimoard): France; Sept. 28 (Nov. 6), 1362 to Dec. 19, 1370. Cult confirmed Mar. 10, 1870.

Gregory XI (Pierre Roger de Beaufort): France; Dec. 30, 1370 (Jan. 5, 1371) to Mar. 26, 1378.

Urban VI (Bartolomeo Prignano): Naples; Apr. 8 (18), 1378 to Oct. 15, 1389.

Boniface IX (Pietro Tomacelli): Naples; Nov. 2 (9), 1389 to Oct. 1, 1404.

Innocent VII (Cosma Migliorati): Sulmona; Oct. 17 (Nov. 11), 1404 to Nov. 6, 1406.

Gregory XII (Angelo Correr): Venice; Nov. 30 (Dec. 19), 1406 to

July 4, 1415 when he voluntarily resigned from the papacy to permit the election of his successor. He died Oct. 18, 1417.

Martin V (Oddone Colonna): Rome; Nov. 11 (21), 1417 to Feb. 20, 1431.

Eugene IV (Gabriele Condulmer): Venice; Mar. 3 (11), 1431 to Feb. 23, 1447.

Nicholas V (Tommaso Parentucelli): Sarzana; Mar. 6 (19), 1447 to Mar. 24, 1455.

Callistus III (Alfonso Borgia): Jativa (Valencia); Apr 8 (20), 1455 to Aug. 6, 1458.

Pius II (Enea Silvio Piccolomini): Siena; Aug. 19 (Sept. 3), 1458 to Aug. 15, 1464.

Paul II (Pietro Barbo): Venice; Aug. 30 (Sept. 16), 1464 to July 26, 1471.

Sixtus IV (Francesco della Rovere): Savona; Aug. 9 (25), 1471 to Aug. 12, 1484.

Innocent VIII (Giovanni Battista Cibo): Genoa; Aug. 29 (Sept. 12), 1484 to July 25, 1492.

Alexander VI (Rodrigo Borgia): Jativa (Valencia); Aug. 11 (26), 1492 to Aug. 18, 1503.

Pius III (Francesco Tedeschini-Piccolomini): Siena; Sept. 22 (Oct. 1, 8), 1503 to Oct. 18, 1503.

Julius II (Giuliano della Rovere): Savona; Oct. 31 (Nov. 26), 1503 to Feb. 21, 1513.

Leo X (Giovanni de' Medici): Florence; Mar. 9 (19), 1513 to Dec. 1, 1521.

Adrian VI (Adrian Florensz): Utrecht; Jan. 9 (Aug. 31), 1522 to Sept. 14, 1523.

Clement VII (Giulio de' Medici): Florence; Nov. 19 (26), 1523 to Sept. 25, 1534.

Paul III (Alessandro Farnese): Rome; Oct. 13 (Nov. 3), 1534 to Nov. 10, 1549.

Julius III (Giovanni Maria Ciocchi del Monte): Rome; Feb. 7 (22), 1550 to Mar. 23, 1555.

Marcellus II (Marcello Cervini): Montepulciano; Apr. 9 (10), 1555 to May 1, 1555.

Paul IV (Gian Pietro Carafa): Naples; May 23 (26), 1555 to Aug. 18, 1559.

Pius IV (Giovan Angelo de' Medici): Milan; Dec. 25, 1559 (Jan. 6, 1560) to Dec. 9, 1565.

St. Pius V (Antonio-Michele Ghislieri): Bosco (Alexandria); Jan. 7 (17), 1566 to May 1, 1572. Canonized May 22, 1712.

Gregory XIII (Ugo Boncompagni): Bologna; May 13 (25), 1572 to Apr. 10, 1585.

Sixtus V (Felice Peretti): Grottamare (Ripatransone); Apr. 24 (May 1), 1585 to Aug. 27, 1590.

Urban VII (Giovanni Battista Castagna): Rome; Sept. 15, 1590 to Sept. 27, 1590.

Gregory XIV (Niccolo Sfondrati): Cremona; Dec. 5 (8), 1590 to Oct. 16, 1591.

Innocent IX (Giovanni Antonio Facchinetti): Bologna; Oct. 29 (Nov. 3), 1591 to Dec. 30, 1591.

Clement VIII (Ippolito Aldobrandini): Florence; Jan. 30 (Feb. 9), 1592 to Mar. 3, 1605.

Leo XI (Alessandro de' Medici): Florence Apr. 1 (10), 1605 to Apr. 27, 1605.

Paul V (Camillo Borghese): Rome; May 16 (29), 1605 to Jan. 28, 1621.

Gregory XV (Alessandro Ludovisi): Bologna; Feb. 9 (14), 1621 to July 8, 1623.

Urban VIII (Maffeo Barberini): Florence; Aug. 6 (Sept. 29), 1623 to July 29, 1644.

Innocent X (Giovanni Battista Pamfili): Rome; Sept. 15 (Oct. 4), 1644 to Jan. 7, 1655.

Alexander VII (Fabio Chigi): Siena; Apr. 7 (18), 1655 to May 22, 1667.

Clement IX (Giulio Rospigliosi): Pistoia; June 20 (26), 1667 to Dec. 9, 1669.

Clement X (Emilio Altieri): Rome; Apr. 29 (May 11), 1670 to July 22, 1676.

Bl. Innocent XI (Benedetto Odescalchi): Como; Sept. 21 (Oct. 4), 1676 to Aug. 1689.

Alexander VIII (Pietro Ottoboni): Venice; Oct. 6 (16), 1689 to Feb. 1, 1691.

Innocent XII (Antonio Pignatelli): Spinazzola; July 12 (15), 1691 to Sept. 27, 1700.

Clement XI (Giovanni Francesco Albani): Urbino; Nov. 23, 30 (Dec. 8), 1700 to Mar. 19, 1721.

Innocent XIII (Michelangelo dei Conti): Rome; May 8 (18), 1721 to Mar. 7, 1724.

Benedict XIII (Pietro Francesco-Vincenzo Maria-Orsini): Gravina (Bari); May 29 (June 4), 1724 to Feb. 21, 1730.

Clement XII (Lorenzo Corsini): Florence; July 12 (16), 1730 to Feb. 6, 1740.

Benedict XIV (Prospero Lambertini): Bologna; Aug. 17 (22), 1740 to May 3, 1758.

Clement XIII (Carlo Rezzonico): Venice; July 6 (16), 1758 to Feb. 2, 1769.

Clement XIV (Giovanni Vincenzo Antonio-Lorenzo-Ganganelli): Rimini; May 19, 28, (June 4), 1769 to Sept. 22, 1774.

Pius VI (Giovanni Angelo Braschi): Cesena; Feb. 15 (22), 1775 to Aug. 29, 1799.

Pius VII (Barnaba-Gregorio-Chiaramonti): Cesena; Mar. 14 (21), 1800 to Aug. 20, 1823.

Leo XII (Annibale della Genga): Genga (Fabriano); Sept. 28 (Oct. 5), 1823 to Feb. 10, 1829.

Pius VIII (Francesco Saverio Castiglioni): Cingoli; Mar. 31 (Apr. 5), 1829 to Nov. 30, 1830.

Gregory XVI (Bartolomeo Alberto-Mauro-Cappellari): Belluno; Feb. 2 (6), 1831 to June 1, 1846.

Pius IX (Giovanni M. Mastai Feretti): Senegallia; June 16 (21), 1846 to Feb. 7, 1878.

Leo XIII (Gioacchino Pecci): Carpineto (Anagni); Feb. 20 (Mar. 3), 1878 to July 20, 1903.

St. Pius X (Giuseppe Sarto): Riese (Treviso); Aug. 4 (9), 1903 to Aug. 20, 1914. Canonized May 29, 1954.

Benedict XV (Giacomo della Chiesa): Genoa; Sept. 3 (6), 1914 to Jan. 22, 1922.

Pius XI (Achille Ratti): Desio (Milan); Feb. 6 (12), 1922 to Feb. 10, 1939.

Pius XII (Eugenio Pacelli): Rome; Mar. 2 (12), 1939 to Oct. 9, 1958.

John XXIII (Angelo Giuseppe Roncalli): Sotto il Monte (Bergamo); Oct. 28 (Nov. 4), 1958 to June 3, 1963.

Paul VI (Giovanni Battista Montini): Concessio (Brescia); June 21 (30), 1963 to Aug. 6, 1978.

John Paul I (Albino Luciani): Forno di Canale (Canale d'Agordo); Aug. 26 (Sept. 3), 1978 to Sept. 28, 1978.

John Paul II (Karol Wojtyla): Wadowice (Poland); Oct. 16 (22), 1978. Currently reigning.

FOOTNOTES FOR THE PRECEDING

1. Up to the time of St. Eleutherius (175–189), the years indicated for the beginning and end of pontificates are not absolutely certain. Also, up to the middle of the 11th century,

there are some doubts about the exact days and months given in the chronological tables. Research is being done on these matters.

2. All the popes before St. Sylvester I were martyrs.

3. He should be called Felix II, and his successors of the same name should be numbered accordingly. The discrepancy in the numerical designations of popes named Felix was caused by the erroneous insertion in some lists of the name of St. Felix of Rome, Martyr.

4. The first pope to change his name on ascending the papacy. His name was Mercury.

5. St. Silverius was violently deposed in March, 537 and abdicated Nov. 11, 537. Virgilius, who ascended the papacy after the violent deposition of St. Silverius, was not recognized as pope by all the Roman clergy until the abdication of St. Silverius.

6. He was elected during the exile of St. Martin I, who is believed to have endorsed him as pope.

7. After the death of St. Zachary, a Roman priest Stephen was elected but died (four days later) before his consecration as bishop of Rome, which would have marked the beginning of his pontificate. His name is not included in all the lists of the popes for this reason, but the numerical order of later popes named Stephen was affected by its inclusion in some lists. In view of this historical confusion, the *Catholic Almanac* lists the true Stephen II, with the ordinal (III) in parenthesis; the true Stephen III (IV), etc.

8. Confusion exists concerning the legitimacy of claims to the pontificate by Leo VII and Benedict V. John XII was deposed on Dec. 4, 963, by a Roman council held at St. Peter's basilica. If this deposition was invalid, Leo was an antipope until after the end of Benedict's reign. If the deposition of John was valid, Leo was the legitimate pope and Benedict an antipope.

9. The custom of changing one's name on ascending to the papacy is generally considered to date from the time of Sergius IV. Before his time several popes had changed their names. After his time this became a regular practice, with few exceptions (Adrian VI and Marcellus II).

10. If the triple removal of Benedict IX (in 1044, 1046 and the December synod) was not legitimate, Sylvester III, Gregory VI and Clement II were antipopes.

11. Elimination was made of the name of John XX in an effort to rectify the numerical designation of popes named John. The error dates back to the time of John XV.
12. The names of Marinus I (882–884) and Marinus II (942–946) were construed as Martin. In view of these two pontificates and the earlier reign of St. Martin I (649–655), this pontiff was called Martin IV.

ILLUSTRATIONS

Cover Photos: St. Peter — U. Pfistermeister, Regensburg (1340); Pope John Paul II — Brother Ed Donaher, S.S.P., Author's Photo: Frank J. Korn.

Page 93: Pope Leo XIII — NC

Page 101: Pope St. Pius X — RNS

Page 107: Pope Benedict XV — RNS

Page 115: Pope Pius XI

Page 133: Pope Pius XII with Francis Cardinal Spellman, Archbishop of New York

Page 161: Pope John XXIII and First Communicant — Felici

Page 193: Pope Paul VI in an Ecumenical Encounter — Felici

Page 237: Pope Paul VI with Albino Cardinal Luciani (Pope John Paul I)

Page 251: Pope John Paul II with the Family of Romualdo Miralli, a member of the Vatican Guard and close friend of the author